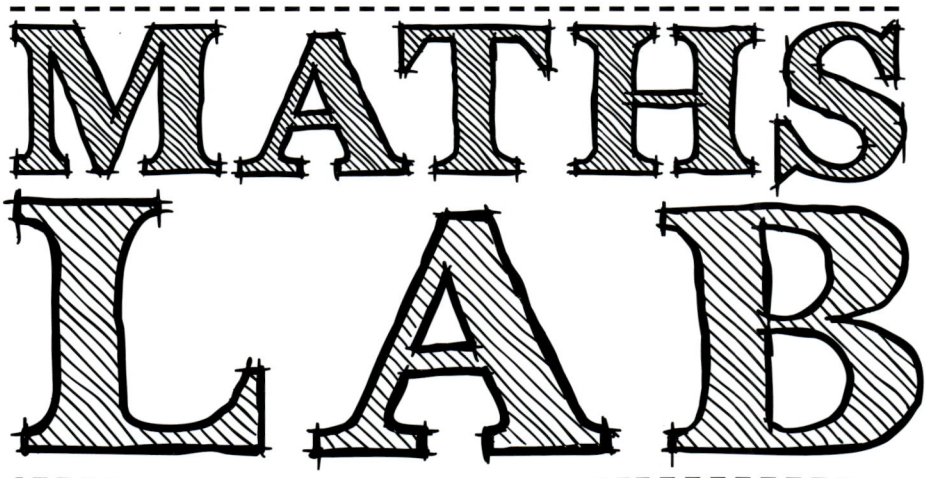

Senior editors Michelle Crane, Sam Kennedy
Senior designer Stefan Podhorodecki
Editor Rachel Thompson
Designers Mik Gates, Jim Green
Illustrator Simon Tegg

Managing editor Fran Baines
Managing art editor Phil Letsu
Production editor Kavita Varma
Senior production controller Samantha Cross
Jacket designer Tanya Mehrotra
Design development manager Sophia MTT
Managing jackets editor Saloni Singh
Jackets editorial coordinator Priyanka Sharma
Jacket DTP designer Rakesh Kumar
Picture researcher Myriam Megharbi

Publisher Andrew Macintyre
Associate publishing director Liz Wheeler
Art director Karen Self
Publishing director Jonathan Metcalf

Consultant Branka Surla
Photographers Stefan Podhorodecki, Michael Wicks

First published in Great Britain in 2021
by Dorling Kindersley Limited
DK, One Embassy Gardens, 8 Viaduct Gardens,
London, SW11 7BW
The authorised representative in the EEA is Dorling Kindersley
Verlag GmbH. Arnulfstr. 124, 80636 Munich, Germany

Copyright © 2021 Dorling Kindersley Limited
A Penguin Random House Company
10 9 8 7 6 5 4 3 2 1
001–318165–June/2021

All rights reserved.
No part of this publication may be reproduced, stored in or introduced into a retrieval system, or transmitted, in any form, or by any means (electronic, mechanical, photocopying, recording, or otherwise), without the prior written permission of the copyright owner.

A CIP catalogue record for this book
is available from the British Library.
ISBN: 978-0-2414-3232-7

Printed and bound in China

For the curious
www.dk.com

This book was made with Forest Stewardship Council ™ certified paper – one small step in DK's commitment to a sustainable future.
For more information go to
www.dk.com/our-green-pledge

MATHS LAB

EXCITING PROJECTS FOR BUDDING MATHEMATICIANS

DK

CONTENTS

6	**NUMBERS**	42	**SHAPES**
8	Number fridge magnets	44	Symmetrical pictures
12	Make your own abacus	50	Picture ball
18	Times table fortune-tellers	56	Wrapping paper and gift bag
22	Maths bingo	62	Scaling up pictures
26	Fibonacci spiral collage	68	Origami jumping frog
32	Dreamcatcher	72	Tessellating patterns
38	Bake and share a pizza	78	Impossible triangle
		82	Pop-up cards

MATHEMATICS FACTS
This symbol highlights extra information that explains the maths behind each project.

WARNING
This symbol identifies a task that might be dangerous. Be sure to get adult supervision.

A WORD ABOUT GLUES

Several of the projects in this book require the use of glue. We have suggested that you use ordinary PVA glue or glue sticks, but in some cases it will be easier to use a glue gun if you have one, as this glue dries much faster. A glue gun should only ever be used by an adult, and they must be sure to follow the manufacturer's guidelines.

88 MEASUREMENTS

90 Speed trials
98 Friendship bracelets
106 Fun fruit drinks
110 Chocolate truffles
114 Chocolate box
118 Popcorn sale tray

126 Shadow puppets
130 Lucky dip
134 Marble run
140 Optical illusions
144 Make your own clock
150 Lolly stick bird feeder

158 Glossary
160 Index

NUMBERS

You can't do maths without numbers. There are 10 number symbols, but they can be used to write or count as many numbers as you can imagine. In this chapter, you'll find projects for getting to grips with numbers, from making your own fridge magnets to using the power of fractions to divide a pizza fairly. You'll also make an abacus to help you master complex calculations, and a dreamcatcher that will test your times tables.

FAMILY MATHS CHALLENGE
NUMBER FRIDGE MAGNETS

With some sticky magnetic sheets and coloured card you can make your very own number magnets. Use them to set challenges for your family on the fridge and see who will be the first to figure out the answers to your fiendish questions.

NUMBER FRIDGE MAGNETS   9

HOW TO MAKE
NUMBER FRIDGE MAGNETS

These magnets are quick and easy to make, especially if you have sticky-backed magnetic sheets. You can use different coloured card to make your numbers stand out on the fridge.

MATHS YOU WILL USE
- MEASUREMENT to make sure your numbers are the perfect size.
- EQUATIONS to create devious addition, subtraction, multiplication, and division challenges for your family.
- ALGEBRA to take your fridge maths to the next level.

Time 60 minutes
Difficulty Easy

Zero is a special number. As a digit, it can be used to change the place value of a number.

WHAT YOU NEED

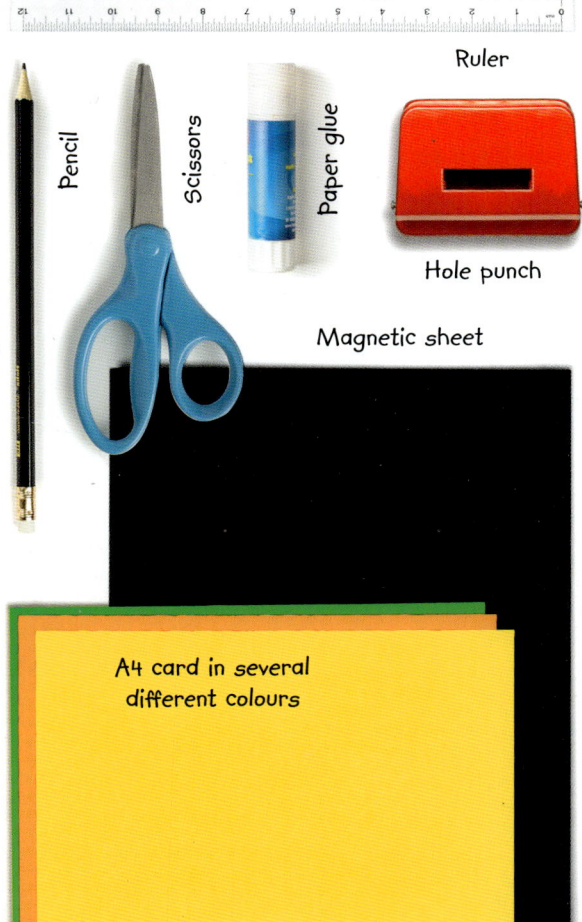

Ruler
Pencil
Scissors
Paper glue
Hole punch
Magnetic sheet
A4 card in several different colours

1 On a piece of coloured card or paper draw a zero, with a rough height of 4.5 cm (1¾ in) and a width of 3.5 cm (1½ in). Make sure the number is bold so that it won't be too flimsy when it's cut out.

2 Carefully cut around the outside of the number with a pair of scissors.

10 NUMBERS

3 Stick your number onto a piece of magnetic sheet with glue or the sheet's sticky backing. Make sure you stick it to the non-magnetic side.

4 Using scissors, carefully cut around the number again, this time cutting the magnetic sheet, too. Ask an adult to help if this is tricky.

You will need to make more than one of each number.

5 To cut the middle out of the zero, use a hole punch to create a hole. You can then push your scissor tips through to continue cutting.

6 Repeat steps 1–5, using different coloured card for digits 1–9. You could stick multiple numbers to one magnetic sheet and cut them out in one go.

7 Repeat steps 1–5, but this time draw the mathematical symbols for addition, subtraction, and multiplication.

The symbols make it fast and simple to write out equations.

8 Next, draw the symbols for division and equals. Draw a thin line linking the different parts of the symbol so the magnet stays in one piece. Repeat steps 2–5 for these symbols.

NUMBER FRIDGE MAGNETS

9 Stick the magnets onto your fridge and use them to create and solve different mathematical problems. Can you work out these cunning calculations?

ALGEBRA ADVENTURES

Make magnets for the letters x and y to create algebra puzzles. In algebra, letters stand for unknown numbers. To solve algebra problems, remember that the values on both sides of the equals sign must balance, like weighing scales. So if the letter is on one side of the equals sign, you can find its value by doing the calculation on the other side. Can you work out the values of x and y in these questions?

1 This puzzle is like a normal maths question, but there is an x to the right of the equals sign. That means x must equal 6 divided by 3, so x = 2.

2 To find out the value of y in this question, you need to subtract 2 from both sides of the equals sign. 8 - 2 is 6, so y must be equal to 6.

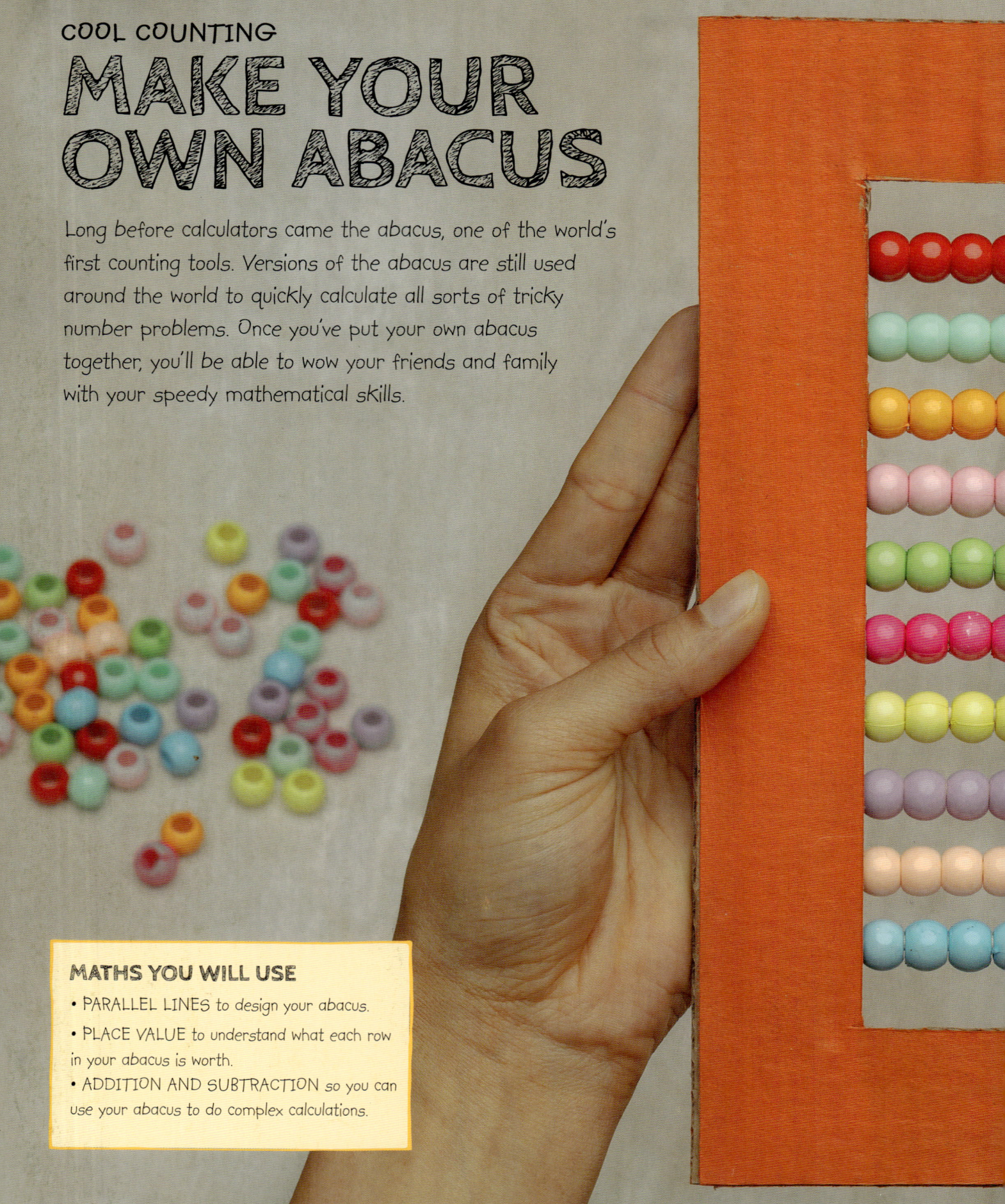

COOL COUNTING
MAKE YOUR OWN ABACUS

Long before calculators came the abacus, one of the world's first counting tools. Versions of the abacus are still used around the world to quickly calculate all sorts of tricky number problems. Once you've put your own abacus together, you'll be able to wow your friends and family with your speedy mathematical skills.

MATHS YOU WILL USE
- PARALLEL LINES to design your abacus.
- PLACE VALUE to understand what each row in your abacus is worth.
- ADDITION AND SUBTRACTION so you can use your abacus to do complex calculations.

Different coloured beads for every row will help you keep track of your calculations.

You can paint the abacus frame in your favourite colour.

NUMBERS

HOW TO MAKE YOUR OWN ABACUS

All you need to make your own abacus is a set of wooden craft sticks, colourful beads, a few pieces of cardboard, and some paint. Make sure you do your measurements carefully so that the rungs are straight and your beads can move freely along them.

Time 45 minutes, plus drying time

Difficulty Medium

WHAT YOU NEED

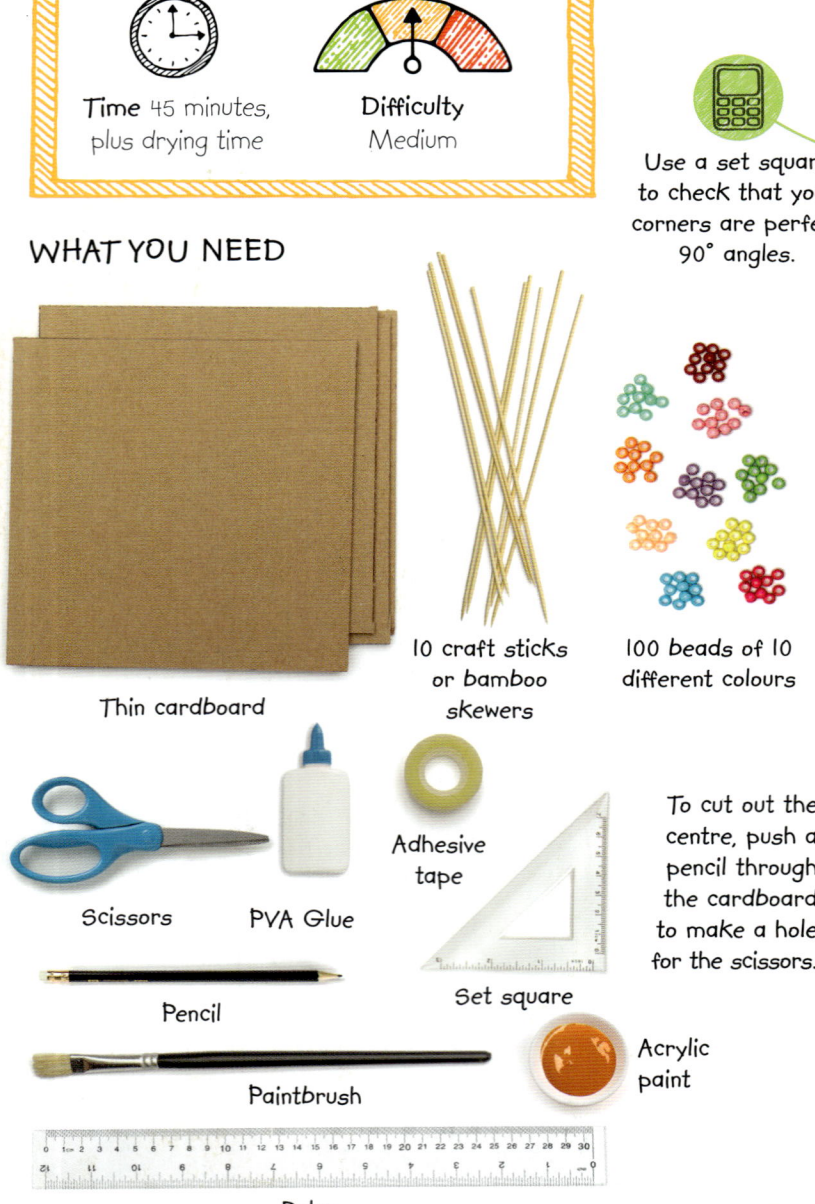

- Thin cardboard
- 10 craft sticks or bamboo skewers
- 100 beads of 10 different colours
- Scissors
- PVA Glue
- Adhesive tape
- Set square
- Pencil
- Paintbrush
- Acrylic paint
- Ruler

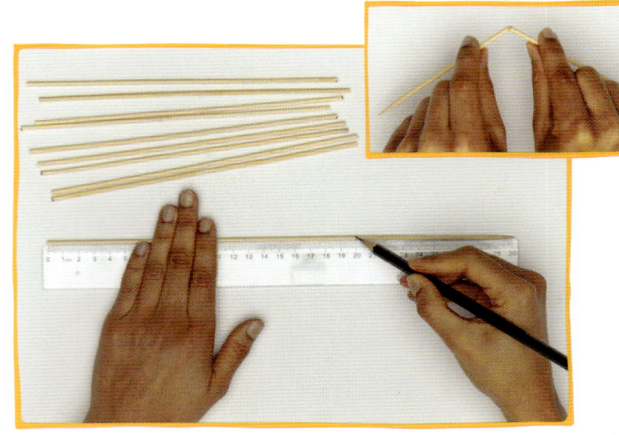

1 Measure 20 cm (8 in) along a stick and mark this point with a pencil. Carefully snap it at the mark. Repeat to make 10 sticks of equal length.

Use a set square to check that your corners are perfect 90° angles.

2 Next, make the frame. Draw a 22.5 cm (9 in) square onto your cardboard. Then measure 3 cm (1¼ in) inside each edge and draw a smaller square inside the first one. Repeat so you have two pieces of cardboard with two identical squares drawn on them.

To cut out the centre, push a pencil through the cardboard to make a hole for the scissors.

3 Cut around the outer square, then cut carefully along the lines of the inner square to remove the centre. Repeat to make two frames.

MAKE YOUR OWN ABACUS   15

4. Using acrylic paint mixed with a very small amount of water so the cardboard doesn't go soggy, paint one side of each frame. Leave to dry.

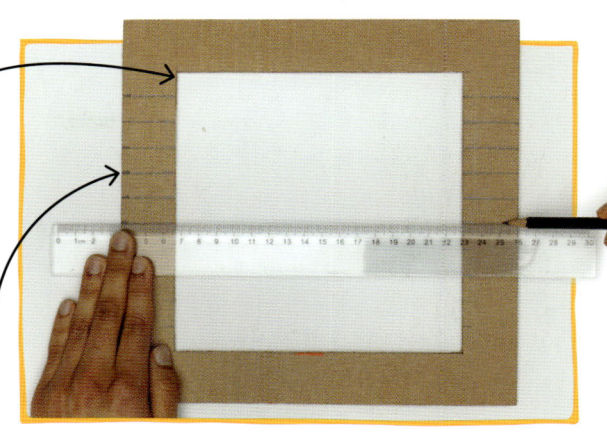

Measure down from the top of the inner frame on both sides.

You will arrange your wooden sticks along these guidelines.

5. Once dry, turn to the unpainted side and mark out 1.5 cm (½ in) intervals along two opposite sides. Then draw a horizontal line through each mark.

The wooden sticks run parallel to each other, which means they will never meet or cross.

6. Thread a bead onto each wooden stick and lay the stick across the lines you have drawn. Check you are happy with the positions of the sticks.

7. Take the top stick from your frame and add another nine beads. Count up to 10 as you thread them on and then place the stick to one side.

10 beads on 10 sticks equals 100 beads in total.

8. Repeat until you have 10 wooden craft sticks with 10 beads of the same colour on each one. Do a final count to make sure you have 10 beads on each stick.

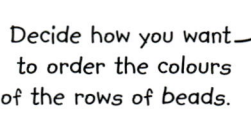
Decide how you want to order the colours of the rows of beads.

16   NUMBERS

PLACE VALUE AND DECIMALS

Each digit in a number has a value based on where it is in the number. For example, the 6 in 42,367.15 represents 6 tens or 60. The numbers left of the decimal point are whole numbers and the numbers to the right are fractions.

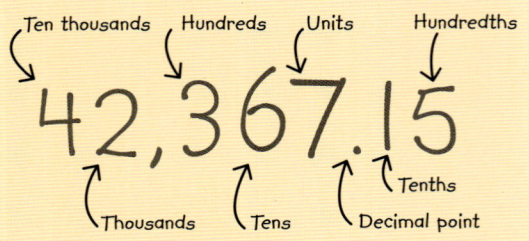

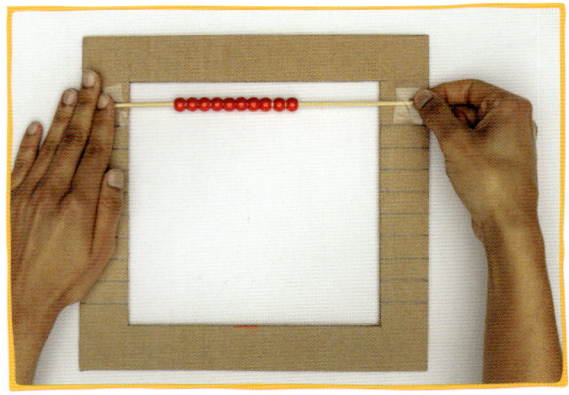

9 Lay the first stick along the top mark of the frame and secure it to the cardboard using adhesive tape at both ends.

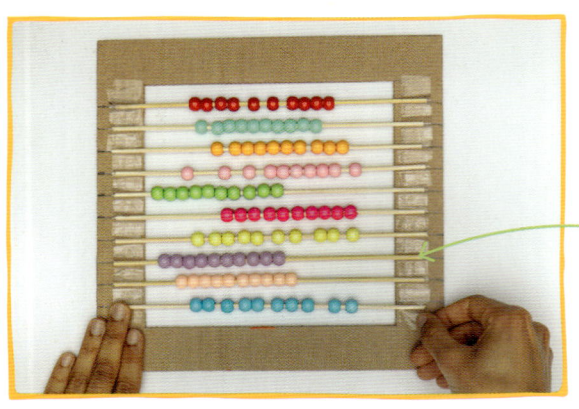

Each row on the abacus represents a different place value.

10 Repeat until you have secured all 10 rows of beads in place. Make sure to press the tape down firmly so the sticks don't move.

11 Make two equal strips of cardboard by drawing and then cutting out two 2.5 x 22 cm (1 x 8¾ in) rectangles.

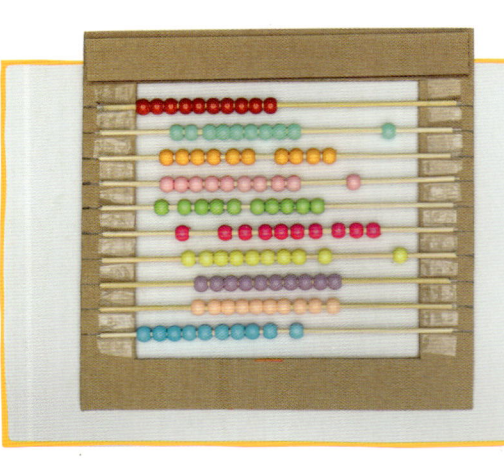

Press firmly and place something heavy on top of the frame while it dries.

12 Dab glue onto the cardboard strips and fix them to the top and bottom of the square frame. The strips should fit just inside the edges of the frame.

13 Add glue to the back of the second square frame and secure it to the back of the frame with the rows of beads. Press gently and allow the glue to dry. Your abacus is complete!

DOING MATHS WITH THE ABACUS

Each rung of the abacus has a different place value – the higher the row, the higher the value. Once you have established these place values, you can use the abacus to quickly do sums of big or complicated numbers.

To read a number on an abacus, start with the top row and work your way down.

1 In this calculation, the bottom row represents tenths, the second row stands for units, the third row stands for 10 and so on. That means the abacus is currently showing the number 317.5.

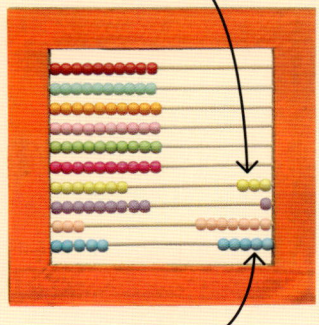

These beads represent tenths.

2 Now add 9 to 317.5 by counting nine beads on the second row, moving them to the right. After counting three beads, this row will be full, so swap the 10 beads on the second row with one from the third row. Keep counting along the second row until you have counted nine beads in total.

Each of these beads represents one hundred, for a total of three hundred.

This bead is equal to ten beads from the row just below it.

3 You can use the abacus to add bigger numbers. To add 1,432.6 to what you have, start from the top and work your way down. Move one bead across the fifth row to represent the thousands, then four beads on the next row and so on.

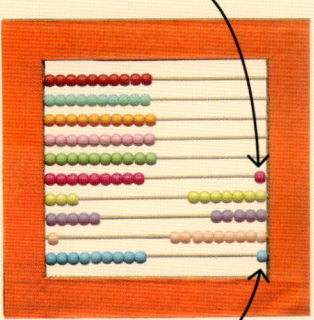

This bead is the same as 10 hundreds from the lower row, or one thousand.

Remember to swap the tenths on the bottom row for ones from the row above.

4 To use the abacus to subtract, you start from the bottom and work up. To subtract 541 from what you have, first move a single bead on the second row back to the left. Then move five beads back on the third row, and finally five beads on the third fourth. What number do you have?

When subtracting, always start with the lowest rows.

REAL WORLD MATHS
HISTORY OF THE ABACUS

The abacus has been in use since ancient times. The oldest tablet counting system discovered so far was found on a Greek island and is more than 2,300 years old. The kind of abacus you have just made, a 100-bead abacus, was commonly used in Europe. Over the centuries, there have been many different types of abacus, each using their own counting system, such as the suanpan, a Chinese abacus, and the version in this picture, which comes from Germany and has fewer rows but more beads per row.

PAPER GAMES
TIMES TABLE FORTUNE-TELLERS

These paper fortune-tellers are quick and easy to fold, and they're a fun way to quiz yourself or your friends and family. We've used this one to practise our times tables, but you can adapt the questions to test almost anything.

MATHS YOU WILL USE
- **MULTIPLICATION TABLES** to answer your fortune-teller's questions.
- **ROTATION** as you turn and fold your fortune-teller.
- **2D SHAPES** to construct your fortune-teller.

TIMES TABLE FORTUNE-TELLERS   19

HOW TO MAKE A FORTUNE-TELLER

To get started with this project, you'll need to make a piece of paper into a square. Follow the instructions to fold your fortune-teller carefully, and then decide what calculations and colours to go for. Fold it all up again, and you're ready to challenge your friends!

Time 15 minutes

Difficulty Easy

WHAT YOU NEED

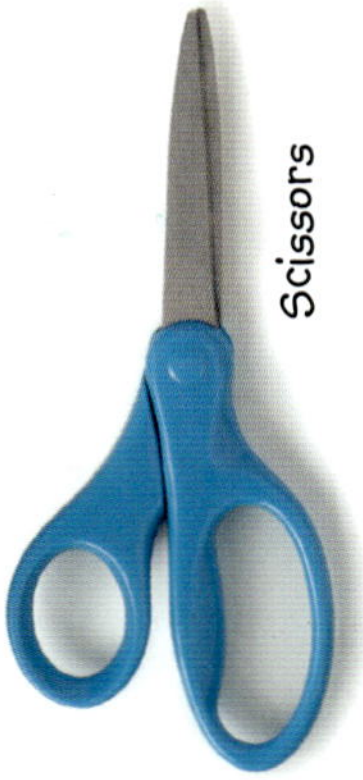

Scissors

Black marker pen

Felt-tip pens

A4 paper

Fold along the purple arrows.

This unusual four-sided shape is called a trapezoid.

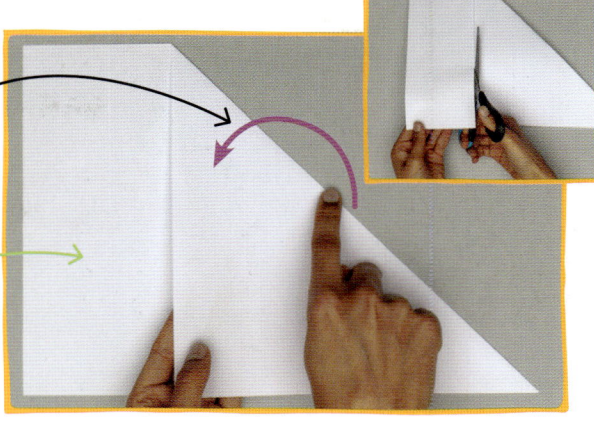

1 Fold down the top-right corner of your piece of A4 paper to meet the bottom edge. Crease along the angle and cut off the rectangular strip.

Fold the square as carefully as you can or your finished fortune-teller won't work smoothly.

2 Open up the paper and you will have a square with a diagonal fold through the middle. Bring the other opposite corners together and fold the crease. Unfold again and you will have two folds marking out four triangles.

A quarter turn can also be called a 90° turn, as 90 is one quarter of 360, and 360° make up a full circle.

3 Fold your square in half, then rotate it a quarter turn and fold in half again. Open it out – you should have six lines crossing through the page.

20 NUMBERS

4 Next, fold each of the square's corners into the middle of the paper to create a diamond shape.

The smaller triangles are called right-angled triangles because their two shortest edges meet at a 90° angle.

5 Turn the paper over and then repeat the previous step, folding all of the corners into the centre of the paper to create a smaller square.

6 Decide what you want your fortune-teller to test. This one is for the three times table. Write a multiplication question in each small triangle. You will have eight questions in total.

Use this step as a chance to memorize your times tables.

7 Flip open the triangles and write the answer to each of the multiplication problems on the underside of the triangle, then fold them back.

8 Turn the fortune-teller over and write the number of the times table you are using on each of the squares. Use felt-tip pens to shade each one in a different colour.

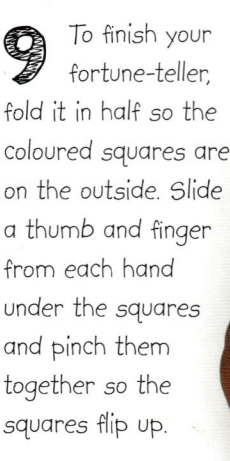

9 To finish your fortune-teller, fold it in half so the coloured squares are on the outside. Slide a thumb and finger from each hand under the squares and pinch them together so the squares flip up.

You're ready to play!

TIMES TABLE FORTUNE-TELLERS   21

MULTIPLICATION MAYHEM

Use your fortune-teller to test a friend's – or your own – knowledge of times tables. Follow the instructions below to find out how to play. You can take it in turns to test each other. No peeking!

1 Ask your friend to pick a colour, and then spell it out, opening the fortune-teller in a different direction for each letter as you say it aloud. When you stop, you will reveal four questions.

2 Ask your friend to choose a question and then answer it! Flip up the triangle to see if they got it right. Keep going until all the questions have been answered.

Open in alternate directions to reveal the two different sets of questions.

Unfold the triangular flap to check and see if the answer was right!

Make a different fortune-teller for each times table.

MORE FORTUNE-TELLER FUN

As well as times tables, you can make fortune-tellers to practise all sorts of maths skills. Here's one with questions about shapes, but you could make one to test addition, subtraction, division, or almost anything else too!

Spell out the name of a shape to reveal the questions.

Write the answers on the inside of each flap.

HOW TO PLAY BINGO

To keep your game of bingo exciting, each player needs their own bingo card with numbers in a random order. That means that even though everyone hears the same questions, you'll all cover different squares and score points at different rates.

MATHS YOU WILL USE
- MEASUREMENT to draw up the bingo cards you'll play on.
- ADDITION, SUBTRACTION, MULTIPLICATION, AND DIVSION to be the fastest to fill your bingo card.

Time 60 minutes

Difficulty Easy

WHAT YOU NEED

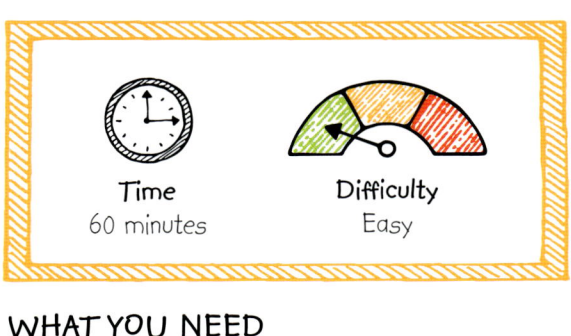

Coloured plastic counters (about 25 per player)

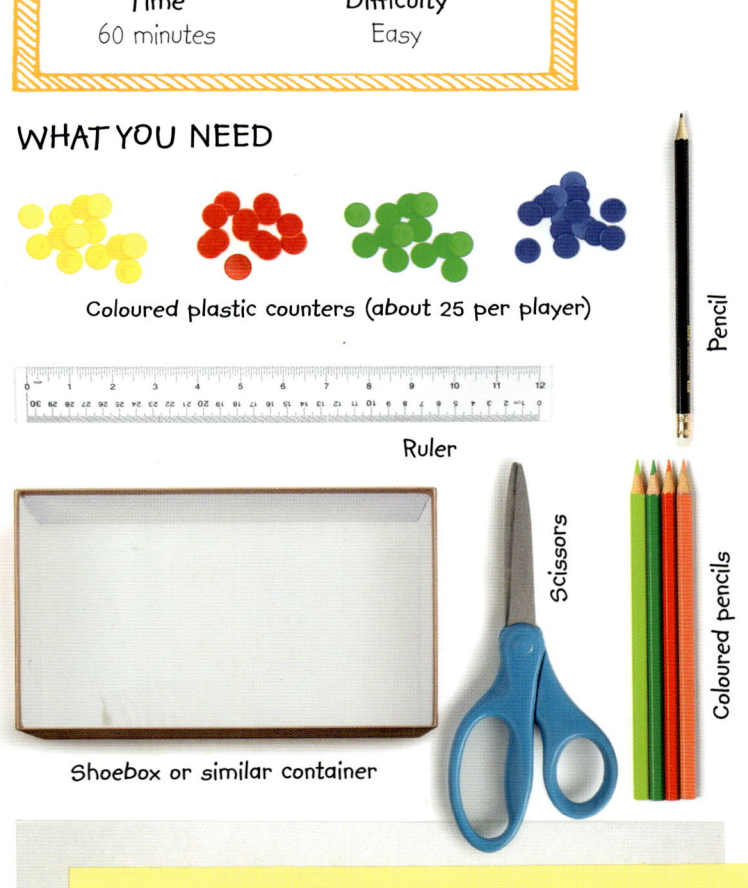

Ruler

Pencil

Scissors

Coloured pencils

Shoebox or similar container

A5 white or coloured card or paper

Measure the full width of your card and divide it by five to make sure you get equal columns.

1 Take a piece of A5 card and create a 5 × 5 grid by drawing four vertical lines from the top to the bottom of the page. Make sure that the lines are equally spaced.

2 Divide the height of the card by five and draw four equally spaced horizontal lines down the page so you have a grid with five columns and five rows.

24 NUMBERS

You could colour each square in the grid a different colour.

3. Number the grid from 1 to 25, starting at the top-left and ending at the bottom-right corner. Repeat steps 1–3 to make more bingo grids, but put the numbers on those grids in a random order.

4. On another piece of card, create a 4 × 3 grid by drawing three equally spaced vertical lines from the top to the bottom of the page and two equally spaced lines crossing the width of the page.

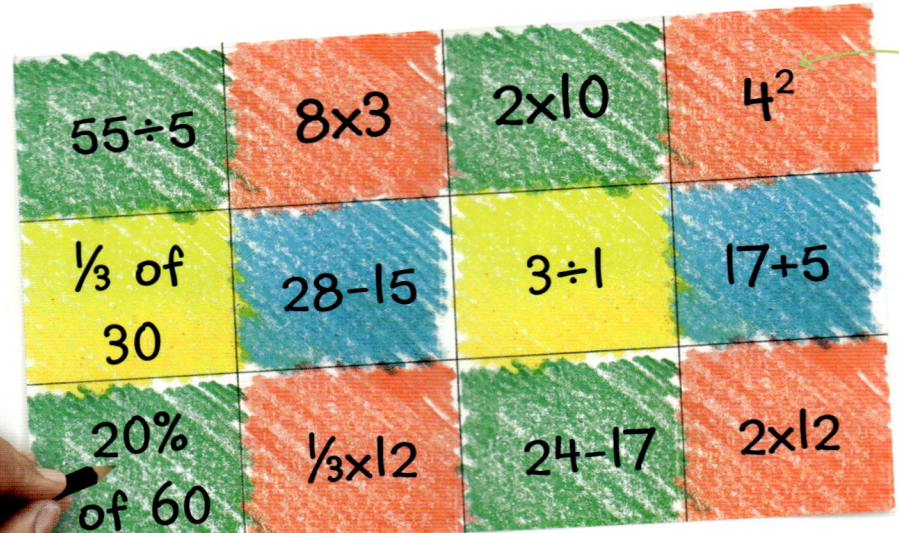

This small 2 is called a power. It tells you how many times to multiply the number below it by itself. To work this out you need to do 4 × 4.

5. Fill each square of the grid with questions then repeat steps 4–5 to create more maths calculations until you have 25 plus a few spare for another game. Make sure that each of the 25 questions has a different answer. Each answer should be between 1 and 25.

Make sure the caller puts the question away after reading it out so there are no repeats.

6. Use a pair of scissors to cut out the questions, then fold them up and place them in a shoebox or similar container.

7. Give every player but one a set of counters and a bingo card. The other player is the "caller", who picks questions from the box and reads them out.

MATHS BINGO   25

If you win, you'll have to prove that your covered answers are all correct!

8 Each time you figure out the answer to a question that the caller reads out, place a counter over the number matching the answer.

9 You can use the examples on the right to work out how to score the game. Keep playing until one person reaches 15 points.

REAL WORLD MATHS
BINGO MACHINES
In a bingo hall, it's important to ensure that the numbers called are completely random. To do that, transparent machines such as this one hold the bingo balls in a chamber that rotates as the handle is turned. This mixes the balls up, before a random ball is scooped out into the tube – or "runway" – below.

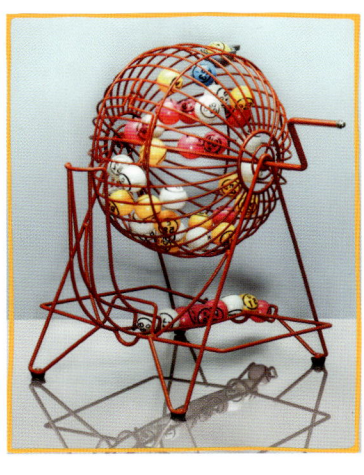

BINGO SCORING
There are two ways to score in this version of bingo: covering all the answers in a column or row, or completing a cross from one corner to the other. A horizontal or vertical line is worth 5 points, while a cross is worth 10 points. The first person to get 15 points or more is the winner!

Column – 5 points

Row – 5 points

Cross – 10 points

SPECTACULAR SEQUENCES
FIBONACCI SPIRAL COLLAGE

Follow in the footsteps of Leonardo da Vinci and create a masterpiece all of your own using the Fibonacci sequence. By fitting together ever-increasing squares, you can draw a perfect spiral and produce a collage fit to hang on your gallery wall.

MATHS YOU WILL USE
- SEQUENCES AND PATTERNS to create ideally sized squares.
- RATIO to draw a perfect rectangle.
- RIGHT ANGLES to ensure your squares fit neatly next to each other.

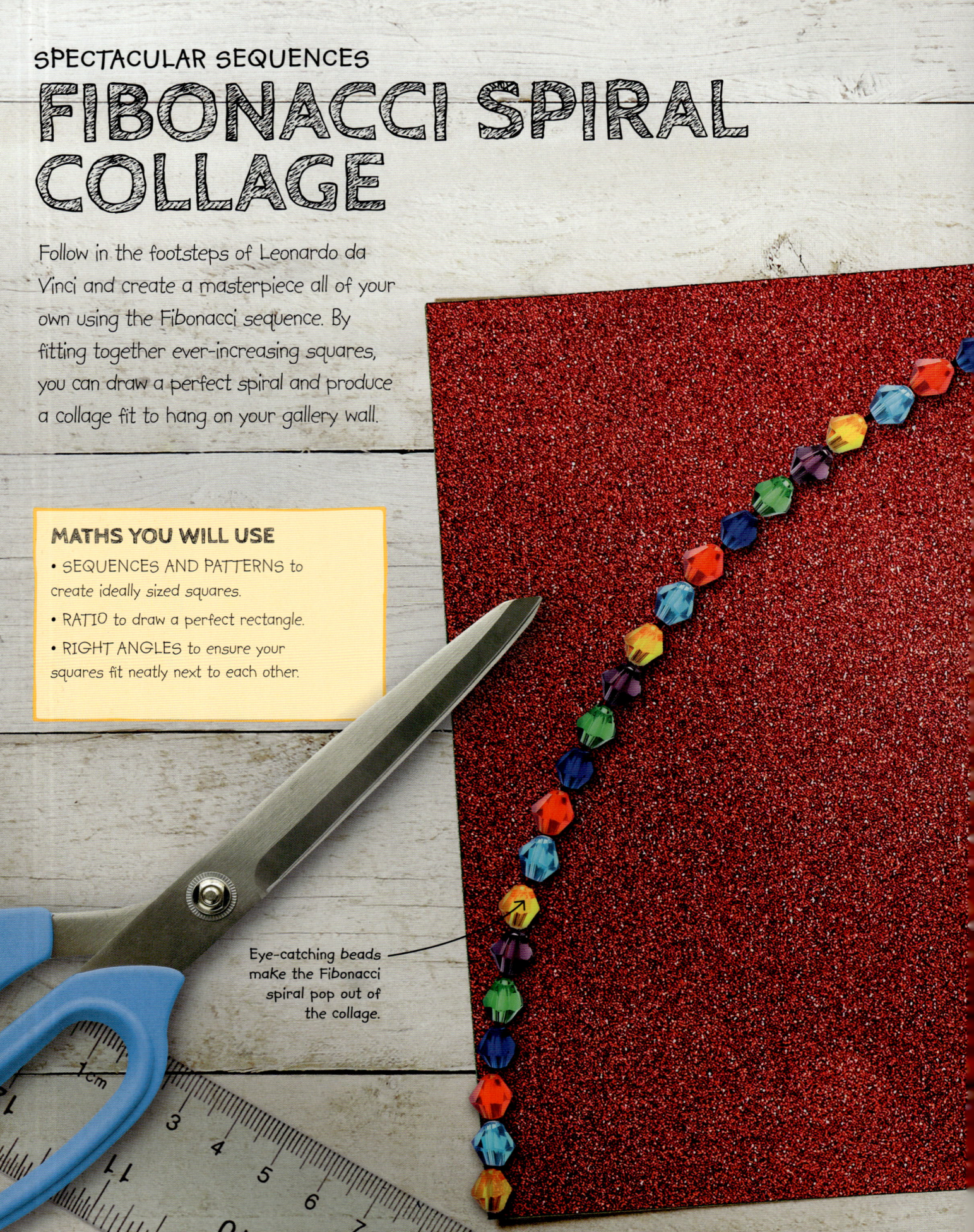

Eye-catching beads make the Fibonacci spiral pop out of the collage.

NUMBERS

HOW TO MAKE A
FIBONACCI SPIRAL COLLAGE

The key to this project is to create the template first by using a number pattern called the Fibonacci sequence to find the size of each square. Fibonacci was an Italian mathematician living 800 years ago who discovered a number sequence common in nature.

Time
120 minutes

Difficulty
Medium

WHAT YOU NEED

Ruler
Scissors
Paper glue
Craft glue
Compass and pencil
Marker pen
Set square
Beads or sequins to decorate
A3 5 mm (¼ in) graph paper
A4 coloured glitter paper or plain coloured paper

FIBONACCI SEQUENCE

The Fibonacci sequence is a pattern of numbers in which the next number in the series is the sum of the two numbers that come before it.

$1 + 1 = \boxed{2}$
$1 + 2 = \boxed{3}$
$2 + 3 = \boxed{5}$
$3 + 5 = \boxed{8}$
$5 + 8 = \boxed{13}$
$8 + 13 = \boxed{21}$
$13 + 21 = \boxed{34}$

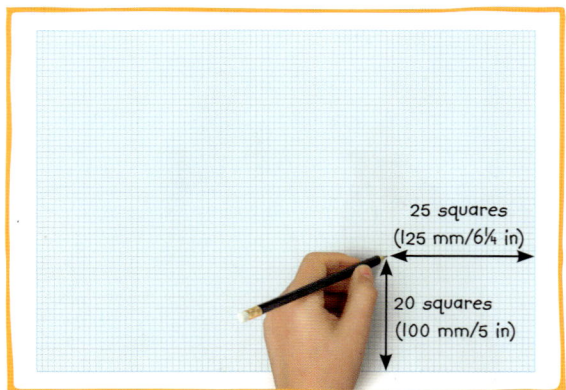

25 squares (125 mm/6¼ in)
20 squares (100 mm/5 in)

1 On an A3 sheet of 5 mm (¼ in) graph paper, make a pencil mark 25 squares left from the right edge and 20 squares up from the bottom edge.

FIBONACCI SPIRAL COLLAGE   29

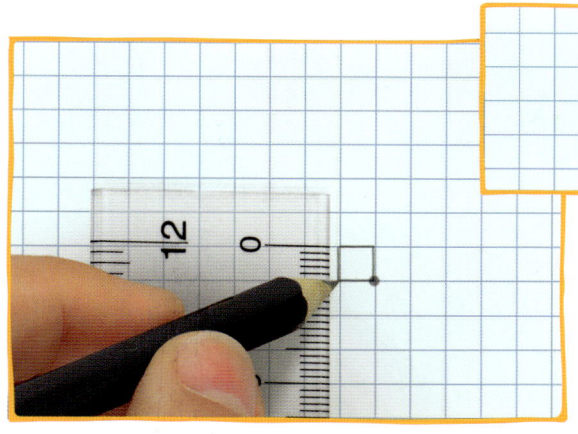

Use the Fibonacci sequence to work out the number of squares needed for the size of the next square.

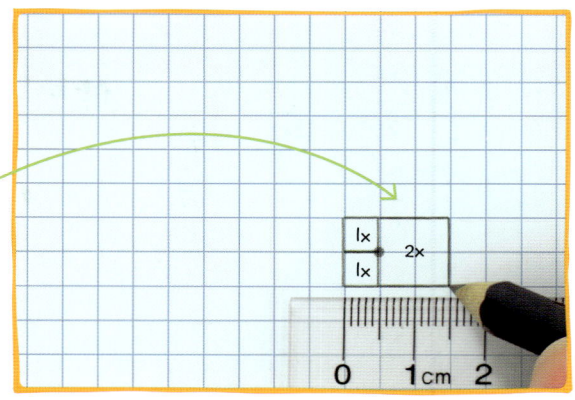

2 Trace a square to the left of the mark. This is a 1 x 1 square because it is one length on each side. Trace another square below the first square, so the mark is between them.

3 The next square needs to be 2 x 2 squares. Draw this square to the right of the two squares you have just drawn.

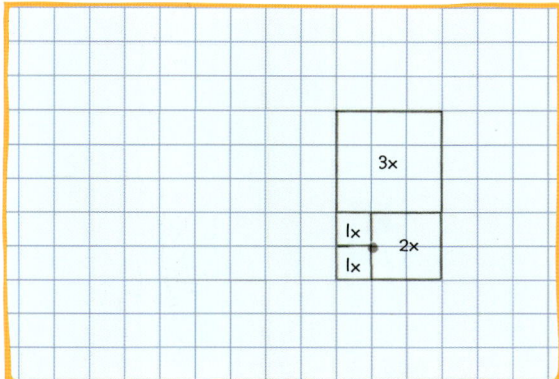

Each time you add a new square, you turn the shape into a larger rectangle.

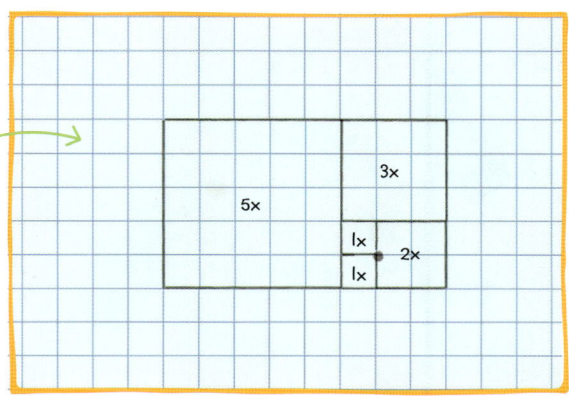

4 The following number in the sequence is 3, so draw a square 3 x 3 immediately above the squares you have already drawn.

5 Five is the next number in the Fibonacci sequence, so draw a square 5 x 5 to the left of the group of smaller squares.

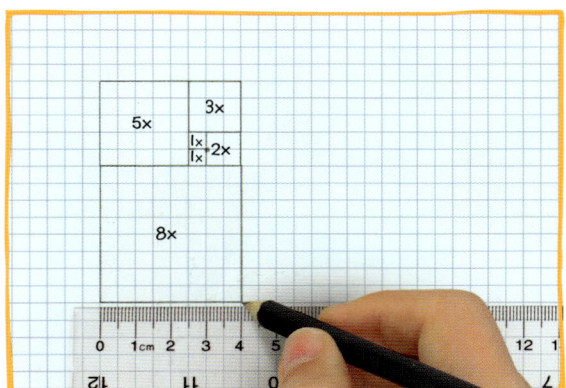

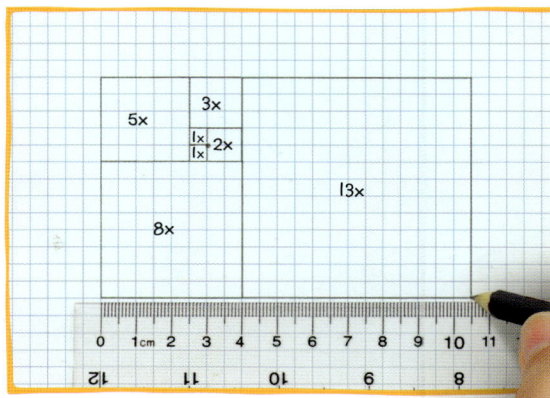

6 Next comes 8, so draw an 8 x 8 square immediately below the rectangle.

7 Thirteen is next, so draw a 13 x 13 square to the right of the rectangle.

30 NUMBERS

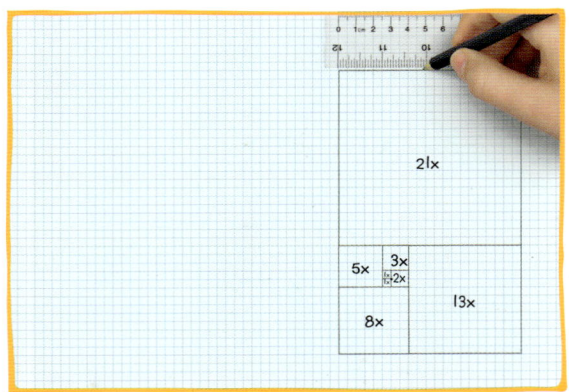

Fibonacci rectangles are special because the ratio of length to width is always 1.6 no matter how big the rectangle is. This is called the Golden Ratio.

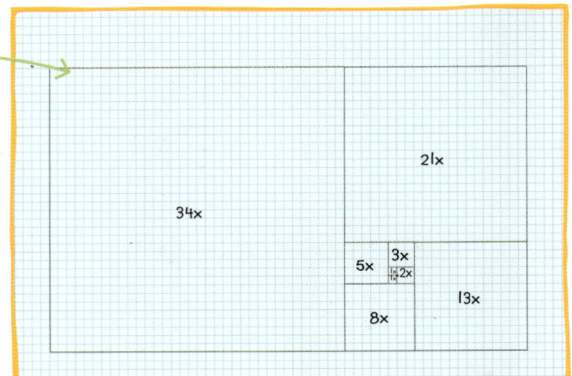

8 And next is 21, so draw a square 21 x 21 immediately above the rectangle.

9 Next up is 34. Draw a square 34 x 34 to the left of the rectangle. Your Fibonacci template is now ready!

You can multiply the Fibonacci numbers by 5 mm (¼ in) to calculate the size of each coloured square to cut.

10 On different coloured paper, measure and cut out squares the same size as the ones you have just drawn. Use a set square and a ruler to ensure the corners are right angles.

11 Glue the squares into position on the template. Start with the smallest squares, then move onto the next biggest until the template is covered. Trim off any excess graph paper.

FIBONACCI SPIRAL
You can use the Fibonacci sequence to draw a spiral by linking the opposite corners of each square with a curved line.

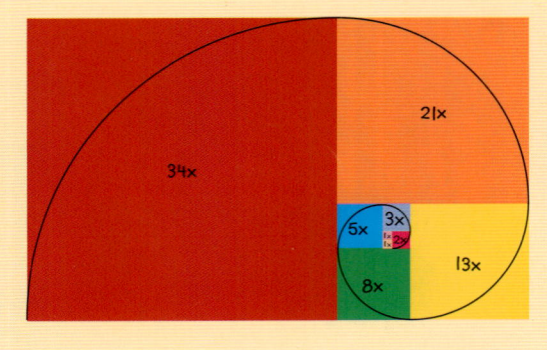

Position the compass point on the very first mark you made in step 1.

12 Set a compass to 5 mm (¼ in) and place it at the top-right corner of the first square. Draw a curve across the two smallest squares.

FIBONACCI SPIRAL COLLAGE   31

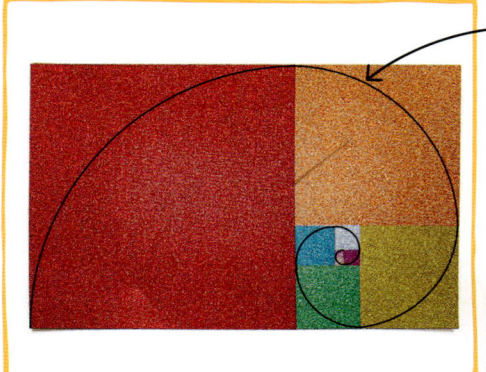

You can use a pencil or black marker pen to draw the curve.

13 Repeat step 13, but each time adjust the compass to the length of the next square and place the compass point on the corner opposite where you will draw your curve. Then use your compass to continue the spiral.

14 Decorate the collage by sticking beads or sequins along the contours of the spiral. Can you create a pattern or sequence using the beads?

REAL WORLD MATHS

FIBONACCI IN NATURE

Fibonacci spirals don't just occur in maths, they are also found in the natural world. Pine cones and pineapples arrange their scales in a Fibonacci spiral, and the number of petals on a flower are often Fibonacci numbers. For example, Michaelmas daisies like these usually have 34, 55, or 89 petals, all of which are Fibonacci numbers.

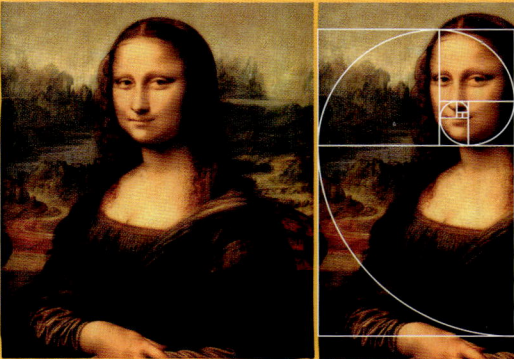

GOLDEN RATIO IN ART

As well as cropping up in nature, the Fibonacci sequence also appears in the art world. As shown above, the famous Italian artist Leonardo da Vinci is thought to have used golden rectangles to make the proportions of some of his most famous paintings, including the *Mona Lisa*, more harmonious.

MULTIPLICATION MOBILE
DREAMCATCHER

Originating from Native American culture, dreamcatchers are thought to keep hold of good dreams and send bad ones packing while you are sleeping. Here, you'll learn how to divide a circle into equal parts and use your times tables skills to create different patterns for the web in the centre of the dreamcatcher. Place your creation over your bed at night and sleep tight. Sweet dreams!

Good dreams trickle down the feathers to the person sleeping below.

MATHS YOU WILL USE
- TIMES TABLES to create different patterns.
- ANGLES to divide a circle into equal parts.
- RADIUS AND DIAMETER to draw a circle inside another circle.

NUMBERS

HOW TO MAKE A
DREAMCATCHER

Making this dreamcatcher is a great way to learn your times tables. All you need is some card, wool, and colourful feathers and beads for decoration. We have used the three times table for our dreamcatcher, but you can also weave different patterns by using any of them.

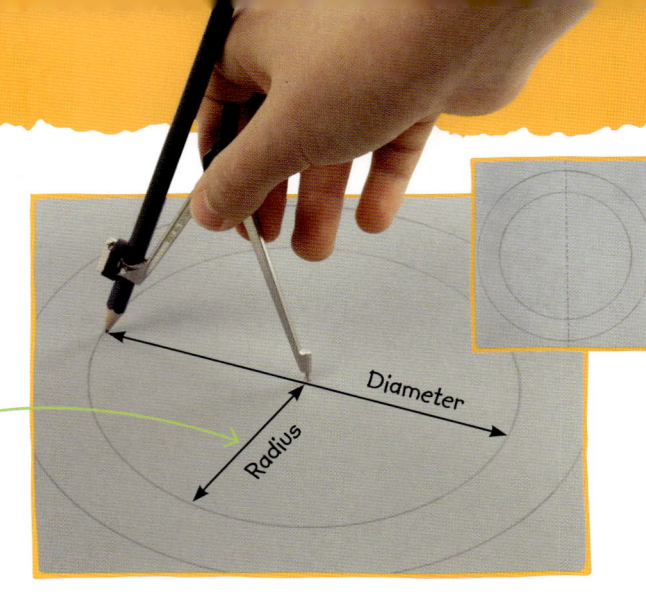

The radius of a circle is half the diameter.

1 Draw a circle with a radius of 10 cm (4 in) on a piece of card. Use the same centre point and draw a smaller circle with a radius of 7.5 cm (3 in) inside it. Then draw a faint line through the centre.

Time: 90 minutes
Difficulty: Medium

WHAT YOU NEED

Ruler, Protractor, Compass and pencil, Scissors, Red wool, Paper glue, Adhesive putty, Coloured feathers, 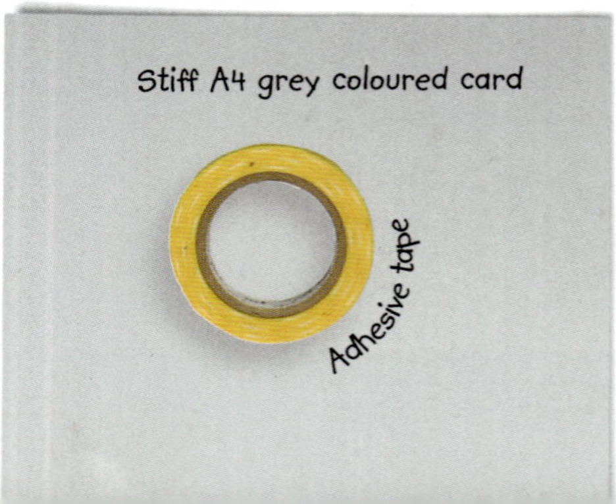 Stiff A4 grey coloured card, Adhesive tape, Beads and stickers or glitter to decorate

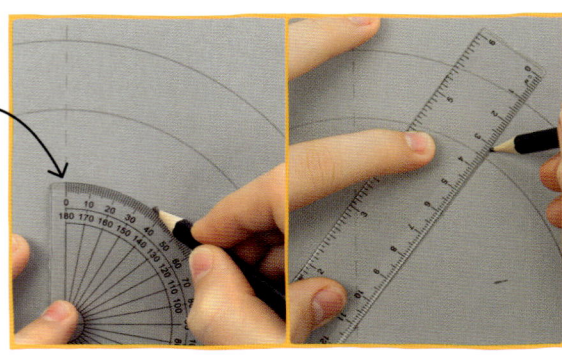

Place the 0° line along the centre line.

2 Use a protractor to mark out 10 segments of 36°. Draw a line connecting each mark with the centre and the smaller circle so that you have something that looks like the spokes of a wheel.

FULL CIRCLE

Angles are measured in degrees (°). There are 360° in a full circle, 180° in a half circle, and 90° in a quarter of a circle.

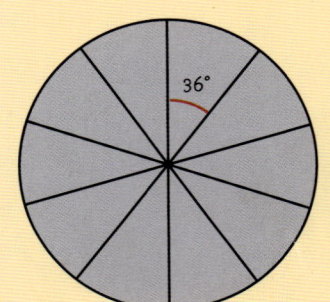

When a circle is divided into 10 equal parts, each segment is 36°.

DREAMCATCHER   35

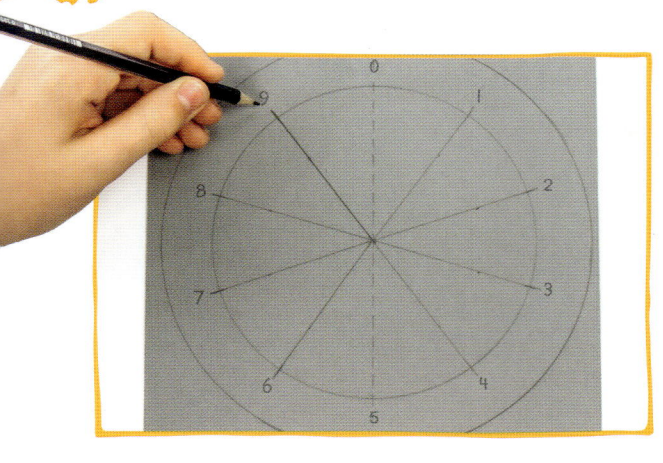

3 Write numbers 0 to 9 above the "spokes" you have drawn. Start with 0 at the top and work your way clockwise around the circle.

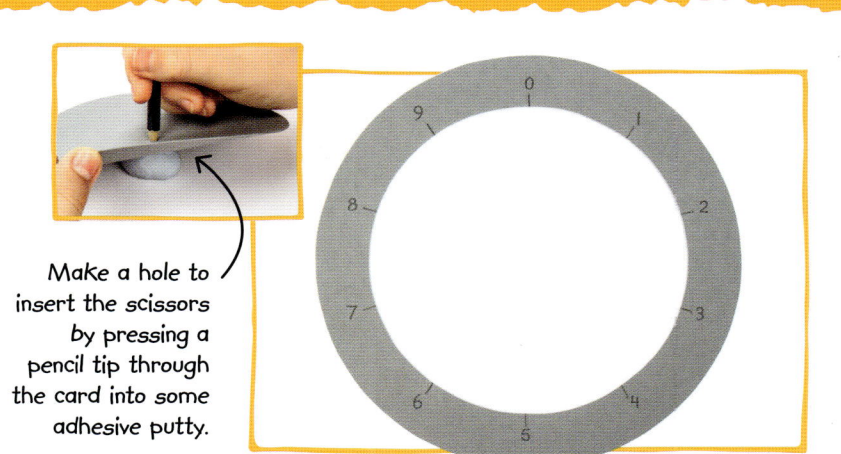

Make a hole to insert the scissors by pressing a pencil tip through the card into some adhesive putty.

4 With scissors, carefully cut out the outer circle and then the inner circle. Repeat steps 1 and 4 only to make a second card circle, needed in step 10.

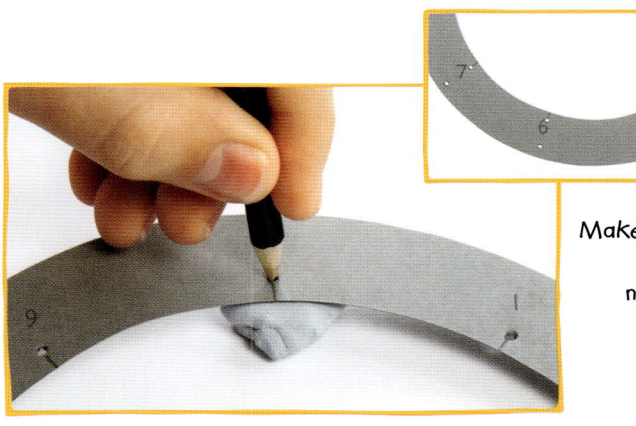

Make extra holes underneath numbers 4, 5, 6, and 7.

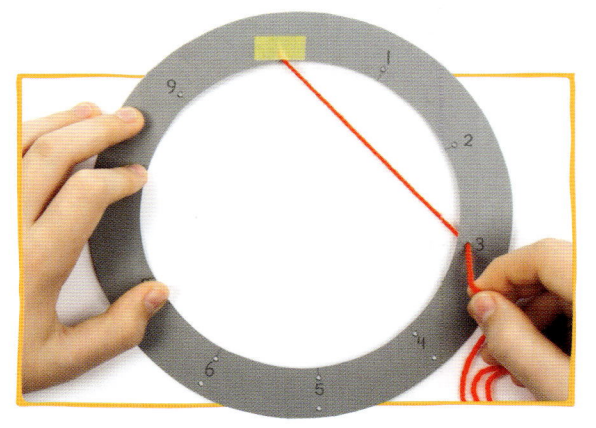

5 Use a pencil and adhesive putty to punch holes by each number, 0.5 cm (¼ in) from the inner rim. Make four extra holes at the bottom of the circle and one at the top between 0 and 1.

This hole will be used to hang up your dreamcatcher.

6 Thread wool through the underside of the hole next to the 0 and attach it with adhesive tape. This dreamcatcher is based on the three times table, so pull the wool across the circle to number 3 and thread it through the hole.

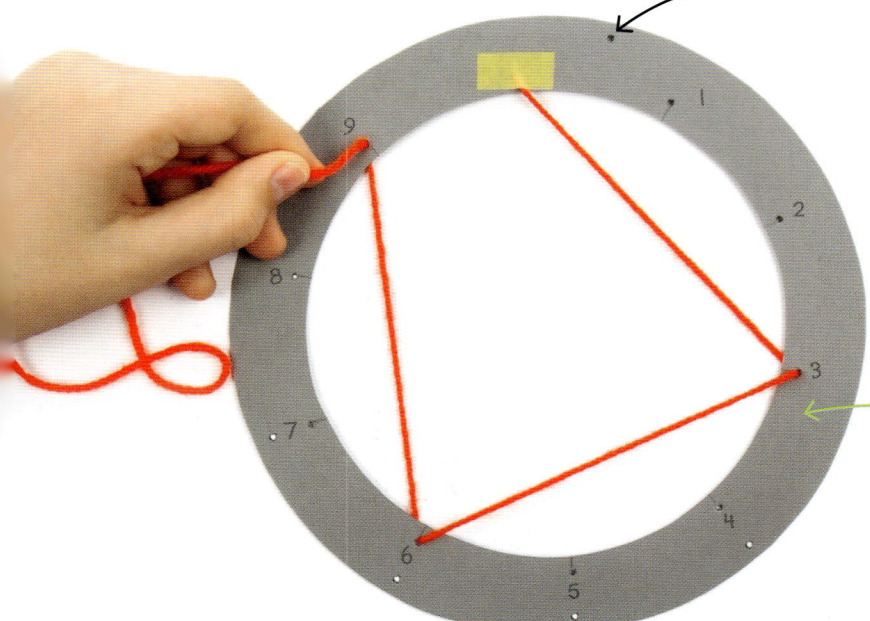

7 Multiply 3 by 2 to work out the next number in the pattern. The answer is 6, so feed the wool from number 3 to number 6 and thread it through. Next, work out 3 times 3 and feed the wool from number 6 across to number 9.

Use the three times table to work out which hole to feed the wool through next.

36 NUMBERS

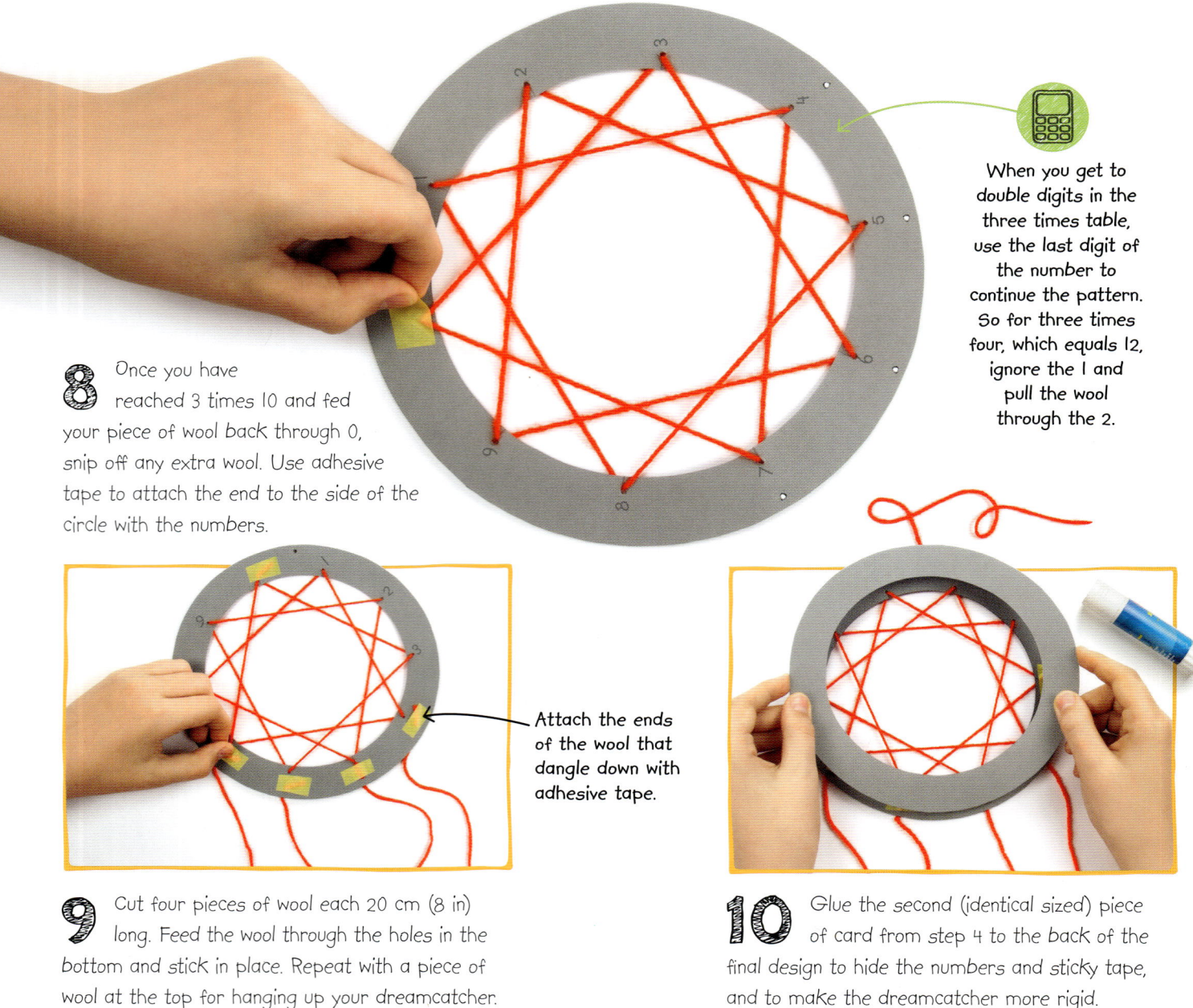

When you get to double digits in the three times table, use the last digit of the number to continue the pattern. So for three times four, which equals 12, ignore the 1 and pull the wool through the 2.

8 Once you have reached 3 times 10 and fed your piece of wool back through 0, snip off any extra wool. Use adhesive tape to attach the end to the side of the circle with the numbers.

Attach the ends of the wool that dangle down with adhesive tape.

9 Cut four pieces of wool each 20 cm (8 in) long. Feed the wool through the holes in the bottom and stick in place. Repeat with a piece of wool at the top for hanging up your dreamcatcher.

10 Glue the second (identical sized) piece of card from step 4 to the back of the final design to hide the numbers and sticky tape, and to make the dreamcatcher more rigid.

11 Thread beads onto each of the four dangling pieces of wool and tie a knot below the last one so that they don't fall off. Push feathers into the bead holes, packing them in tightly so they are secure. Cut off any excess wool.

DREAMCATCHER   37

PATTERN WEAVING

Try using different times tables to see what patterns you weave. You could even try combining times tables using different coloured wool.

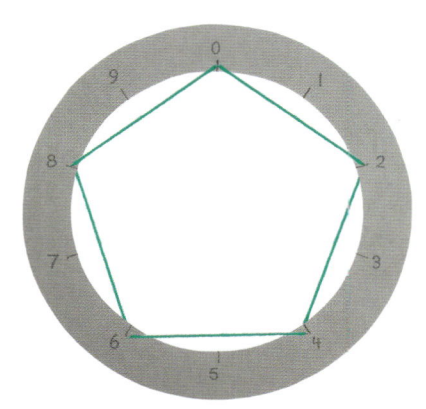

Two times table

Four times table

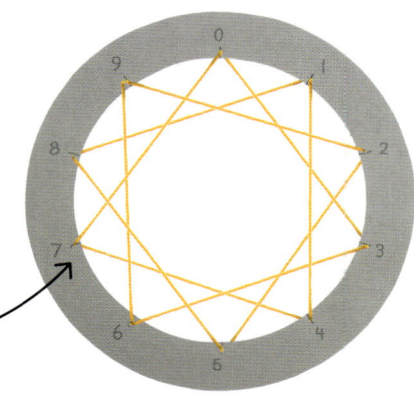

Seven times table

12 Decorate your dreamcatcher with stickers, glitter, or paint and then it is ready to hang up!

Vibrant feathers add colour to your dreamcatcher.

Some times tables will have the same patterns as others. This one matches the three times table.

FRACTIONS FEAST
BAKE AND SHARE A PIZZA

If you are having friends over for tea, why not make them some yummy pizza to share. As you make the dough and the sauce, you will learn how to measure out ingredients, and once your pizza is ready, fractions will help you to work out how much pizza each of your friends will get. Enjoy!

Divide your pizza into equal slices or there may be trouble!

MATHS YOU WILL USE
- MEASUREMENT to get the proportions of ingredients right.
- FRACTIONS to divide your pizza equally between friends.

HOW TO BAKE AND SHARE A PIZZA

Making a pizza is a great way to understand fractions, as you will need to divide up a whole pizza into equal parts so there's some for everyone. This recipe will make enough for two pizzas and you can add toppings of your choice.

Time
30 minutes plus 60 minutes of resting time

Difficulty
Easy

Warning
Hot stuff! Adult supervision required.

FOR TWO PIZZAS YOU NEED

- 450 g (16 oz) strong white bread flour
- 275 ml (9 fl oz) water
- Sugar
- Dried yeast
- Salt
- Two balls of mozzarella
- Red wine vinegar
- Garlic
- Dried basil
- Other toppings of your choice
- Tablespoon and teaspoon
- Fresh basil (optional)
- Tea towel
- 400 g (14 oz) tin of plum tomatoes
- Weighing scales
- Mixing bowl
- Pizza baking tray
- Blender
- Rolling pin

1 Mix 450 g (16 oz) of strong white bread flour with a teaspoon each of salt, sugar, and dried yeast. Make a well in the middle of the mixture and pour in 275 ml (9 fl oz) of water.

2 Use a spoon to stir the water into the flour. When a ball of dough starts to form, use slightly damp hands to bring the mixture together.

3 Sprinkle flour onto your work surface to prevent sticking. Take the ball of dough and start to knead it by pushing and stretching it until it is smooth and less sticky.

40 NUMBERS

5 While the dough is resting, make the tomato sauce. Pour the 400 g (14 oz) tin of tomatoes into a blender. Add a pinch of salt, some pepper and dried basil, the clove of garlic, and a tablespoon of red wine vinegar. Ask an adult to help you whizz the ingredients to form a smooth sauce.

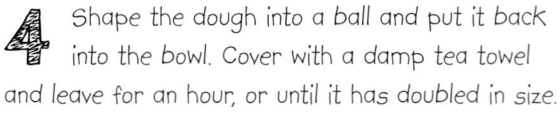

When the dough expands, its volume is increasing.

4 Shape the dough into a ball and put it back into the bowl. Cover with a damp tea towel and leave for an hour, or until it has doubled in size.

There is no need to slice your clove of garlic. Just peel it.

6 Remove the tea towel and knock the air out of the dough by punching it lightly. Tip it out of the bowl and give it a final knead. Split the dough into two equal-sized pieces.

FRACTIONS
A fraction is a portion of something larger. Here, the two balls of dough that you split apart are both fractions – halves – of the larger ball. If you split the ball into three, they would be thirds.

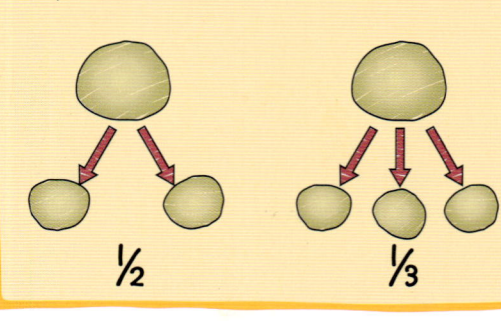

½   ⅓

Temperature is measured in different units, Celsius or Fahrenheit, in different parts of the world.

7 Preheat the oven to 220°C (430°F/Gas 7). Lightly dust your work surface with flour and then roll each piece of dough into a circular shape.

BAKE AND SHARE A PIZZA   41

8 Lift your dough onto the baking tray. Fold the edges over if it is too big – this will make a nice crust. Spread half your sauce over the dough.

9 Tear one ball of mozzarella into pieces and scatter it over the pizza. You can add any other toppings you want, such as onions, peppers, or salami. Repeat to make a second pizza. Ask an adult to put the pizza into the oven and bake for 10–15 minutes.

10 When the cheese is bubbling and golden, take the pizza out. Ask an adult to help you as the oven will be hot. Wait for the pizza to cool down a bit. Divide it up and enjoy!

You could divide your pizza into two halves by putting one topping on half of its surface and another topping on the other half.

DIVIDING UP YOUR PIZZA

Sharing a pizza equally between friends is a useful way to understand how fractions work.

1 If there are three of you sharing a pizza and you each want one slice, the pizza needs to be divided into three equal parts. One divided by three is $\frac{1}{3}$, so split the pizza into thirds.

$$1 \div 3 = \frac{1}{3}$$

2 If three more friends turn up and you all want one slice, then you'll need to divide the pizza into six equal parts. One divided by six is $\frac{1}{6}$, so cut the pizza into sixths. The larger the bottom number of the fraction, the smaller each slice of pizza will be.

$$1 \div 6 = \frac{1}{6}$$

Garnish your pizza with fresh basil if you like.

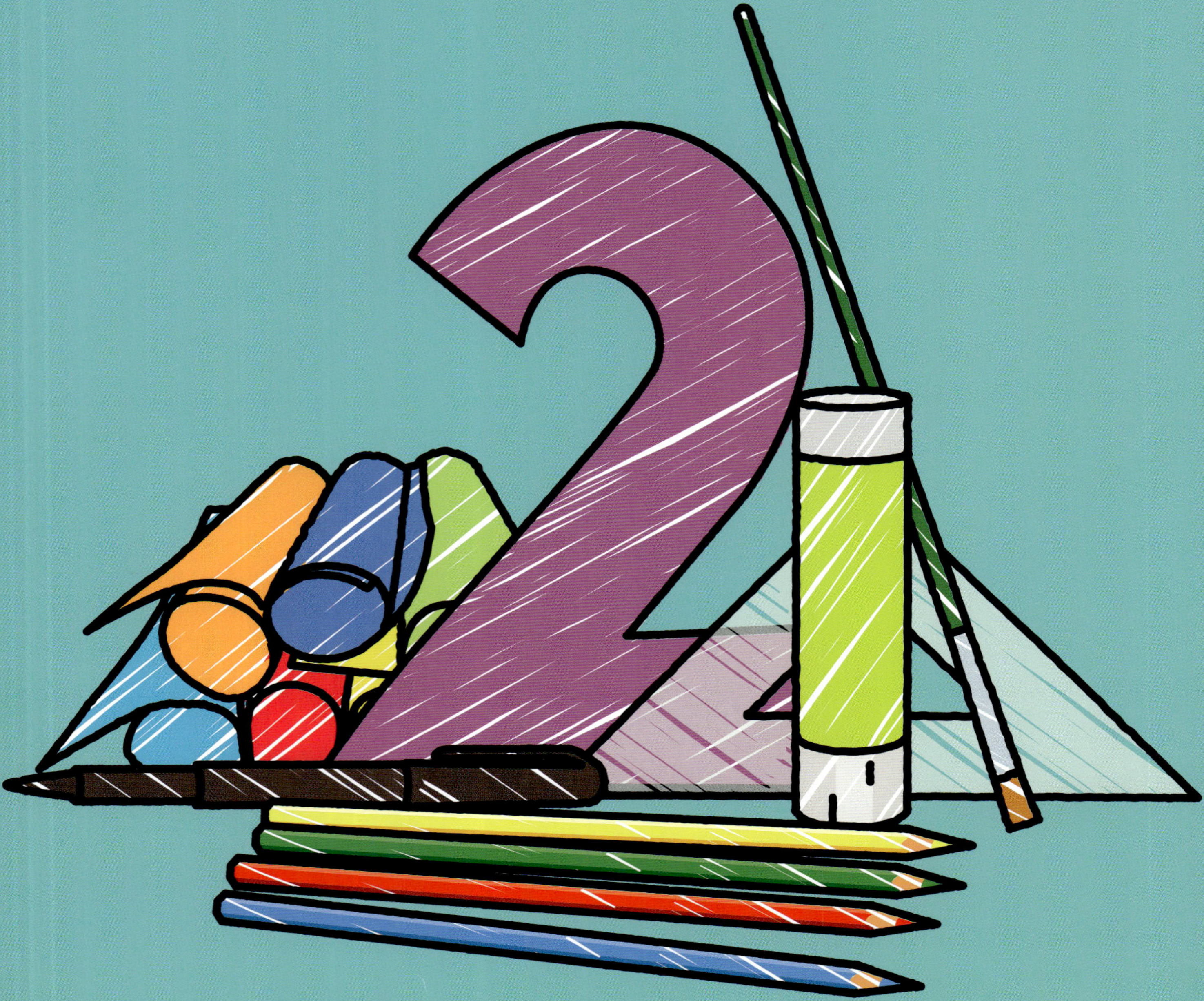

SHAPES

Shapes are like mathematical building blocks that you can use to create all sorts of fantastic things. By making the picture ball project in this chapter, you'll see how 2D shapes can be put together to create 3D objects. You'll also learn how to print repeating patterns and experiment with tessellation to create amazing artworks. Plus you'll have fun exploring how folded shapes can make an origami frog leap and pop-up cards spring to life.

MIRROR IMAGES
SYMMETRICAL PICTURES

Our eyes find images that are symmetrical – with two halves that reflect each other – appealing and attractive, and in this project you're going to make two symmetrical pictures two different ways. You'll also learn how to use coordinates on a grid to structure your art.

← This central line is the key to making a symmetrical painting.

You can use coordinates to make the reflection super precise.

46   SHAPES

HOW TO CREATE SYMMETRICAL PICTURES

There are two artworks to create here, both of which use reflective symmetry. For the first you'll need lots of colourful paint. The second is a little trickier and you'll need to draw a grid first, or you can use squared paper if you have some.

MATHS YOU WILL USE
- REFLECTIVE SYMMETRY so each side of your artwork mirrors the other.
- COORDINATES to make your drawing perfectly symmetrical.
- VERTICES to pinpoint the areas that should reflect on both sides of your drawing.

Time 120 minutes
Difficulty Medium

WHAT YOU NEED

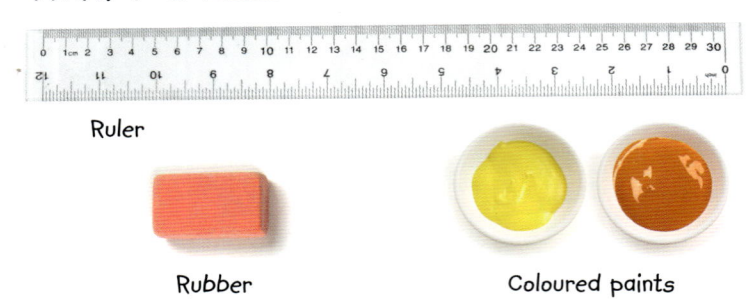

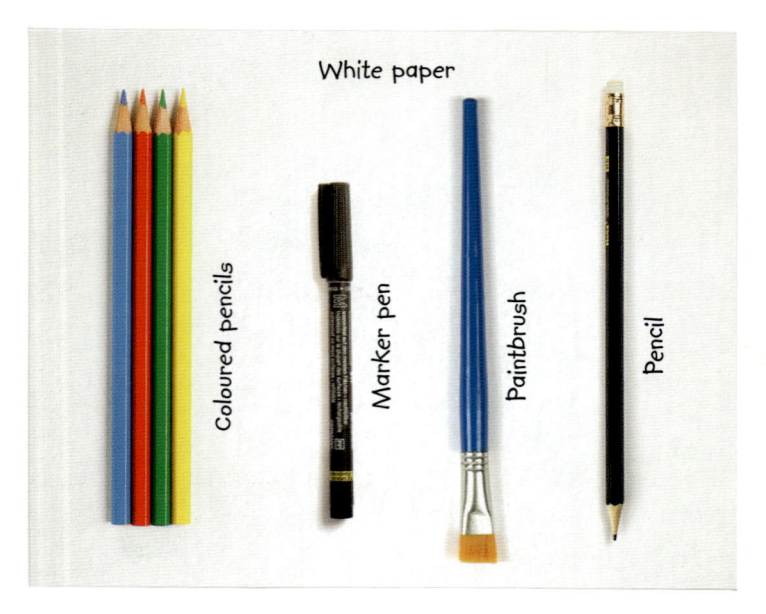

Ruler

Rubber

Coloured paints

White paper

Coloured pencils

Marker pen

Paintbrush

Pencil

PROJECT 1

1 Fold a piece of paper in half and open it up again. Use a pencil and ruler to draw a dotted line vertically down the centre of the page.

2 On one side of the folded paper, draw one half of a butterfly lightly in pencil.

SYMMETRICAL PICTURES   47

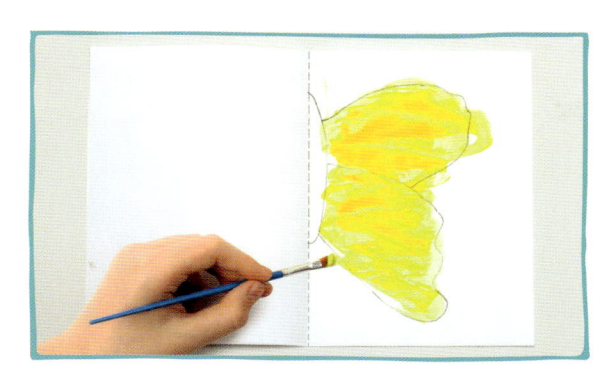

3 Place a spare piece of paper under your drawing then colour in the outline of your butterfly with paint. Use plenty of paint so it will transfer to the other side when you fold the paper.

A line of symmetry is also called an axis of symmetry or a mirror line.

4 Fold the paper in half and press down on it. Open the paper up and you will see that the butterfly has transferred onto the opposite side of the page, creating a symmetrical image.

5 Repeat step 3, using more colour to add detail to your design. Then fold and press the paper again to transfer the paint across to the other side.

REFLECTIVE SYMMETRY
A shape has reflective symmetry if drawing a line through it would divide it into two identical halves that perfectly mirror each other. This line, called the line of symmetry, can go in any direction, not just up and down or left and right. Some shapes may have several lines of symmetry, while others may have none.

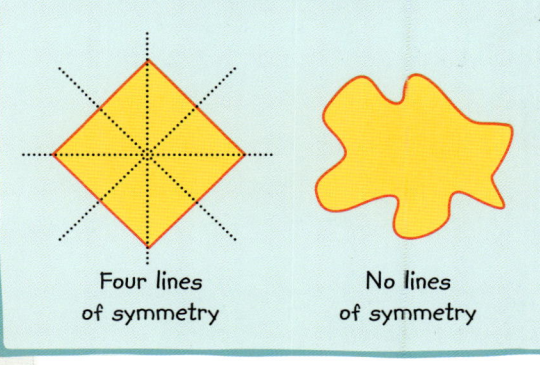

Four lines of symmetry

No lines of symmetry

6 Open up the paper again and you'll see this extra detail reflected on the other side of the fold.

This butterfly has one axis of symmetry.

48 SHAPES

PROJECT 2

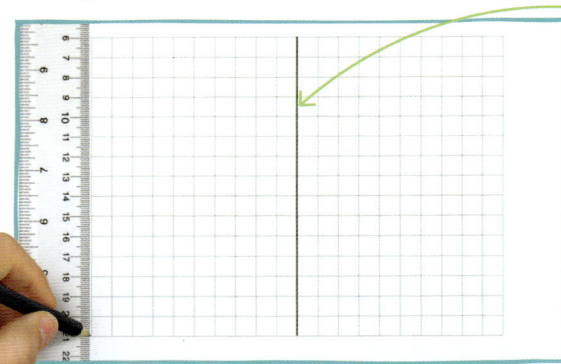

1 With a pencil, draw a rectangle 20 × 15 cm (8 × 6 in) on a piece of paper. Mark every 1 cm (½ in) along each side and connect the lines to make a grid. Draw a thicker line down the centre of your grid.

This vertical line is the y-axis of your grid and will be the line of symmetry.

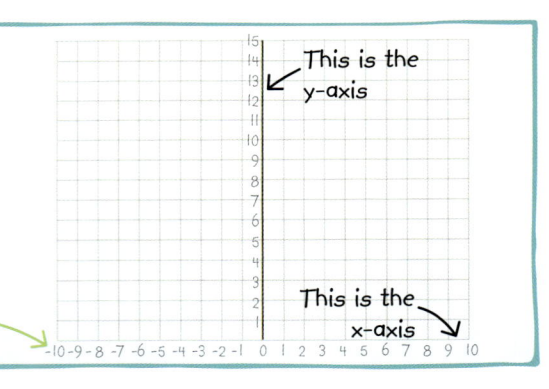

2 Starting from the left and working your way to the right, begin numbering grid lines along the x-axis, starting from -10, until your reach 10. Then number the y-axis up to number 15.

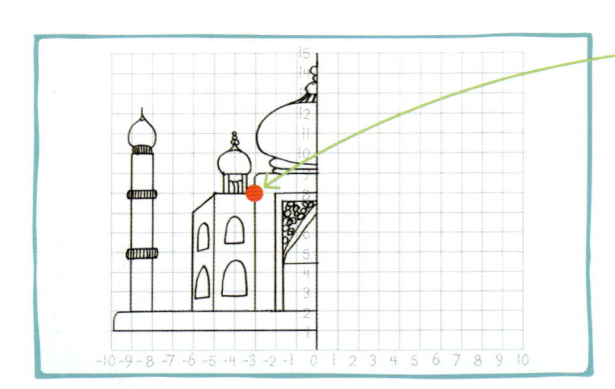

This is the y-axis
This is the x-axis

Numbers to the left of the zero are negative.

3 On the left-hand side of the y-axis, draw one half of a building. Follow the grid where you can. You will use grid numbers to work out coordinates for each point the lines meet. This is called a vertex.

The coordinates of this vertex are (-3,8).

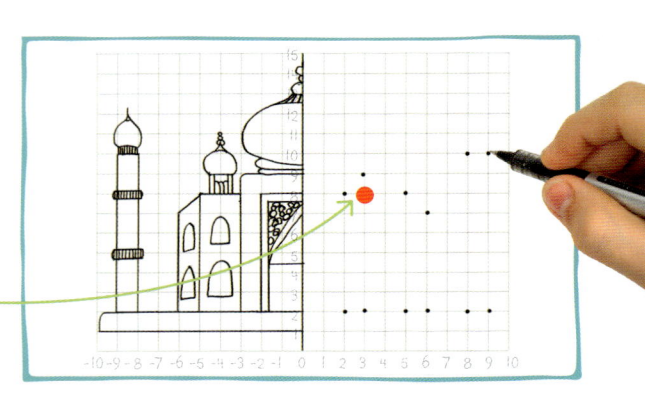

A coordinate with a negative number of -3 becomes 3 when it is plotted in the mirror line.

4 To work out where to draw the reflection of each vertex, convert the first part of each coordinate from a negative to a positive number. Plot these coordinates on the other side of the y-axis.

COORDINATES

The numbers that are used to identify the exact position of something on a grid or map are called coordinates. They are written in brackets, with the first number referring to the x-axis and the second, to the y-axis. A comma always separates the two numbers.

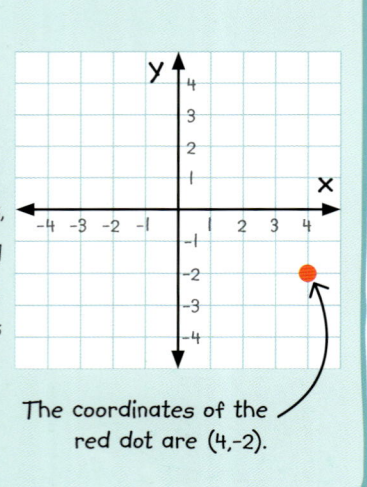

The coordinates of the red dot are (4,-2).

5 Use a pencil to draw lines connecting the vertices and then fill in any additional detail. Once you are happy with your picture, go over the pencil lines in black marker pen.

SYMMETRICAL PICTURES   49

This square is light green on the left of the y-axis so it has to be light green on the right of it, too.

6 Colour in the left-hand side of the picture using different coloured pencils or pens. You can create interesting patterns by using two tones of the same colour, such as light and dark green.

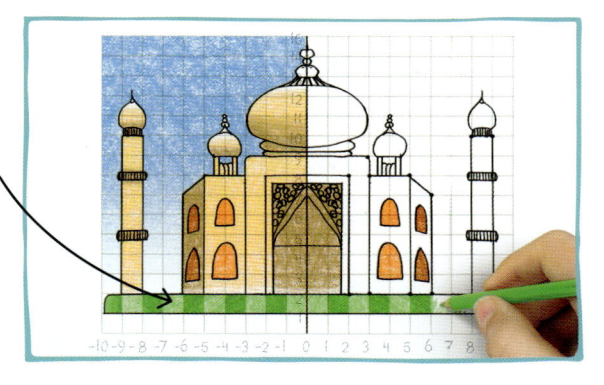

7 Next, carefully repeat the pattern to the right of the line of symmetry by colouring in the opposite squares. Use the coordinates to help you work out what colour should fill each square.

8 Repeat the process until you have coloured in the whole drawing. What other images do you think would make a good symmetrical picture?

REAL WORLD MATHS
SYMMETRY IN ARCHITECTURE

Symmetry is used in the design of buildings, not just to make them strong structures but because our eyes (and brains) find symmetrical things attractive. The structure of the Eiffel Tower in Paris, France, and the patterns of the metal crosses up its sides are both symmetrical.

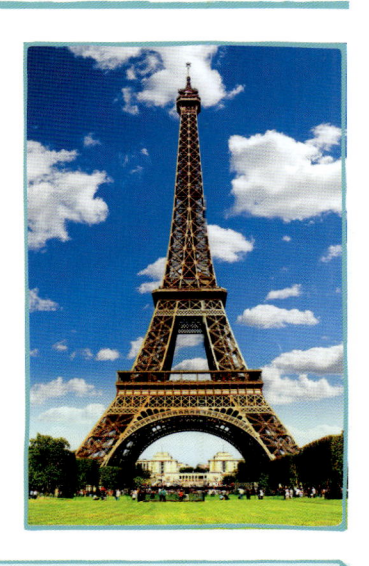

ROTATIONAL SYMMETRY

An object has rotational symmetry if it can be turned around a point called the centre of rotation and look exactly the same. The number of times an object can do this is called the order of rotational symmetry.

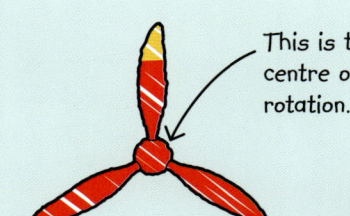

This is the centre of rotation.

1 To help show this propeller's order of rotational symmetry, we have marked the blade at the top of one of the propellers yellow.

2 Rotate the propeller until it matches the position in step 1. You'll see the yellow tip has moved around the central point.

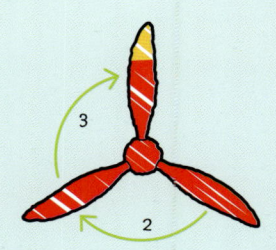

3 Rotate the shape until the yellow tip is back at the top. To do this, it will have repeated the position in step 1 three times, meaning it has a rotational symmetry of 3.

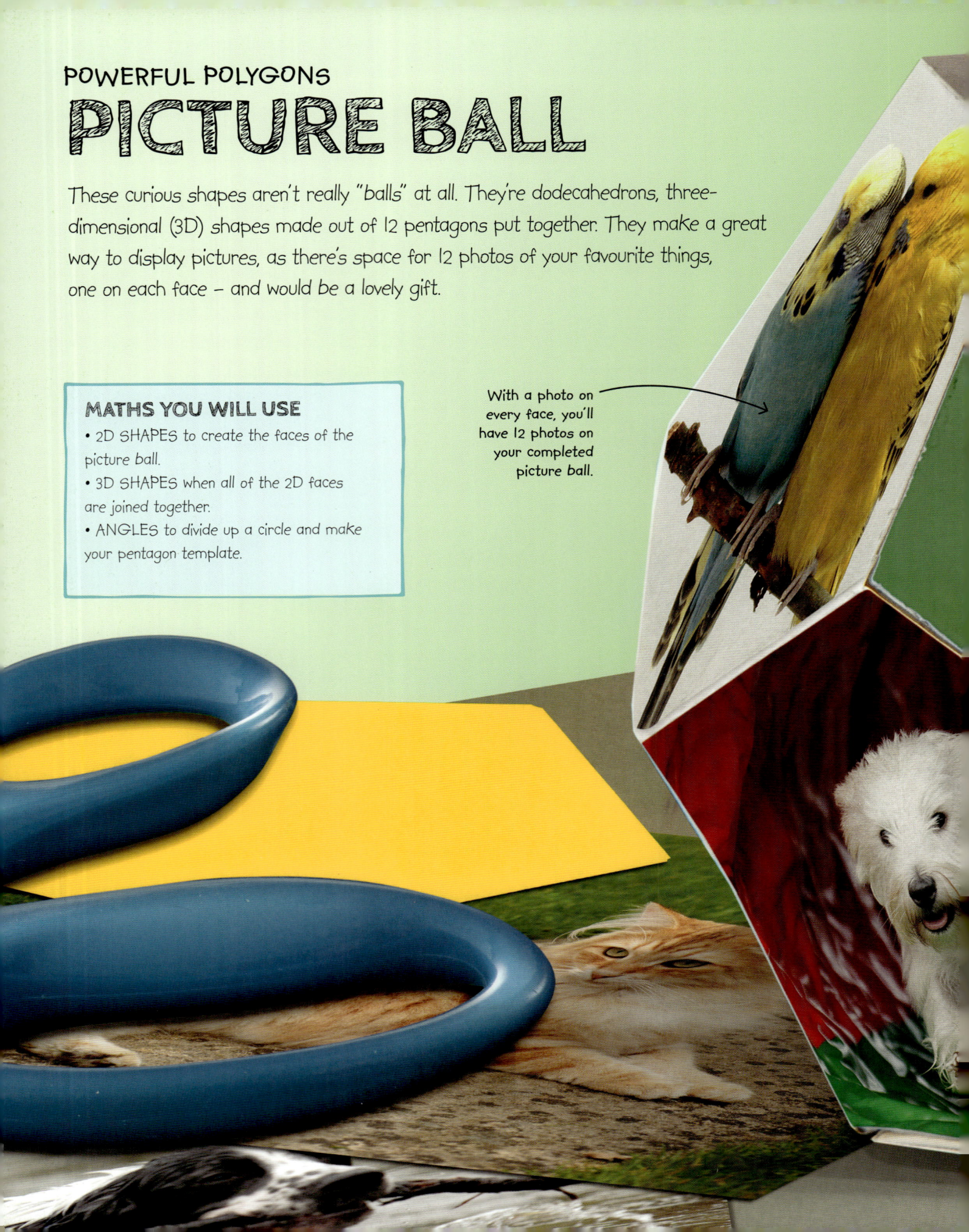

POWERFUL POLYGONS
PICTURE BALL

These curious shapes aren't really "balls" at all. They're dodecahedrons, three-dimensional (3D) shapes made out of 12 pentagons put together. They make a great way to display pictures, as there's space for 12 photos of your favourite things, one on each face – and would be a lovely gift.

MATHS YOU WILL USE
- 2D SHAPES to create the faces of the picture ball.
- 3D SHAPES when all of the 2D faces are joined together.
- ANGLES to divide up a circle and make your pentagon template.

With a photo on every face, you'll have 12 photos on your completed picture ball.

Each face is a flat shape, but they come together to make a 3D structure.

52 SHAPES

HOW TO MAKE A PICTURE BALL

You'll start this project by making a template. Be sure to measure it carefully, as it will affect the size of your final picture ball. Once you've made the 3D shape, you can decorate it with anything you want. Here, we've used pictures of pets, but they could be of holidays, hobbies, or whatever you like.

Time: 45 minutes
Difficulty: Medium

WHAT YOU NEED

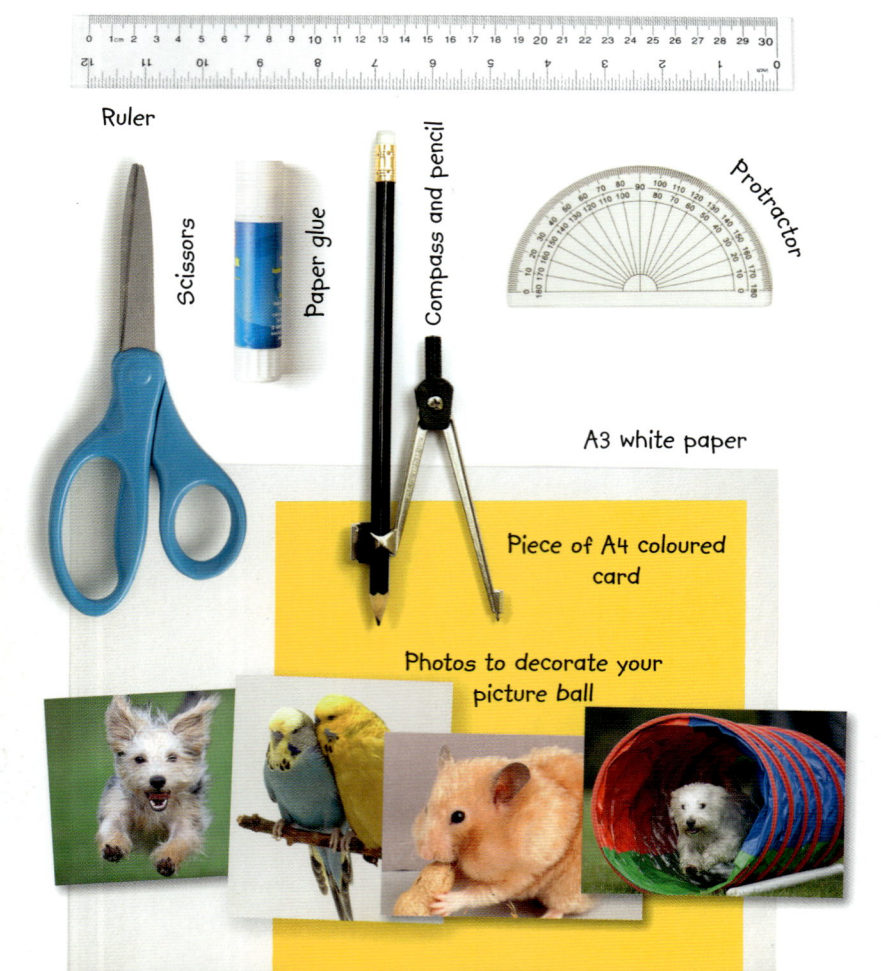

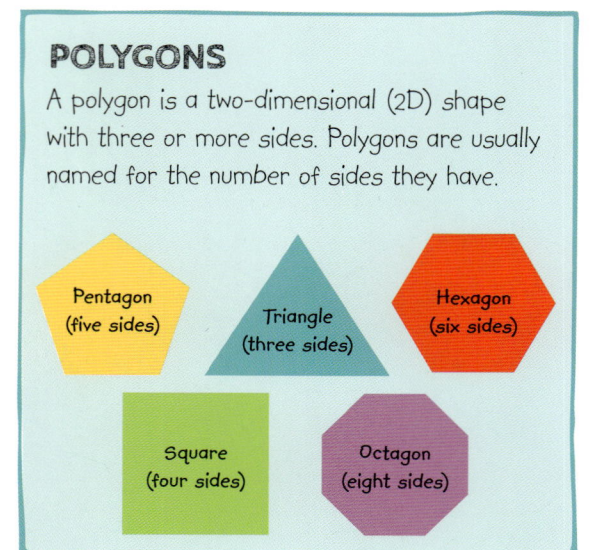

- Ruler
- Scissors
- Paper glue
- Compass and pencil
- Protractor
- A3 white paper
- Piece of A4 coloured card
- Photos to decorate your picture ball

The diameter cuts a circle in half through the middle. The radius runs from the edge of a circle to its centre.

1 Set your compass to 3 cm (1¼ in), and then use it to draw a circle on a piece of A4 card. The circle will have a radius of 3 cm (1¼ in) and a diameter of 6 cm (2½ in).

360 divided by five is 72, so making marks every 72° gives a five-sided shape.

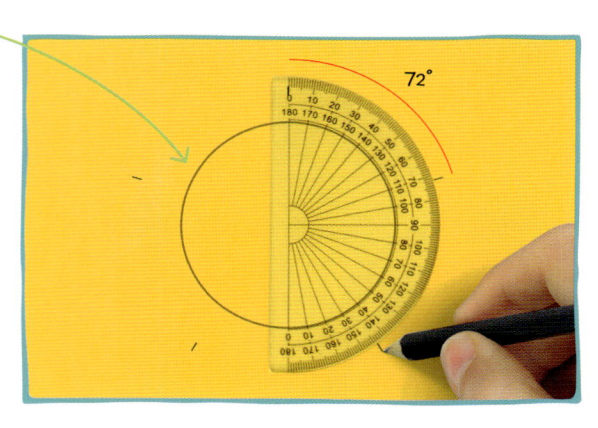

2 Place your protractor in the centre of the circle. Starting from the top of the circle, make a mark at 0°, 72°, 144°, 216°, and 288°. You will need to rotate your protractor.

POLYGONS

A polygon is a two-dimensional (2D) shape with three or more sides. Polygons are usually named for the number of sides they have.

- Pentagon (five sides)
- Triangle (three sides)
- Hexagon (six sides)
- Square (four sides)
- Octagon (eight sides)

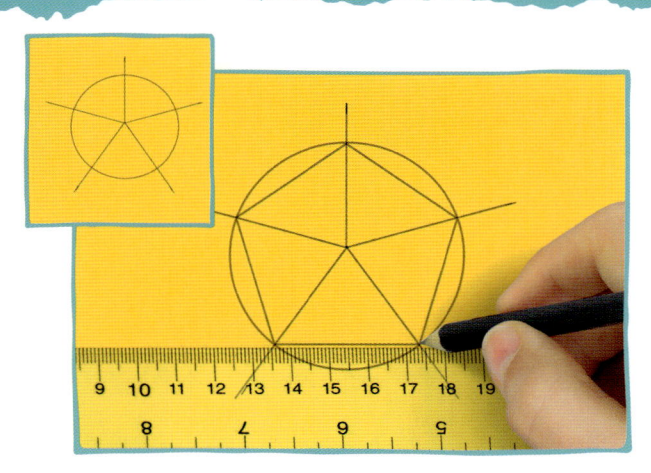

PICTURE BALL   53

3 Use a ruler to draw lines connecting the five pencil marks you just made to the centre of the circle. Draw straight lines between the points where each line meets the circle to create a pentagon.

After cutting out the pentagon, flip it over so the pencil lines don't distract you.

4 Carefully cut out the pentagon using scissors. This will be the template for making your picture ball, so take extra care to make sure the sides are nice and straight.

5 Place the pentagon on the left-hand side of an A3 sheet of paper, making sure you have at least 8 cm (3 in) surrounding it on all sides, then draw around its edges with a pencil and number it 1.

Numbering the pentagons will make it easier to follow later instructions.

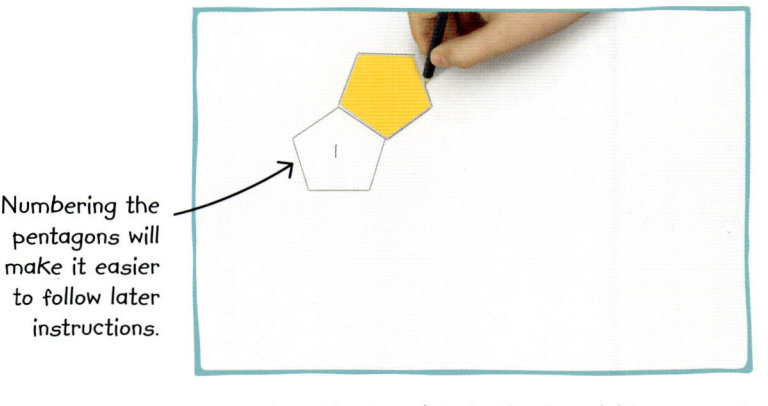

6 Move the template to the top-right corner of the outline you just drew, trace around it, and number it 2. The bottom left of the second pentagon should align with the top right of the first one.

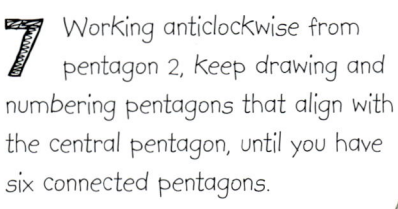

7 Working anticlockwise from pentagon 2, keep drawing and numbering pentagons that align with the central pentagon, until you have six connected pentagons.

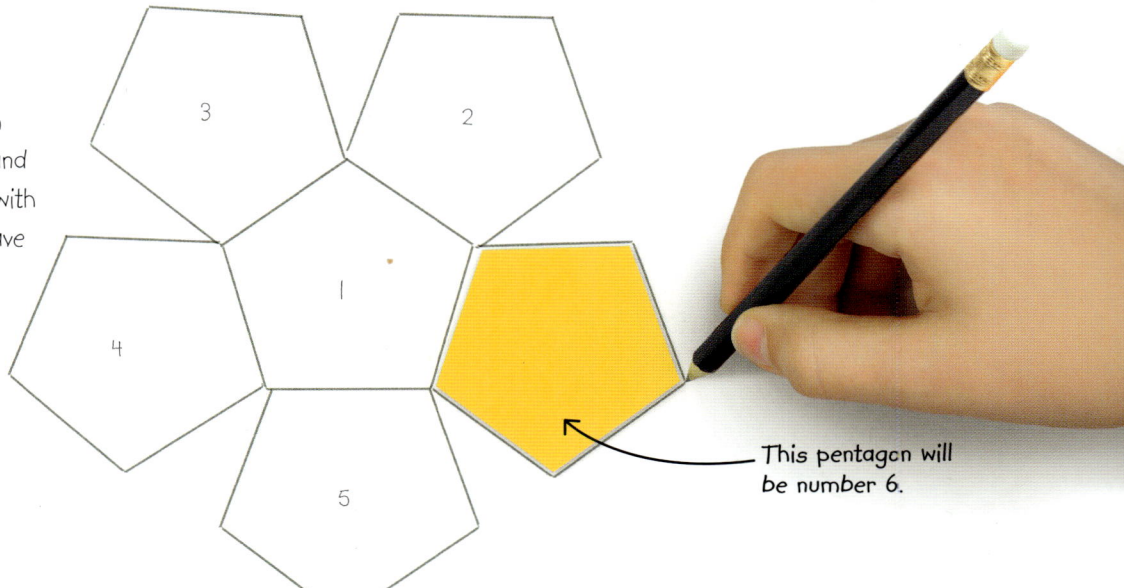

This pentagon will be number 6.

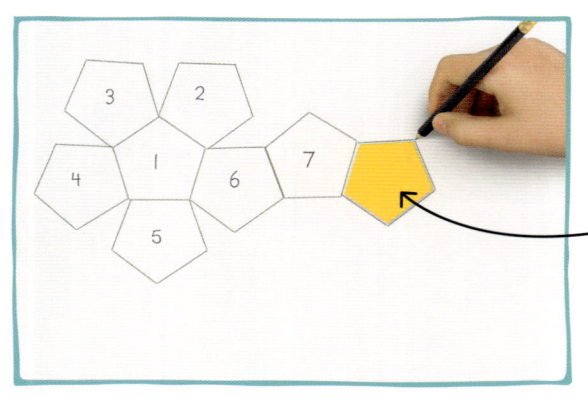

54   SHAPES

This will be pentagon number 8.

POLYHEDRONS
3D shapes with faces made from polygons are called polyhedrons. The five polyhedrons below are known as regular polyhedrons because their faces are all the same size and shape.

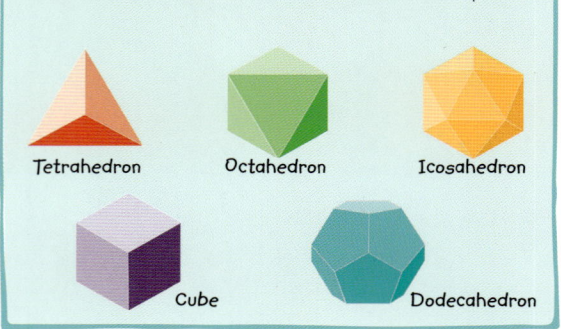

Tetrahedron   Octahedron   Icosahedron

Cube   Dodecahedron

8 Extend the pattern by drawing a new pentagon (number 7), aligning with the right-hand edge of pentagon 6. Then draw a second pentagon (8), connecting to the right-hand edge of pentagon 7.

This will be pentagon number 12.

9 Draw four more pentagons around pentagon 8, numbering as you go. You should get a shape mirroring the one you completed in step 7.

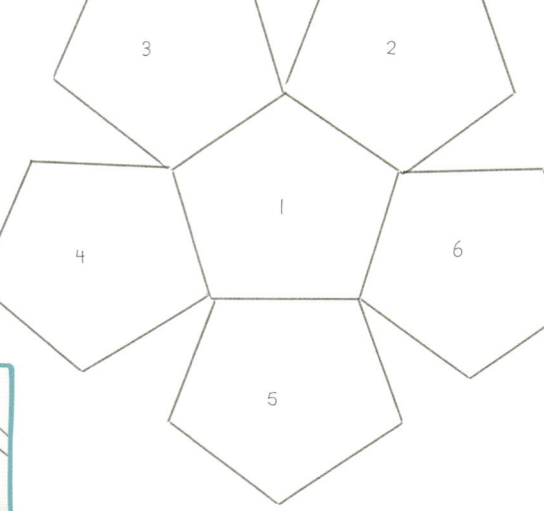

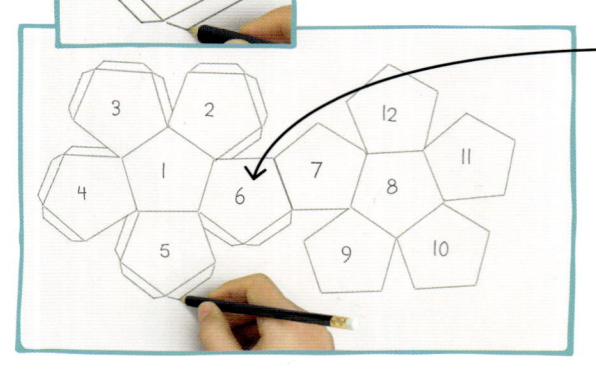

This pentagon will only have space for two tabs.

When folded together, this net of polygons will form a dodecahedron, a polyhedron with 12 faces.

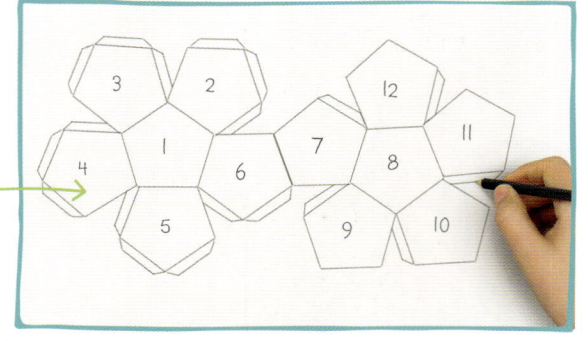

10 Draw a 0.5 cm (¼ in) high tab on the bottom-right side of pentagon 2. Then, working anticlockwise, continue adding tabs to each side of pentagons 2–6, skipping every fourth tab.

11 Draw a single tab on the top-right side of pentagon 7. Working clockwise, skip three sides and then draw a tab on the bottom-right side of pentagon 12. Repeat until you reach pentagon 9.

PICTURE BALL   55

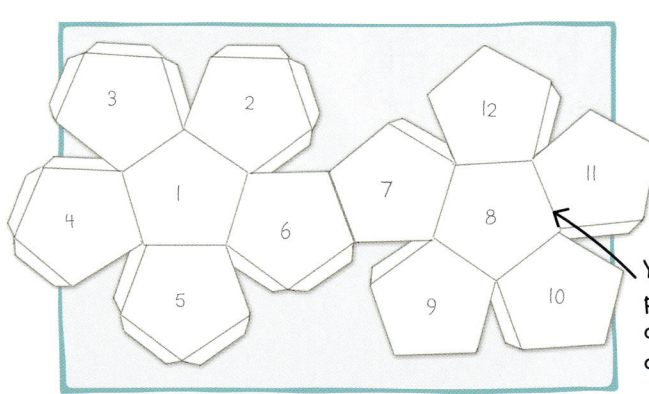

You can use the point of a pencil and a ruler to score along the fold lines.

12 Cut around the entire shape, making sure you don't cut through the middle. Score along all of the pencil lines so they fold neatly.

13 Flip your pattern over so the pencil lines are not visible. Use the pentagon template to cut out printouts of your pets or family and stick one picture onto each of the faces.

15 Fold along all other scored lines to bring the shape together, then press firmly to stick the tabs underneath each pentagon.

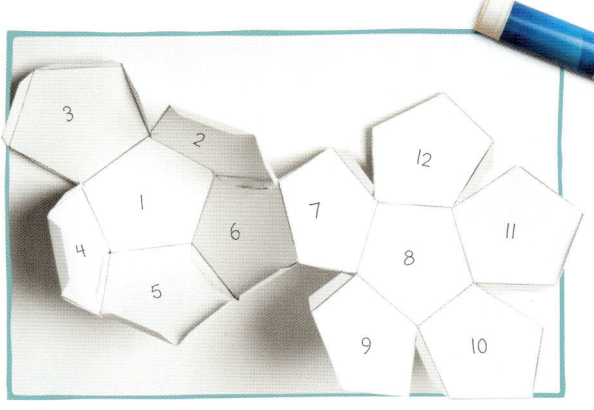

Each face should stick onto the tabs on the face below.

14 Flip the pattern over again and fold and crease along the scored lines so the tabs bend easily. Then apply paper glue to each tab.

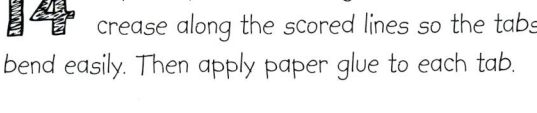

REAL WORLD MATHS
FOOTBALL

A ball is a sphere, a circular 3D shape with one face. However, footballs are made out of two different types of polygon – five-sided pentagons and six-sided hexagons – stitched together to make a single, smooth face.

PAPER PACKAGING
WRAPPING PAPER AND GIFT BAG

Everyone loves receiving presents in gift wrap or a party bag to take home, and these homemade prints are sure to impress your friends. Artists often use mathematical sequences to create their designs, and you can do the same by decorating your wrapping paper with a repeating pattern.

Why not make a matching gift tag too?

Create a great gift bag and fill it with your friend's favourite treats.

MATHS YOU WILL USE

- REPEATING PATTERNS to decorate your wrapping paper and gift bag.
- ANGLES to make sure you fold your gift bag precisely.
- MEASUREMENT to work out the shape and size of your gift wrap, bag, and handles.

WRAPPING PAPER AND GIFT BAG 57

HOW TO BLOCK PRINT PAPER

To print the pattern on your gift wrap, this project uses a potato as a stamp. We have used a fish to make our pattern, but you can choose any shape you like. Be sure you have plenty of paper because it's fun to use some to make gift bags.

Time 90 minutes
Difficulty Medium
Warning Sharp Knife! Adult supervision required

WHAT YOU NEED

- Ruler
- Pencil
- Set square
- Blue and green acrylic paint
- Scissors
- Adhesive tape
- Chopping board
- Kitchen knife
- Butter knife
- Potatoes
- Paper glue
- Paintbrush
- Felt-tip pen
- Roll or large sheet of brown paper
- White paper
- A4 red card

MAKE WRAPPING PAPER

1 Ask an adult to cut a raw potato in half using a kitchen knife and a chopping board.

2 Draw a fish shape with a pen on some paper and cut it out. Place the fish on the potato and ask an adult to help you make cuts 0.5 cm (¼ in) deep roughly around the template. Then cut around the edge of the template to the same depth. You may find it easier to do this by drawing round the template.

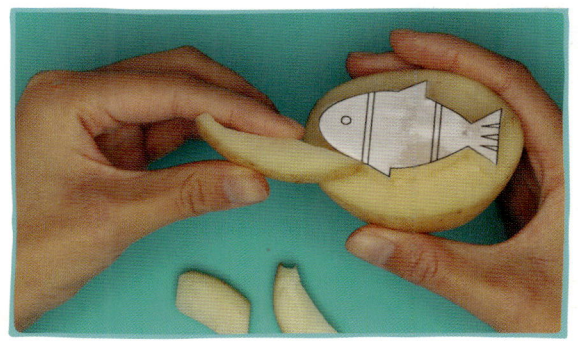

3 Prise off the loose potato with your fingers, leaving the shape of the fish. Repeat steps 1–3 to make a second fish, but facing the other way.

58   SHAPES

Use the lines as guides when moving your potatoes across the paper.

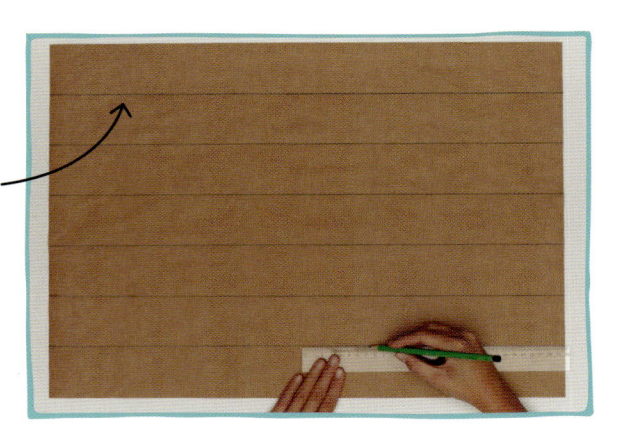

4. With a butter knife, cut some stripes into the body and tail. Use a pencil point to carve out eyes and complete your printing block.

5. Measure the height of your potato stamp. Then mark points the same height up the sides of the sheet of brown paper. Use a ruler to draw faint lines joining the marks across the sheet.

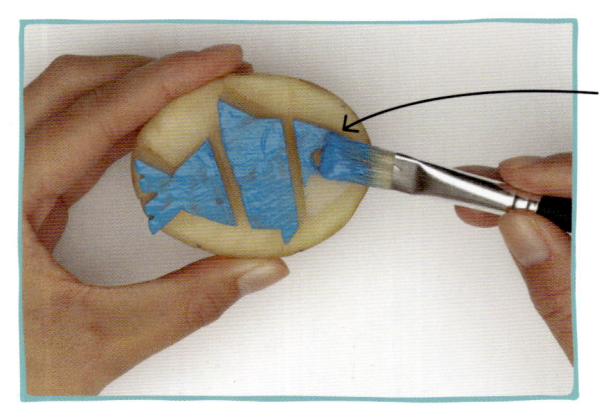

Don't put too much paint on the potato stamp or your design's details will not show through.

6. Mix some acrylic paint with a small amount of water. Brush paint onto your potato stamp. You will need more paint after printing every two fish or so.

7. Press the stamp onto the paper in the top left-hand corner, leaving an imprint. Continue printing until you have filled one line with blue fish.

Repeating patterns can work horizontally, vertically, or diagonally. They can also alternate every few lines, like this one does.

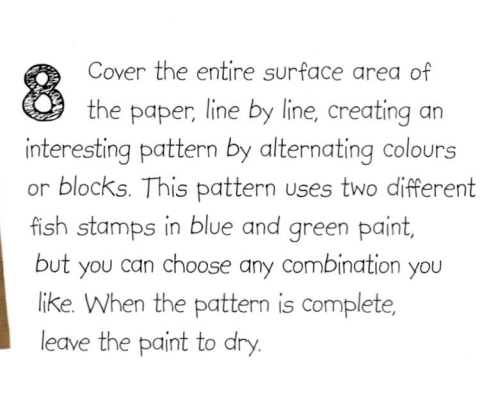

8. Cover the entire surface area of the paper, line by line, creating an interesting pattern by alternating colours or blocks. This pattern uses two different fish stamps in blue and green paint, but you can choose any combination you like. When the pattern is complete, leave the paint to dry.

WRAPPING PAPER AND GIFT BAG

MAKE A GIFT BAG

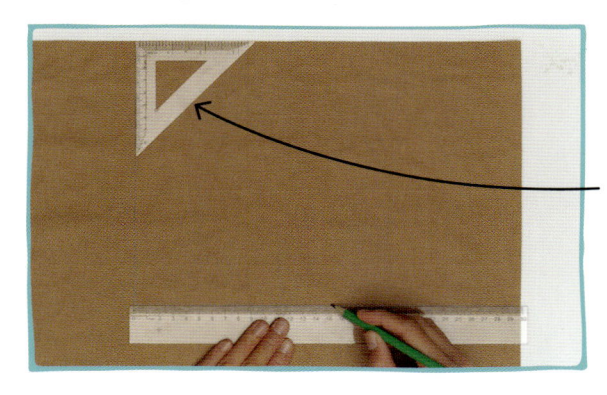

Use a set square to check the corners are at right angles. Then cut out the rectangle with scissors.

1 On the back of your wrapping paper, use a pencil and ruler to measure out a rectangle with a width of 21 cm (8¼ in) and a length of 30 cm (11¾ in). Cut out the rectangle with scissors.

REPEATING PATTERNS
Patterns that repeat follow a sequence over and over again. You can create repeating patterns with shapes, colours, or numbers.

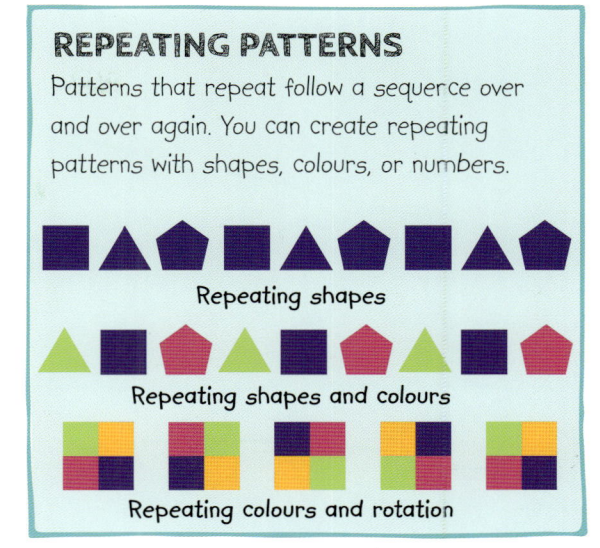

Repeating shapes

Repeating shapes and colours

Repeating colours and rotation

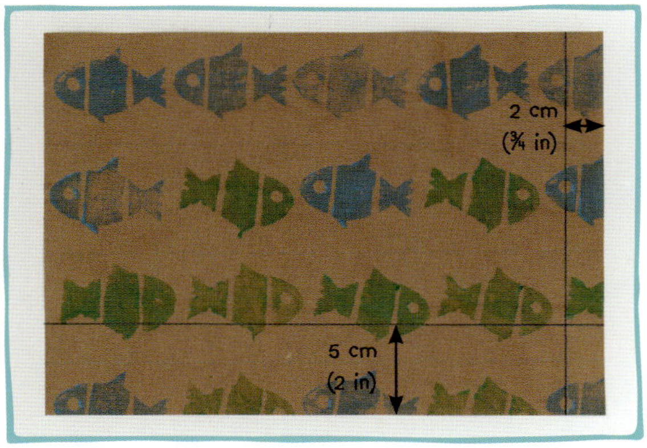

2 With a pencil, lightly draw a vertical line 2 cm (¾ in) in from the right-hand edge and a horizontal line 5 cm (2 in) in from the bottom.

Use the glue on the printed side of the tab to stick both sides of the sheet together.

3 Fold along the 2 cm (¾ in) line to create a tab, then turn the paper over. Glue the tab, then take the right-hand side of the paper, fold it over, and press firmly so it sticks to the tab.

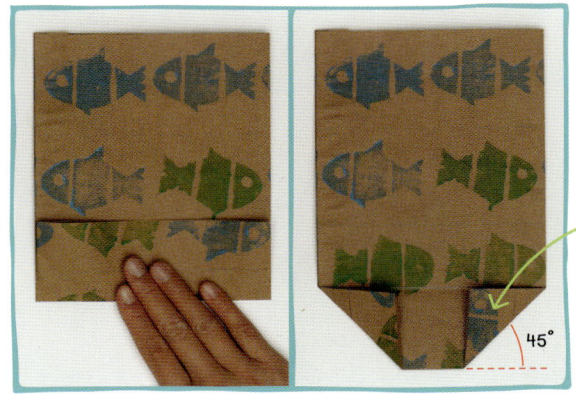

4 Fold along the 5 cm (2 in) line you drew in step 2, then flatten it out. Fold the bottom corners up to meet the pencil line and press the folds.

Fold the corners in at an angle of 45° to create a triangle shape on both sides.

5 Open up the bottom of the bag at the fold line and press the sides towards the centre. Flatten the edges to create two large triangle shapes.

60   SHAPES

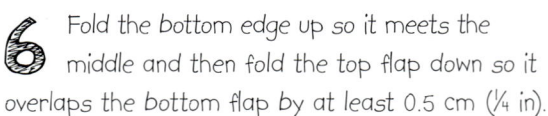

These 90° right angles are created by the folds.

Use adhesive tape along the centre to stick the two flaps down.

6 Fold the bottom edge up so it meets the middle and then fold the top flap down so it overlaps the bottom flap by at least 0.5 cm (¼ in).

7 Rotate the bag by 90° and fold the long sides inwards to create right angles in the left-hand corners. Crease along the folds, then unfold again.

The folds of the crease lines give the bag shape.

Mark the inside of the bag.

8 Open up the bag, place your hand inside, and carefully push the bottom of the bag out. Then crease along the folds you have made.

9 At the opening, use a pencil to mark 2 cm (¾ in) in from both edges of the longer sides. These marks are where the bag's handles will attach.

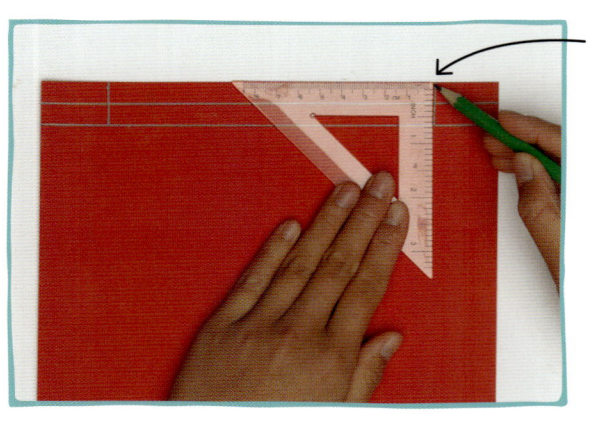

At the 3 cm (1¼ in) marks, use a set square to draw vertical lines at right angles to the horizontal lines already drawn.

Only add glue to one end before sticking to your bag.

10 To make the handles, measure and draw two 21 x 1 cm (8¼ x ½ in) strips on a piece of coloured card. Then draw a line across the rectangles 3 cm (1¼ in) in from each end.

11 Cut out the two rectangular strips of card and make a crease along the pencil lines to form tabs. Dab some paper glue onto one end of each of the tabs.

WRAPPING PAPER AND GIFT BAG   61

12 Place the glued end of one of the handles inside the bag where you made the pencil mark in step 9 and press it down firmly. Then twist the strip and glue the other end in position too. Turn the bag over and repeat with the other handle.

13 Turn the bag upright and fill it with treats to give to a friend. Why not make more bags and fill them with gifts to hand out at the end of a party.

The alternating fish pattern gives the gift bag a stylish look.

REAL WORLD MATHS
TEXTILE PRINTING

The process of transferring colour and pattern onto a piece of fabric is known as textile printing. Repeating patterns can be printed onto fabric using lots of different methods, including rollers, wooden blocks, stencils, or silkscreens.

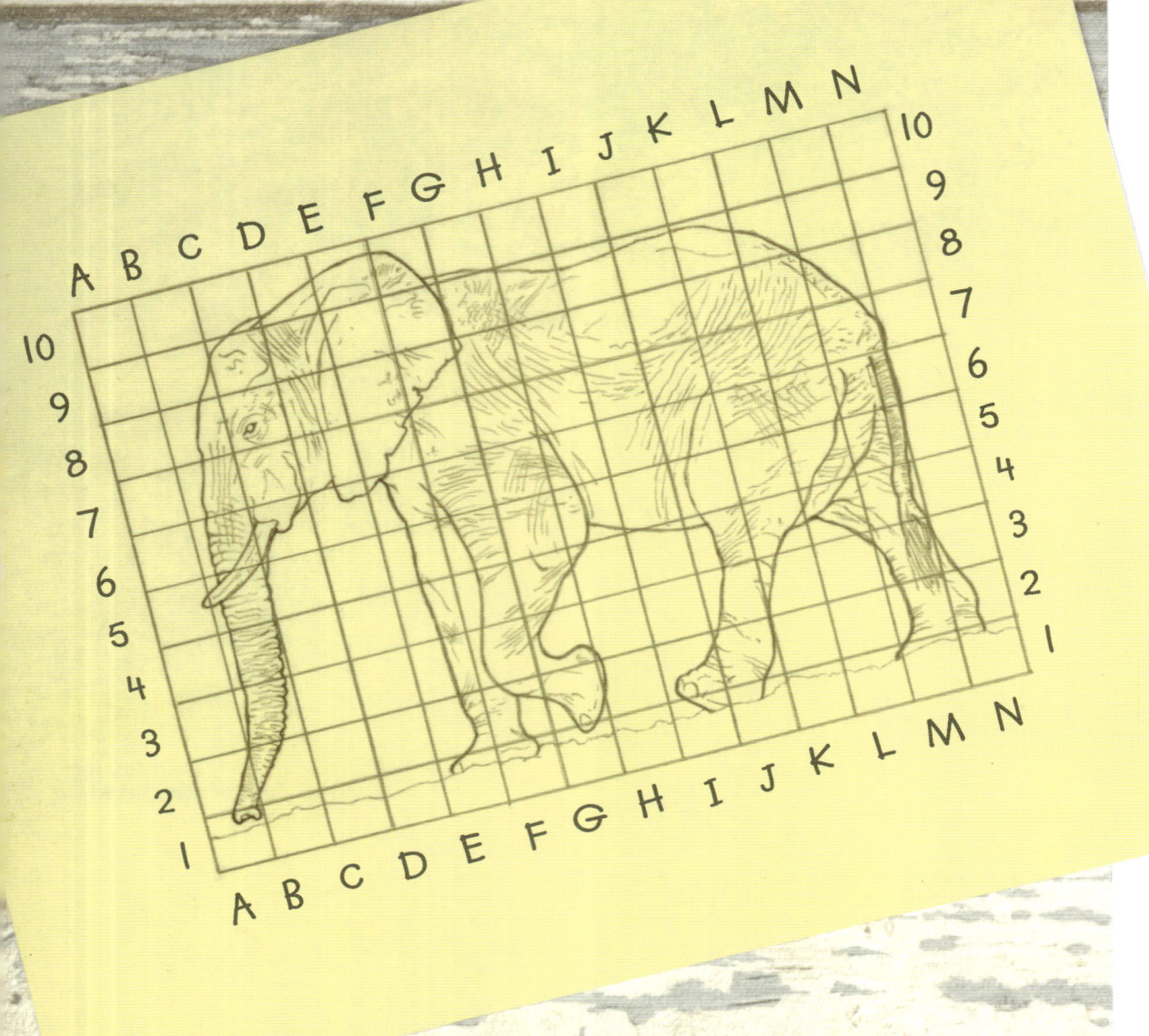

ENORMOUS IMAGES
SCALING UP PICTURES

Using a grid is a handy way of enlarging a picture accurately while keeping the proportions the same. You can even make artworks big enough to hang on your wall – just choose your picture and prepare to go large.

A large image will give you space to add more detail.

MATHS YOU WILL USE

• MEASUREMENT to help you draw an accurate grid.

• SCALE FACTOR to understand how size may change but proportions remain the same.

• GRID REFERENCES so that you can copy your drawing at a new scale.

HOW TO SCALE UP A PICTURE

For this project, you will need two separate grids. The difference in size between them is the scale – the larger the scale, the bigger the difference. You could copy your starting image from a book by making your first grid on tracing paper. Clip or stick the grid to the book so it doesn't move and then trace the picture.

Time 120 minutes
Difficulty Medium

WHAT YOU NEED

- Ruler
- A picture to copy
- Rubber
- Black felt-tip pen
- Pencil
- Scissors
- A3 white paper
- Set square

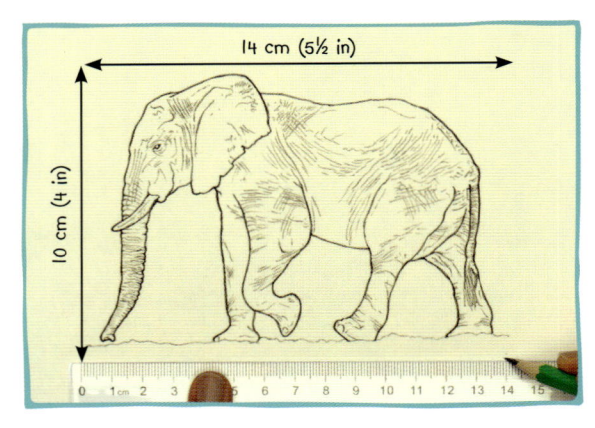

1 Choose an image you would like to enlarge and use a ruler to measure its height and width. Our image is 10 cm (4 in) in height and 14 cm (5½ in) in width.

Use a set square to ensure that your corners are right angles (90°).

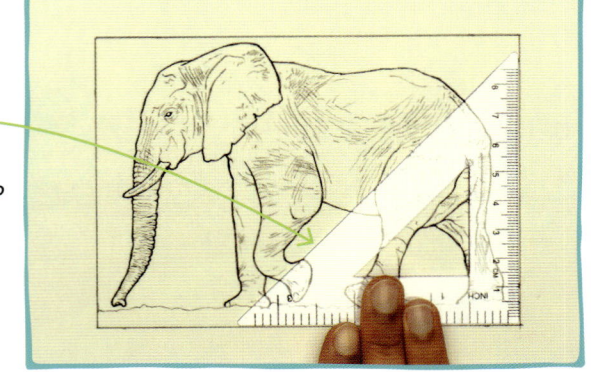

2 Draw a rectangle around the outside of your image. Leave a bit of space above, below, and to the sides of your drawing.

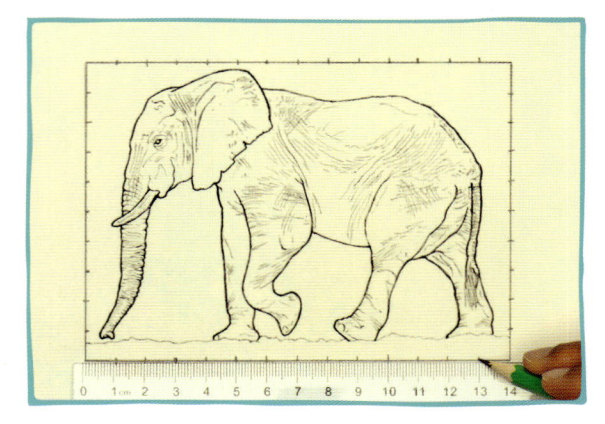

3 Use a ruler and pencil to make marks every 1 cm (½ in) along each side of the rectangle. Because of the size of our image, we have 14 marks along the top and bottom, and 10 along the sides.

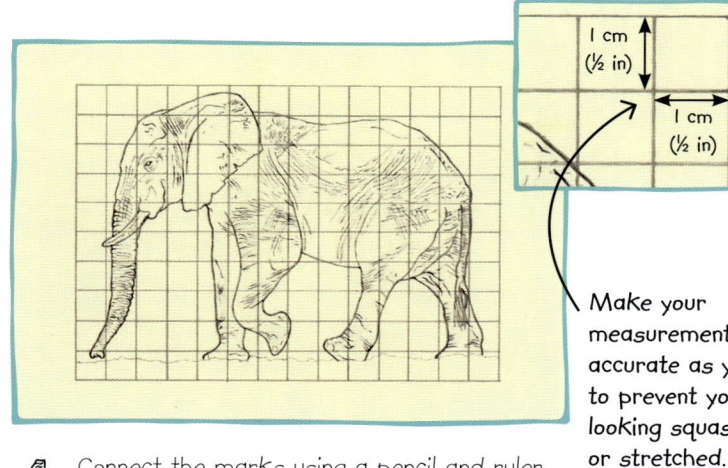

SCALING UP PICTURES   65

1 cm (½ in)
1 cm (½ in)

Make your measurements as accurate as you can to prevent your image looking squashed or stretched.

4 Connect the marks using a pencil and ruler to draw horizontal and vertical lines across the picture. You should now have a grid of 140 squares overlaying the original image.

5 Number the squares running up the sides of the grid from 1–10, then label the squares along the top and bottom A–N, as shown below. These labels are called grid references, and they will help you to find specific squares on your image.

The grid for your pictures can have any number of squares, as long as they're equally sized.

SCALE FACTOR
Scaling is making something larger or smaller while keeping everything in proportion. The scale factor is the amount you increase or decrease the size by.

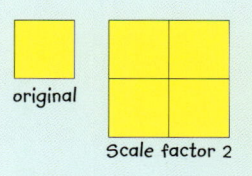

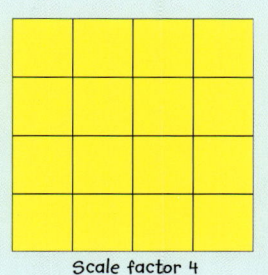

original
Scale factor 2
Scale factor 4

At scale factor 2, the length of each side is doubled.

Doubling the dimensions of the original image is equivalent to enlarging it by a scale factor of 2.

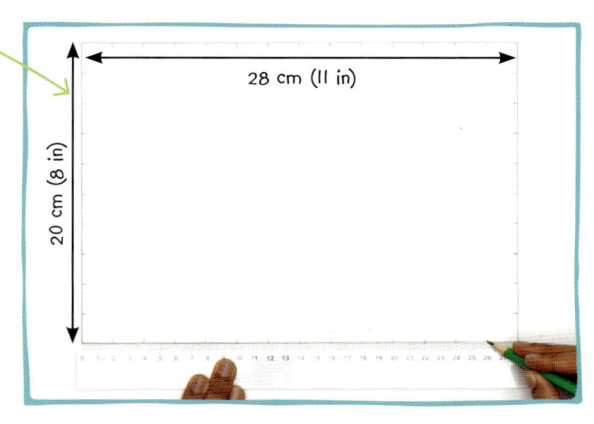

28 cm (11 in)
20 cm (8 in)

6 To double the size of the image, multiply both the height and width by two. On a blank piece of A3 paper, draw a rectangle with the new dimensions of 20 × 28 cm (8 × 11 in).

2 cm (¾ in)
2 cm (¾ in)

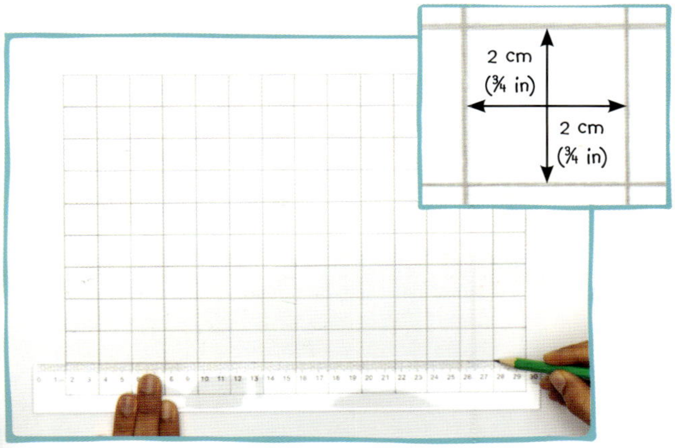

7 Repeat step 3 to create a new grid, but enlarging the squares by a factor of 2 – to 2 × 2 cm (¾ × ¾ in).

66   SHAPES

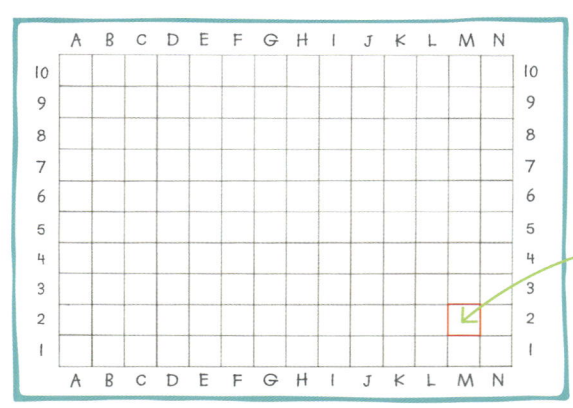

8 Add grid references to the columns and rows, as you did in step 5. You are now ready to copy the smaller elephant onto your larger grid.

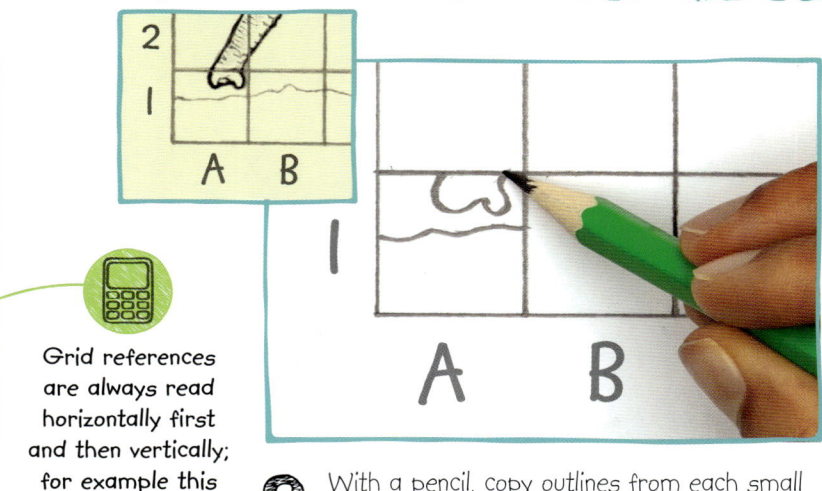

Grid references are always read horizontally first and then vertically; for example this would be M2.

9 With a pencil, copy outlines from each small grid square to the same position on your large grid square, starting at A1.

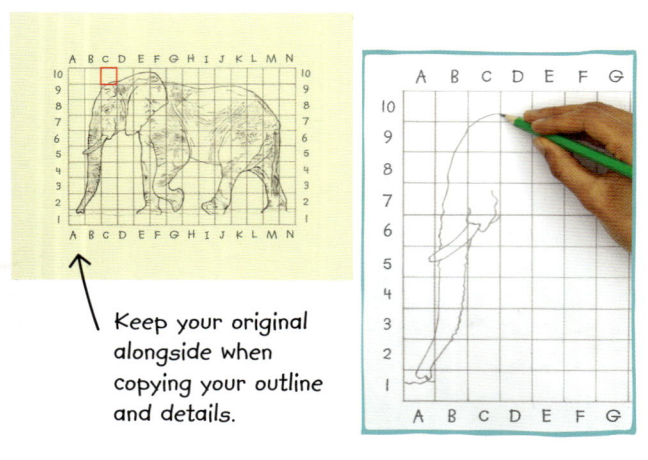

Keep your original alongside when copying your outline and details.

10 Work your way up and down the columns to transfer the picture to the larger grid. Keep it simple by starting with the outline image, and use the grid references to keep track of what you need to draw in each square.

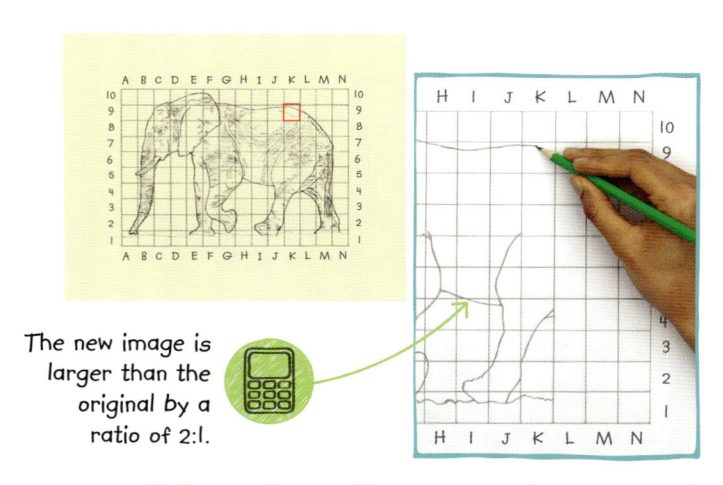

The new image is larger than the original by a ratio of 2:1.

11 Continue working across the large grid until you have transferred the whole outline from the smaller image. Check back over the squares to make sure you haven't missed any lines.

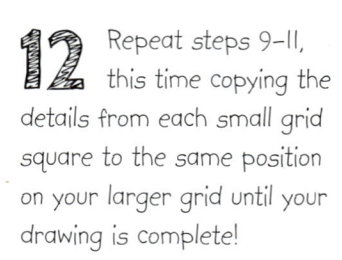

12 Repeat steps 9–11, this time copying the details from each small grid square to the same position on your larger grid until your drawing is complete!

It is much easier to add detail and features once the outline is in place.

SCALING UP PICTURES   67

Use scissors to cut around the outer rectangle of your final image, to separate your drawing from the labelled grid.

13 Once you're happy with your drawing, go over the pencil lines with a *black* felt-tip pen. Rub out all of the pencil lines and then cut around the rectangle you drew in step 2.

SCALING 3D SHAPES
Scale factor can also be applied to 3D objects. In addition to height and width, this also affects the depth of an object.

The length of each of the larger cube's sides has been extended to three cubes.

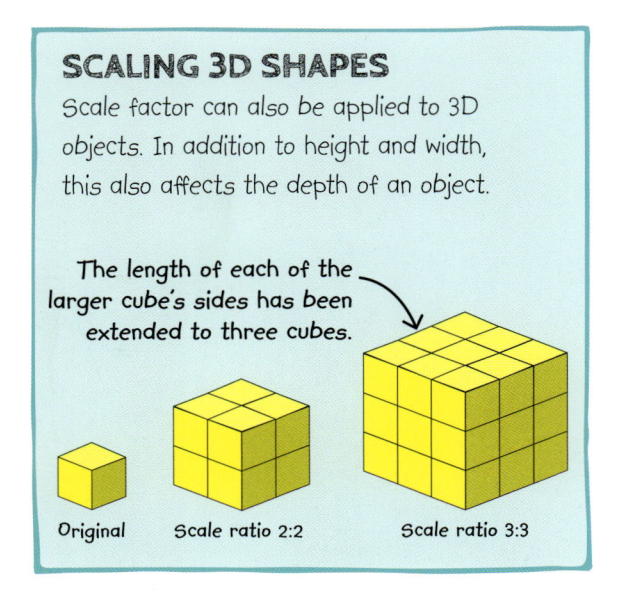

Original   Scale ratio 2:2   Scale ratio 3:3

REAL WORLD MATHS
MINIATURE DOLL'S HOUSE
A doll's house is an example of a toy that is a detailed model of a real house, but shrunk to a fraction of the original size. To make the house and its objects look as realistic as possible, the scale has to be kept in proportion.

Push down on the back of your frog to send it leaping through the air!

MATHS YOU WILL USE
- ANGLES and bisection to ensure your origami folds are precise.
- SQUARES, RECTANGLES, AND TRIANGLES to create intricate origami shapes.

Give your frog some extra camouflage by drawing dots on its back.

Add googly eyes so your frog can be on the watch for flies.

Using brightly coloured paper will give your frog an exotic look.

FOLDING FUN
ORIGAMI JUMPING FROG

Use origami – the ancient Japanese art of paper folding – to make your own jumping frog. The length of its leap could put any self-respecting amphibian to shame, so set up a track to measure how far you can get your frog to jump. Now hop to it!

HOW TO MAKE AN ORIGAMI JUMPING FROG

To make this frog, you'll need to start with square paper, and step 1 shows you how to make that from an ordinary A4 sheet. You can also buy thin, square paper designed for origami at craft shops. As you fold, make sure your creases are precise so that the frog looks just right.

Time 20 minutes

Difficulty Medium

WHAT YOU NEED

- Pencil
- Googly eyes
- Scissors
- PVA glue
- Ruler
- Thin A4 green and blue paper

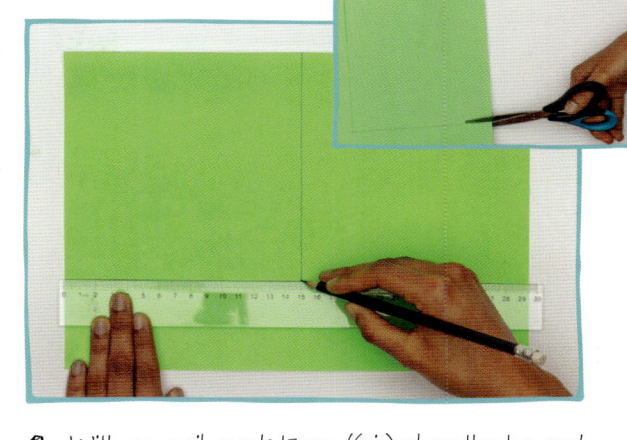

1 With a pencil, mark 15 cm (6 in) along the top and left edges of the A4 paper. Draw straight lines along the marks to make a square, then cut it out.

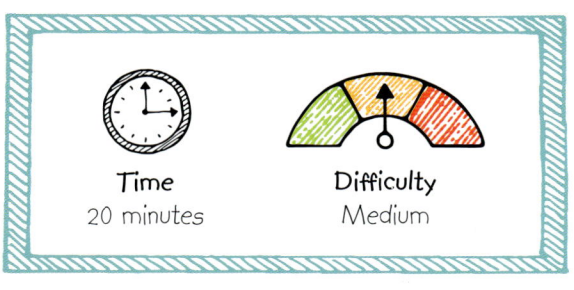

Run your finger along the crease to create a neat, sharp fold.

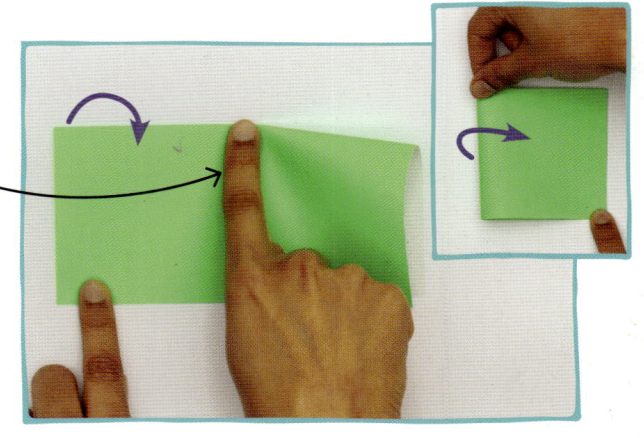

2 Fold the square in half so you have a green rectangle. Fold it again to create a small square, then unfold it so you have two squares.

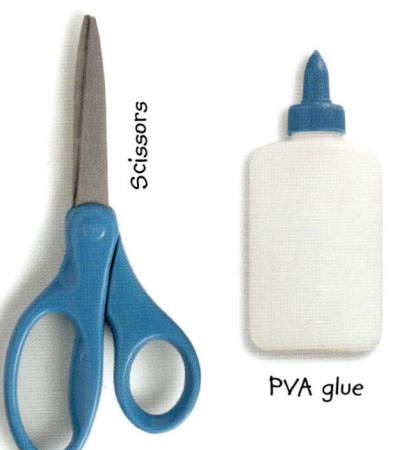

Here, you are folding a right angle in half, or bisecting it.

3 Fold the top corner of each square to the opposite corner, then unfold and do the same with the bottom corners. When you unfold the bottom corners, you will have crossed folds in both squares.

70 SHAPES

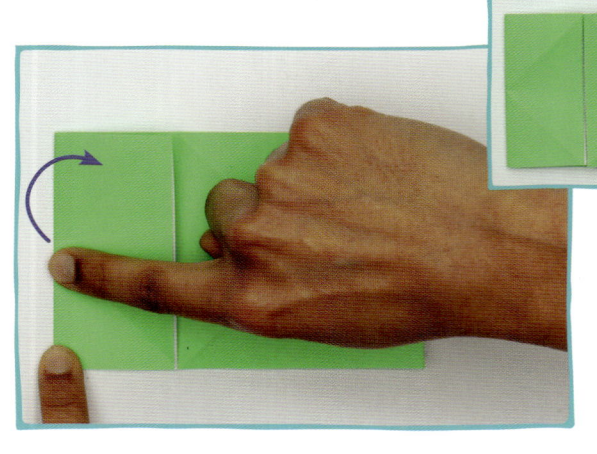

Look closely at the creases. How many shapes can you see within your unfolded piece of paper?

4 Flip the paper over and fold each square in half lengthwise through the centre of each cross to make a square that is open in the middle.

5 Flip the paper over again and repeat the same folds as in step 4. Once opened out, the triangles at the top and bottom of the paper should pop up.

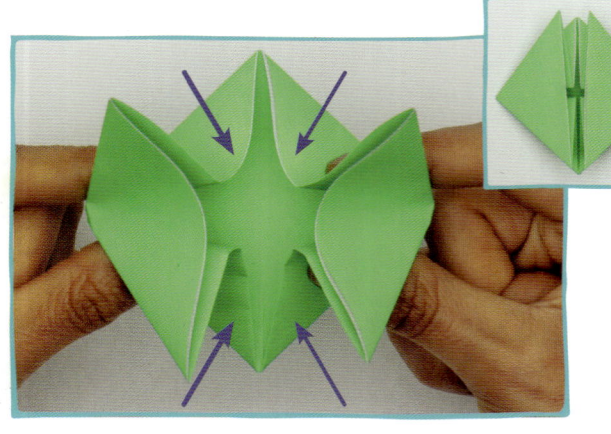

You are bisecting these triangles by folding them in half.

6 Push the outer three triangles on both sides together. As your paper collapses inwards, it will form a diamond shape.

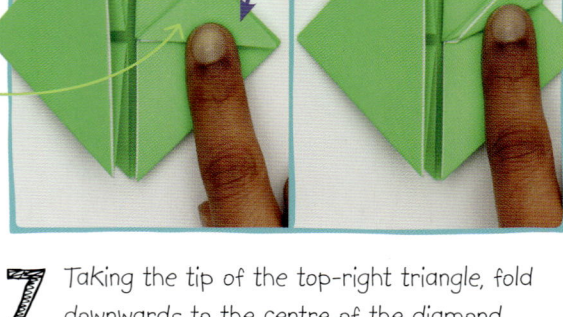

7 Taking the tip of the top-right triangle, fold downwards to the centre of the diamond. Then fold it upwards on itself to create a smaller triangle. Repeat on the left-hand top triangle.

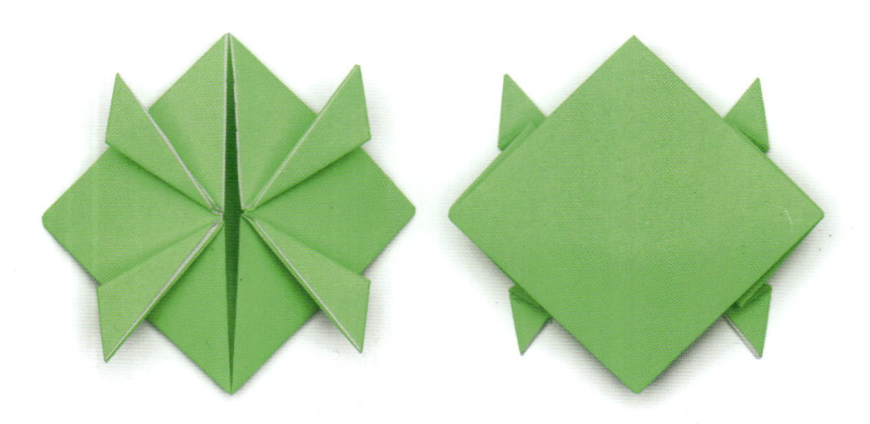

8 Repeat step 7 for the bottom two triangles, but first fold upwards and then downwards to create a mirror image of the folds you just did. Turn the frog over so the flat side is facing upwards.

BISECTION
Bisecting means to cut or divide something into two equal parts. This angle has been bisected, giving two equal 20° angles.

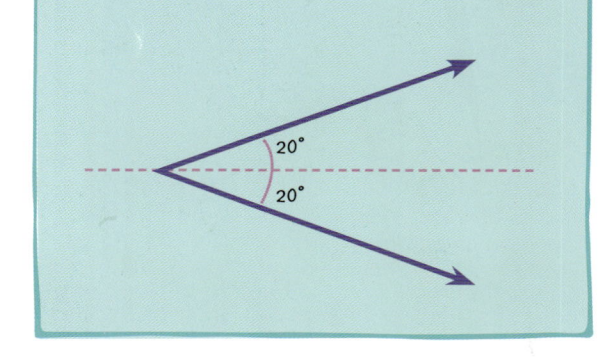

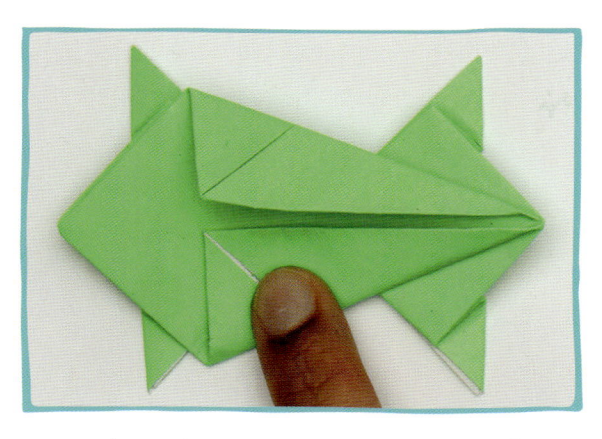

ORIGAMI JUMPING FROG   71

9 Fold the bottom edge of the diamond along the centre line of the frog. Repeat on the other side to create a kite shape.

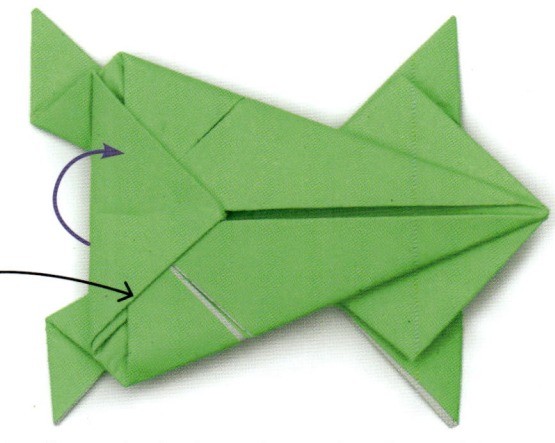

10 Fold the left edge of the diamond to form a triangle. Tuck the inner tips of the kite into the pockets of the triangle you just made.

Make sure the tips are tucked into the pockets of the triangle.

Fold the tips of the front legs in and down to raise the frog's body and head.

11 Turn your frog over and rotate it 90° so the point is at the top. Then fold the frog in half through the middle so that the back feet touch the front feet.

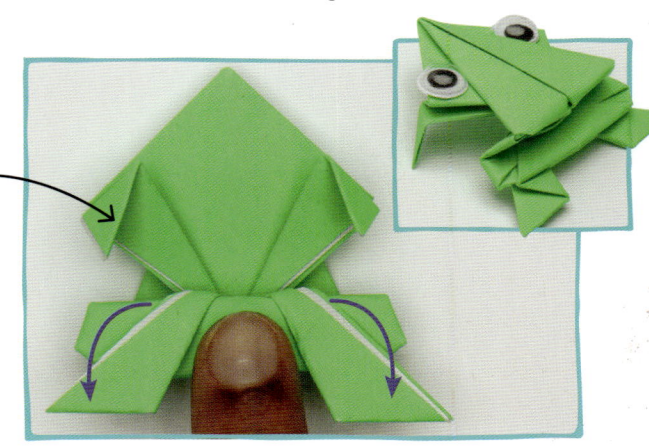

12 Fold the back legs in half towards you to make the spring. Then make small folds in the front feet to raise the head, before turning your frog over and adding googly eyes with PVA glue.

13 Place your finger on the spring, then pull back and release it to make your frog jump! You can use a piece of blue paper as a river to measure how far your frog can leap.

Mark where your frog lands and then use a ruler to measure how far it leapt from the starting point.

Press down on the spring and then release your finger to fire the frog.

MATHS YOU WILL USE
- TESSELLATION to create an interlocking pattern of 2D shapes that fit perfectly together.
- ROTATION as you position each shape to fit tightly with the following one.
- MEASUREMENT to create a grid with equal-sized squares.

The beauty of tessellating patterns is that the picture will look good whichever way up you hang it!

PLAYFUL PICTURES
TESSELLATING PATTERNS

A tessellation pattern is made up of identical shapes that fit together without any gaps or overlap. Have you ever noticed that honeycomb built by bees is made up of tessellated hexagons, fitting neatly together with spectacular effect? Have a go at making your own eye-catching masterpiece using tessellating patterns – what shape will you choose?

We've chosen a smiley face for our tessellating pattern. Even simple designs can create detailed tessellations.

74 SHAPES

HOW TO MAKE
TESSELLATING PATTERNS

This art project creates an impressive end result. To get started, decide on the shape you want to tessellate and make a template. We'll show you how to create a template that will match our smiley face pattern, but you could use this technique to make an artwork of your own by tweaking the template in step 2.

TESSELLATING SHAPES
Shapes tessellate if they fit together perfectly with no gaps or overlapping. How many tessellating shapes can you think of?

Triangles tessellate

Squares tessellate

Circles don't tessellate

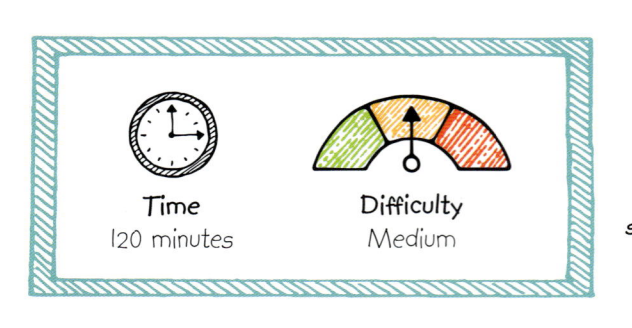

Time 120 minutes

Difficulty Medium

Make sure you measure your square accurately, so all the sides are equal.

WHAT YOU NEED

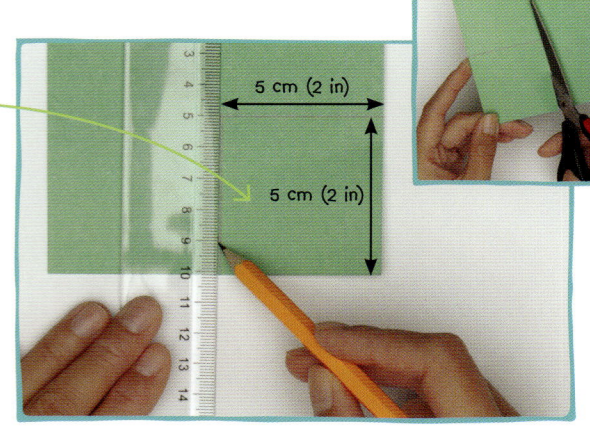

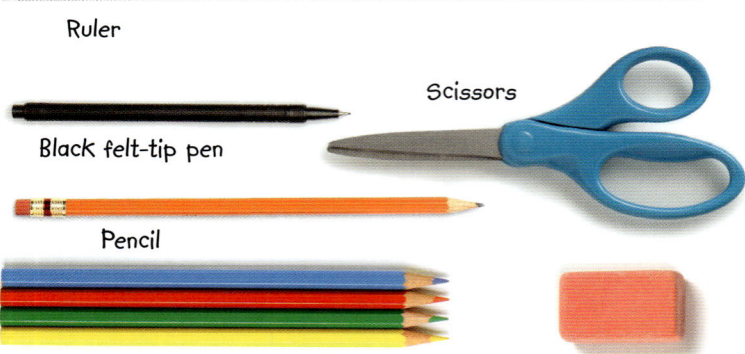

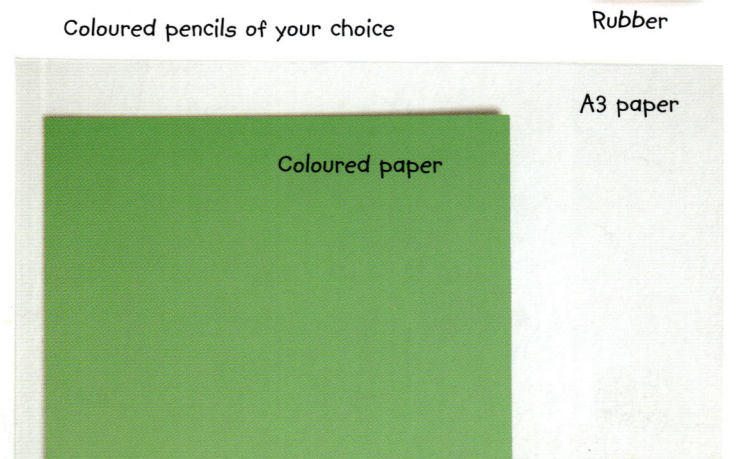

- Ruler
- Black felt-tip pen
- Scissors
- Pencil
- Coloured pencils of your choice
- Rubber
- A3 paper
- Coloured paper

1 Use a ruler to measure out a 5 x 5 cm (2 x 2 in) square on your card and then carefully cut it out with a pair of scissors.

2 Copy the shapes shown here, drawing lines between the corners on two edges of the square. If you are designing your own pattern, make your line wavy or jagged, but not too detailed as this will make it difficult to cut out.

TESSELLATING PATTERNS   75

Rotate the separate pieces of card by an angle of 270°.

270°

Trim the tape that hangs over the shape's edge.

3 Using a pair of scissors, carefully cut along the lines you have drawn. You will be left with three separate pieces.

4 Rotate the pieces you have cut out and place them on the outside of the adjacent sides of the shape. Use tape to stick the shapes together.

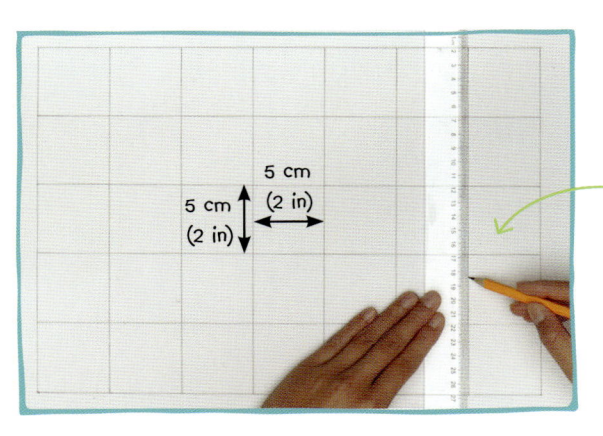

5 cm (2 in)
5 cm (2 in)

The grid will be made up of squares measuring 5 × 5 cm (2 × 2 in).

5 On an A3 sheet of paper, use a pencil and ruler to mark out 5 cm (2 in) intervals along all four sides. Then draw horizontal and vertical lines connecting the marks to create a grid.

Align the shape's vertical and horizontal lines with those on the grid.

6 Place your shape in one of the squares in the centre of the grid. Use one hand to keep the shape in position while you carefully trace around it in pencil to give the outline of the shape.

76   SHAPES

7 Consider what you could draw in your shape to bring it to life. We have gone for a happy face. Draw these details on your pencil outline.

ROTATION
When an object moves around a centre point it rotates. The distance we move the shape is called the angle of rotation.

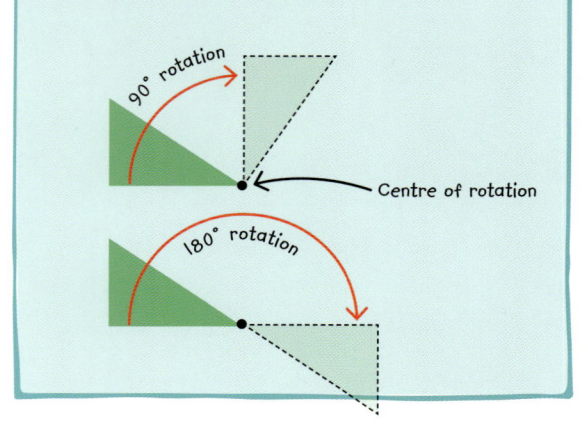

90° rotation
Centre of rotation
180° rotation

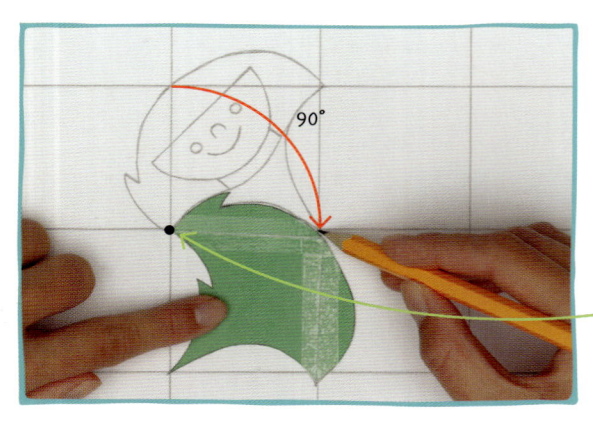

8 Rotate the card by 90° onto an adjacent square and trace around it again. See how the shapes interact with each other like puzzle pieces.

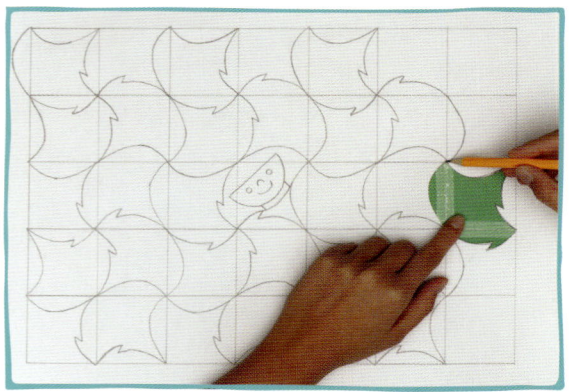

Keep one corner of your shape fixed on this point – the centre of rotation – as you turn it.

9 Continue drawing around your card template, turning it 90° each time until you have filled the entire grid with tessellating shapes.

10 Now draw a face or repeat your pattern on all the shapes, until each one has the same design as your very first one.

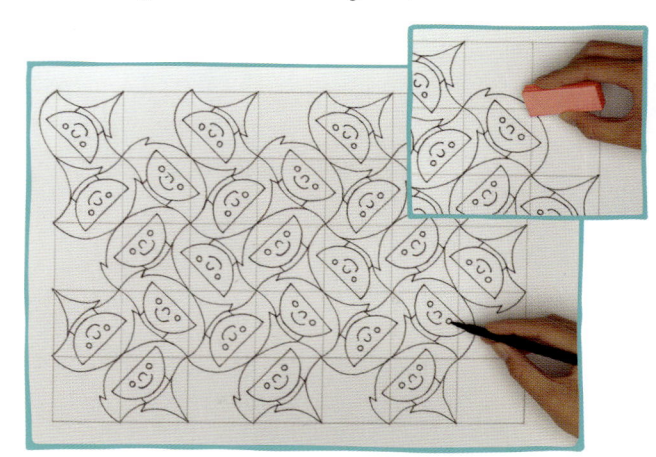

You may find it easier to rotate your paper as you add detail to the shapes.

11 Using a black felt-tip pen, carefully go over your pencil lines to make your tessellation more defined and then rub out all the pencil grid lines.

TESSELLATING PATTERNS 77

12 Now colour in your tessellating pattern using coloured pencils or felt-tips.

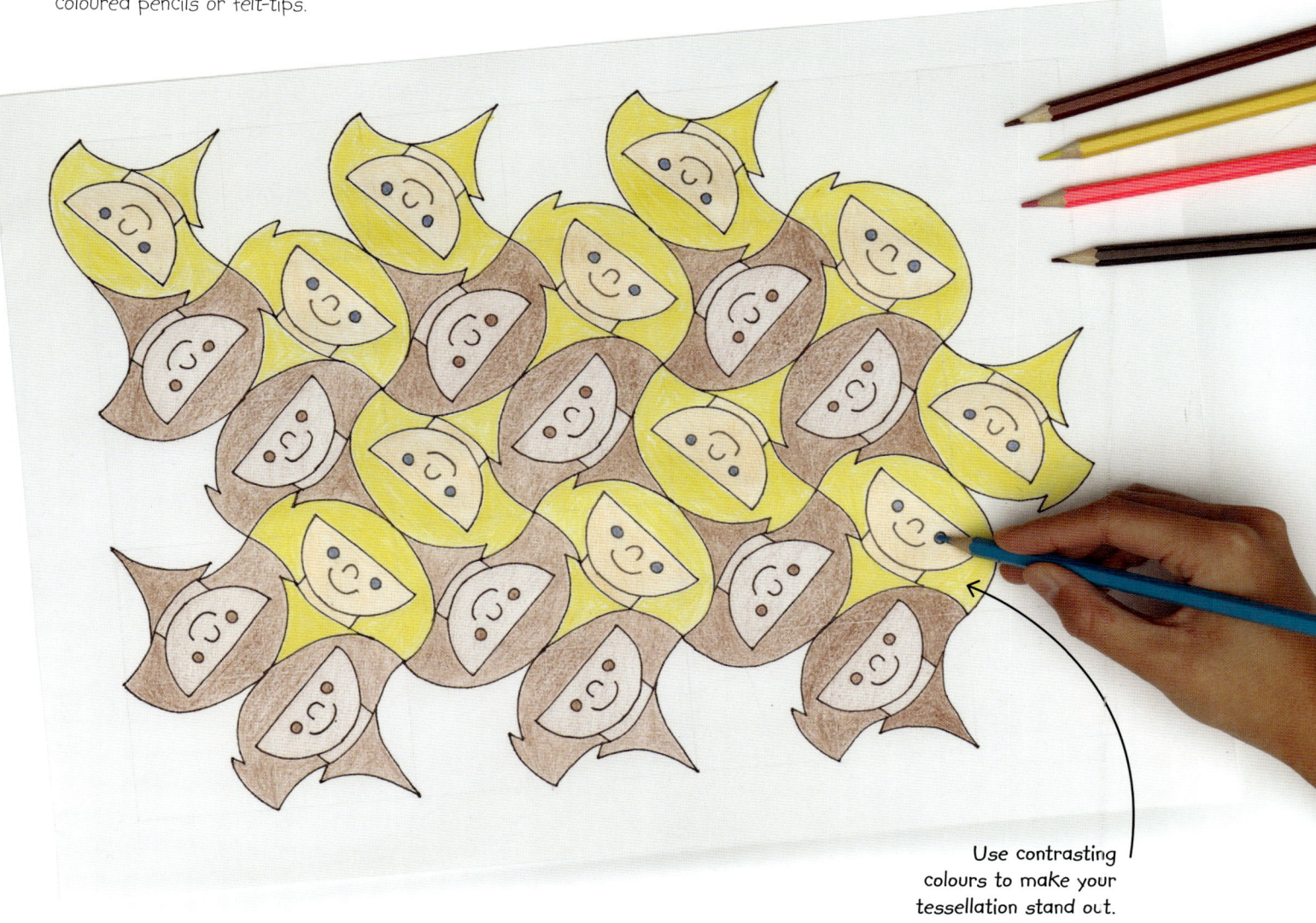

Use contrasting colours to make your tessellation stand out.

MORE COMPLEX TESSELLATIONS

Once you've mastered the basics of creating tessellations, why not have a go at more complex patterns. These use the same technique that you've just learned but start with more complex versions of the template you draw in step 2. You can also experiment with colour to make your pattern look even deeper and more detailed.

MIND-BOGGLING SHAPES
IMPOSSIBLE TRIANGLE

Impress your friends by drawing this tricky triangle. It's a shape that can't exist in three dimensions, which is why it's called impossible, but the clever angles fool your brain into believing that it could work in real life.

MATHS YOU WILL USE
- MEASURING to make sure your triangle has sides of equal length.
- COMPASS SKILLS to mark out where to draw the outline of the triangle.
- 3D SHAPES to make your triangle stand out on the page.

You can mount your triangle in an arty picture frame for your bedroom or to give as a present.

Go large! Try doubling or trebling the measurements to draw a super-sized triangle.

HOW TO MAKE AN IMPOSSIBLE TRIANGLE

A perfect impossible triangle needs to have equal internal angles, which is why your compass comes in handy. You can experiment with colours and shading at the end to make your shape look like it's 3D.

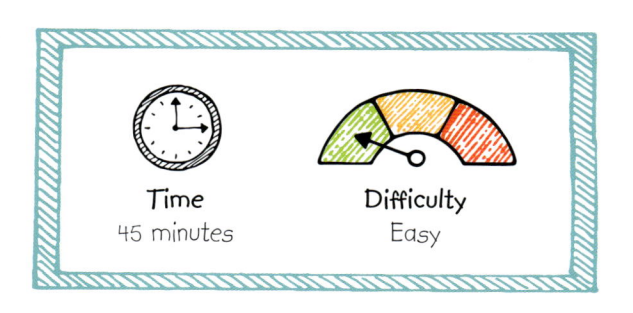

Time 45 minutes

Difficulty Easy

WHAT YOU NEED

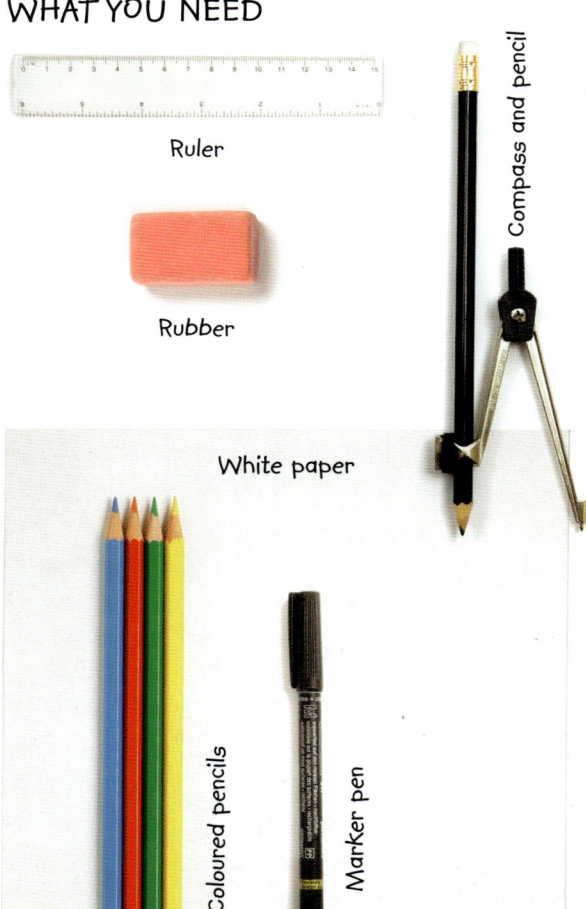

- Ruler
- Rubber
- Compass and pencil
- White paper
- Coloured pencils
- Marker pen

EQUILATERAL TRIANGLE

An equilateral triangle has three equal sides and its interior angles all measure 60°.

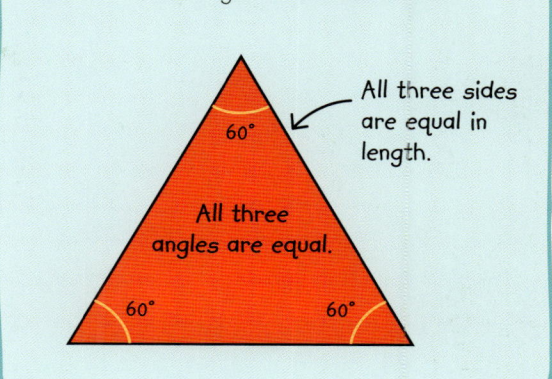

All three sides are equal in length.

All three angles are equal.

Be careful to fix your compass to 9 cm (3½ in) or your triangle won't be equal on all sides!

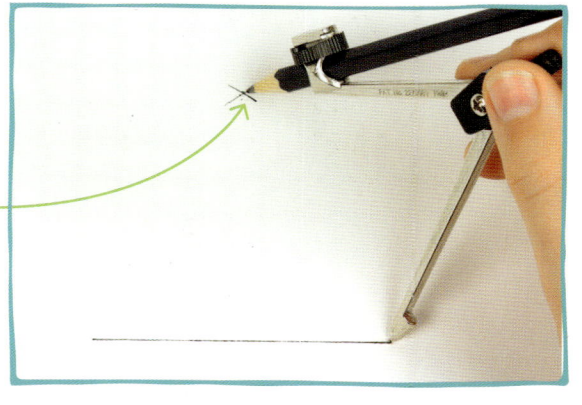

1 Start by using a pencil and ruler to draw a 9 cm (3½ in) line. Set your compass to 9 cm (3½ in), place the point at one end of the line, and draw a faint arc. Repeat at the other end of the line.

Press lightly with your pencil, as you'll be rubbing these lines out later.

2 With a pencil and ruler, join both ends of the line at the centre of the two arcs to form a triangle with three equal sides and angles.

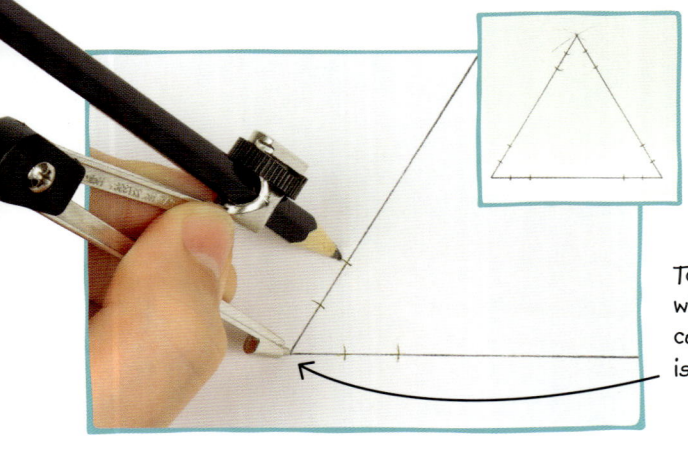

SHAPES

3 Next, set your compass to 1 cm (½ in) and mark this distance from each corner. Then repeat with your compass set to 2 cm (1 in).

Take care when using your compass – the end is very sharp!

4 In each corner, use your ruler to draw a line connecting the 1 cm (½ in) points to make three small equilateral triangles.

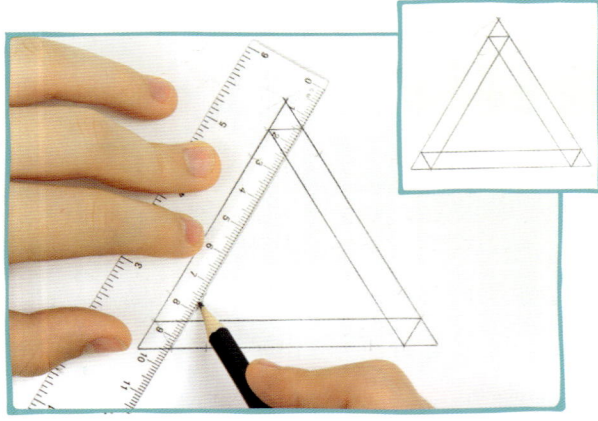

5 Draw a parallel line above the base line that joins the 1 cm (½ in) points. Repeat for the other two sides, creating a smaller triangle inside the first one.

Your three sets of parallel lines should form three perfect equilateral triangles.

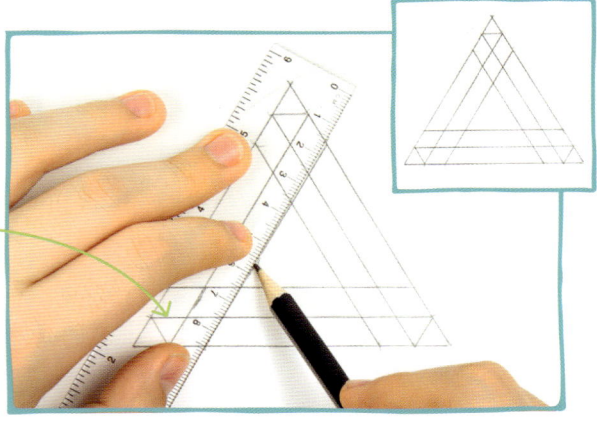

6 Use your pencil and ruler to draw three more lines, this time connecting the 2 cm (1 in) points to create an even smaller triangle inside the second one.

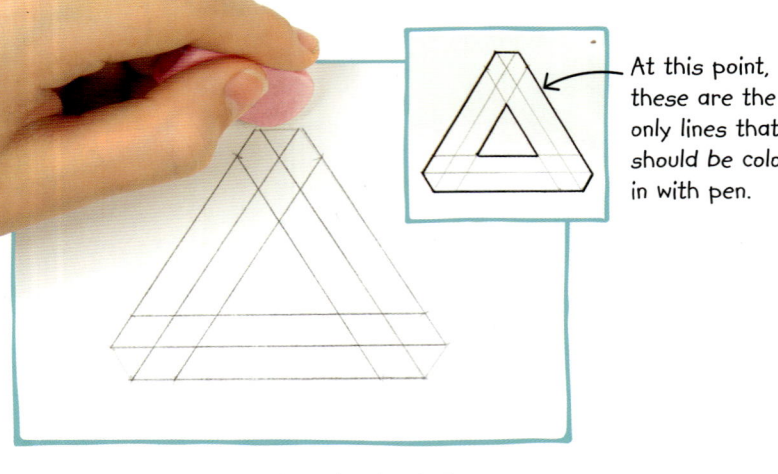

At this point, these are the only lines that should be coloured in with pen.

7 Rub out the three tiny triangles in the corners and draw around the shape's outline in black pen. Go over the inside triangle in black pen, too.

8 Next, go over the three lines that are 1 cm (½ in) in from the outer triangle, but stopping at the line that is 2 cm (1 in) in from the edge.

IMPOSSIBLE TRIANGLE   81

This is one of the lines that makes the illusion work.

Add shade to the places that would be in shadow on a 3D shape.

9 Complete your impossible triangle by joining up the 1 cm (½ in) lines to the inner triangle in three places and then rubbing out the pencil lines you don't need.

10 Now for some final colouring tricks! Adding shadow will make your triangle look even more 3D.

LEVEL UP

To make your impossible triangle even more mind-boggling, why not construct it entirely out of cubes? Although it looks complicated, this version uses lines drawn at only three angles. You won't need a compass for this, so if you don't have one to hand this is a good alternative way to make the impossible triangle.

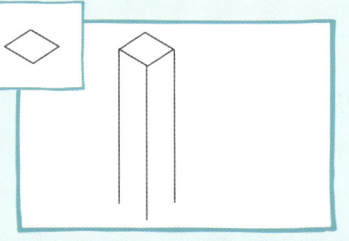

1 Draw a diamond shape, slightly wider than it is tall. Draw three parallel lines running down from the diamond.

2 Join the three lines with wide V shapes to create a tower of five cubes. Extend the bottom three Vs to the right.

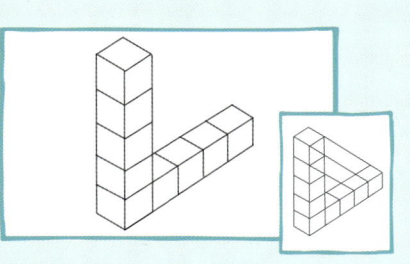

3 Repeat step 2 to divide these parallel lines into cubes. Extend the final three Vs to join the first diamond shape.

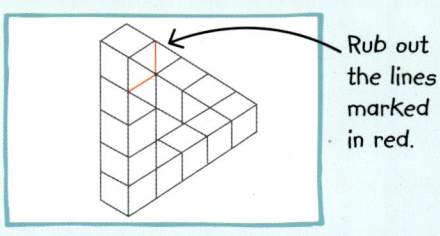

4 Add more Vs to turn these three parallel lines into cubes, then rub out the extra lines on the final cube.

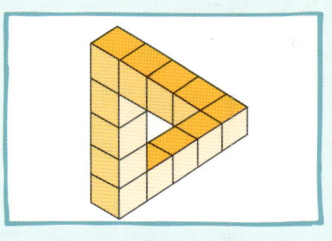

Rub out the lines marked in red.

5 Use different shades to colour in your shape and improve the 3D illusion of your impossible cubed triangle.

A grassy green makes a colourful background for a lion card.

A cardboard tongue adds character to this frog.

MATHS YOU WILL USE
- ANGLES to give your cards a strong structure and make your pop-ups pop.
- MEASURING to get the shape and size of your pop-up just right.

AMAZING ANGLES
POP-UP CARDS

Surprise your friends and family with these cardboard creations. Using a few mathematical skills, you'll be able to create cards that come to life as you open them. Along the way you'll learn how to measure angles and build a paper structure that bursts off the page. Birthdays will never be the same again!

SHAPES

HOW TO MAKE A POP-UP CARD

The key to this project is getting the angles right. If you measure them carefully, everything will come together smoothly. Just make sure you really crease your card to get even folds. Once you've mastered the lion, you can experiment with all sorts of pop-ups.

Time: 30 minutes
Difficulty: Medium

WHAT YOU NEED

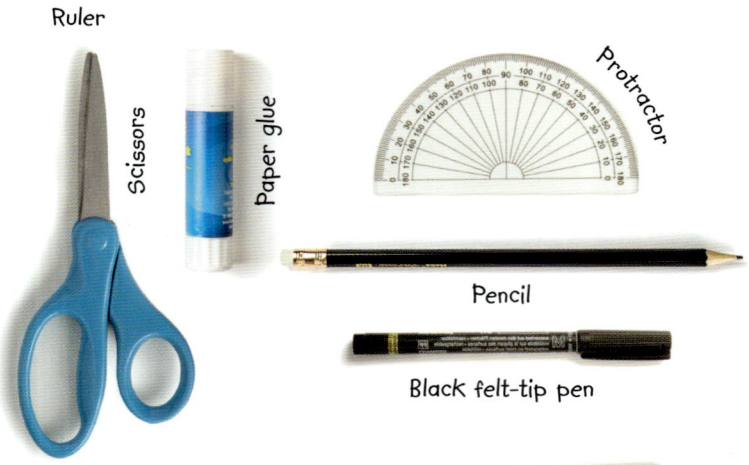

- Ruler
- Scissors
- Paper glue
- Protractor
- Pencil
- Black felt-tip pen
- Several sheets of A4 coloured card
  For this lion we used:
  1 x green
  2 x yellow
  1 x orange

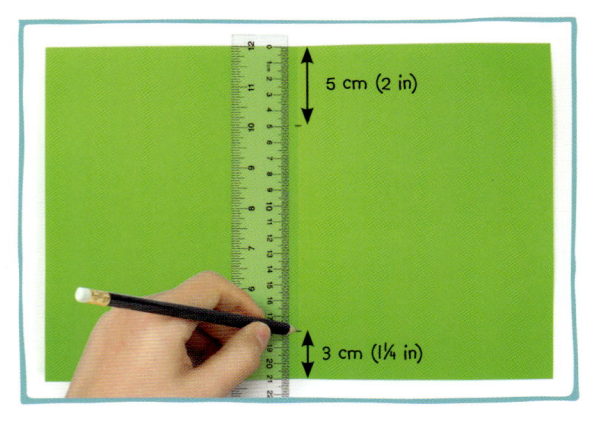

1 Fold an A4 sheet of card and press along the fold. Open it up and mark the crease 5 cm (2 in) from the top and 3 cm (1¼ in) from the bottom.

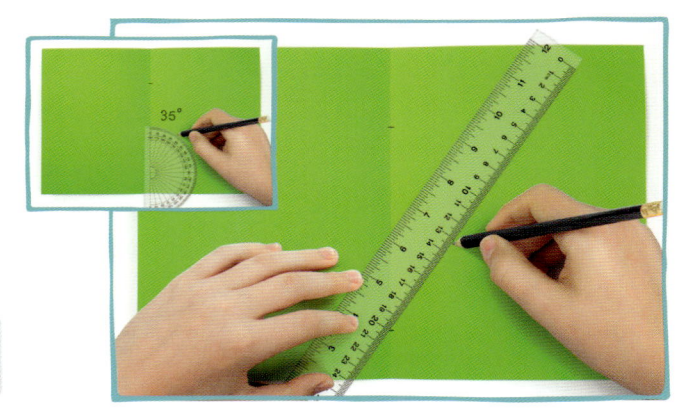

2 Place your protractor at the 3 cm (1¼ in) mark so the 0° lines up with the crease. Measure a 35° angle and draw a line 8 cm (3 in) long linking it to the 3 cm (1¼ in) mark you made on the crease.

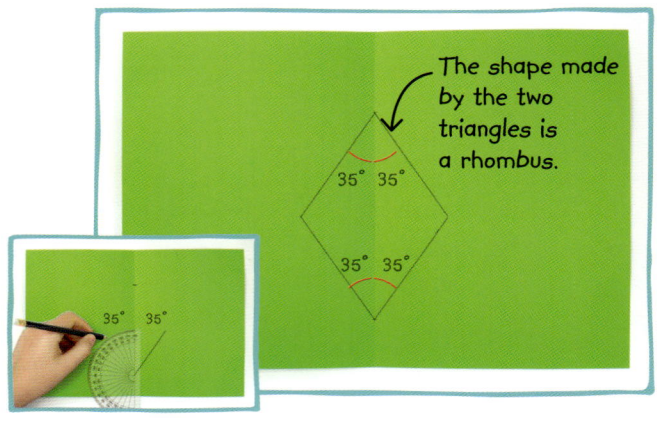

The shape made by the two triangles is a rhombus.

3 Repeat step 2 on the other side of the crease, then again at the 5 cm (2 in) mark with the angles facing down the page. You should have two 70° angles facing each other.

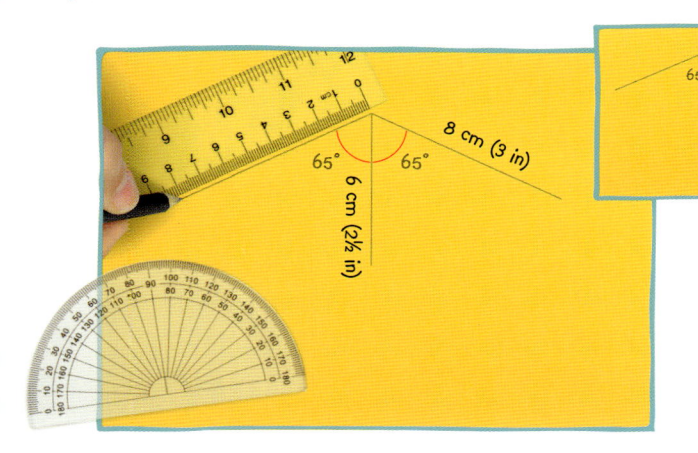

POP-UP CARDS   85

4 For the muzzle, draw a 6 cm (2½ in) line on a piece of yellow card. Draw two 8 cm (3 in) lines coming off the top of this line at 65° angles.

The angles at the bottom are double the size of the angles at the top.

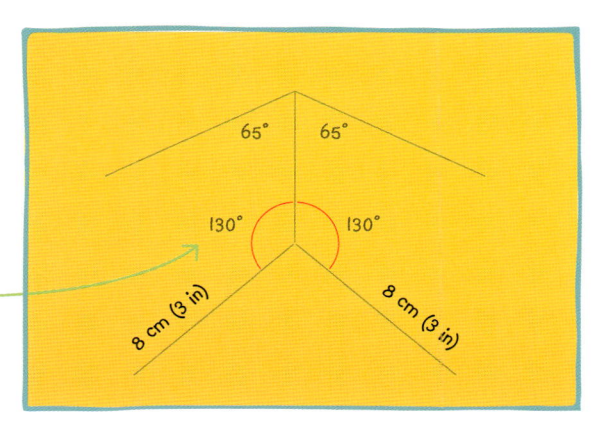

5 At the bottom of the 6 cm (2½ in) line, use the protractor to measure two 130° angles, then draw an 8 cm (3 in) line along each of these angles.

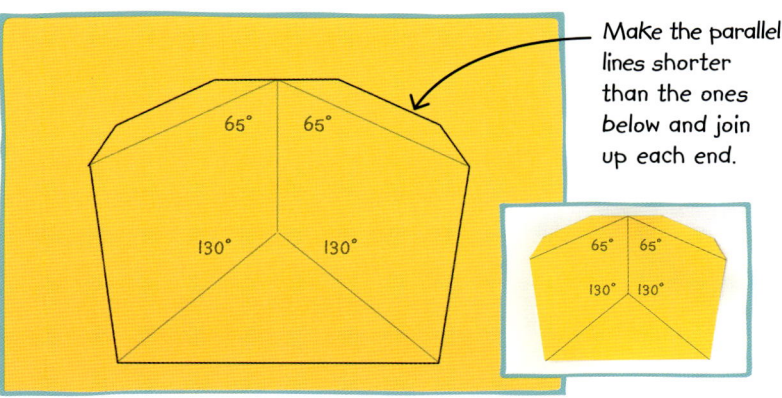

Make the parallel lines shorter than the ones below and join up each end.

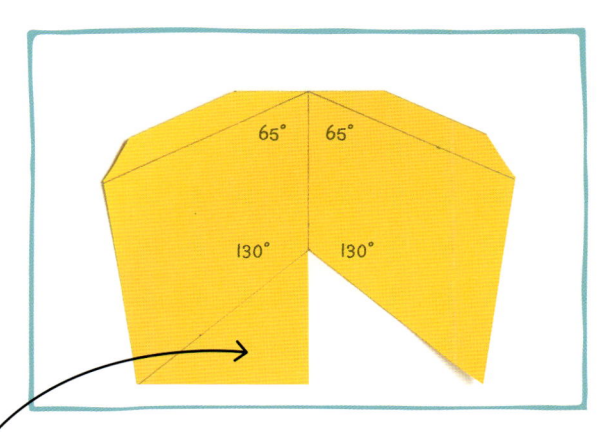

The reverse side of this tab will be where you glue.

6 Draw parallel lines 1 cm (½ in) above the two top lines to make a tab. Use a pen to join up the points, creating a shape with a triangle at the base. Cut out the shape along the lines.

7 Cut the triangle at the base in half, as shown above, to create a tab. Score and fold tightly along all the pencil lines, then glue under the tab.

USING A PROTRACTOR

Align the protractor with the angle's baseline, then look along its edge to find the number matching the angle you're looking for.

Be careful which set of numbers you use.

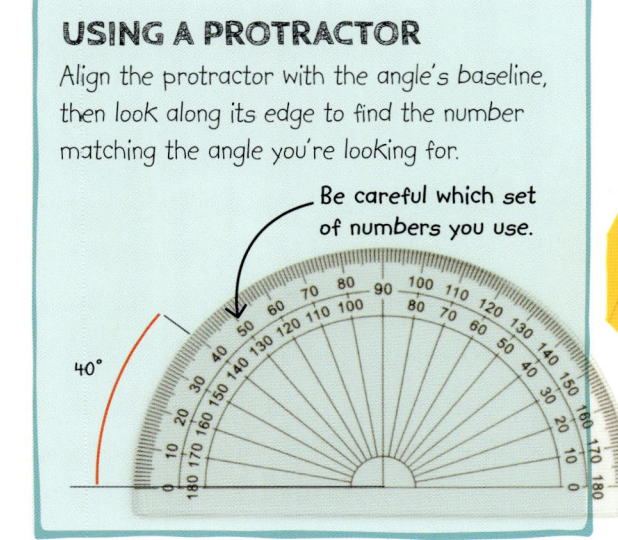

8 Turn the card over, then fold the glued triangular tab under the opposite side so both 8 cm (3 in) lines meet. This is the top of your lion's muzzle.

Triangular tab sticks under here with glue.

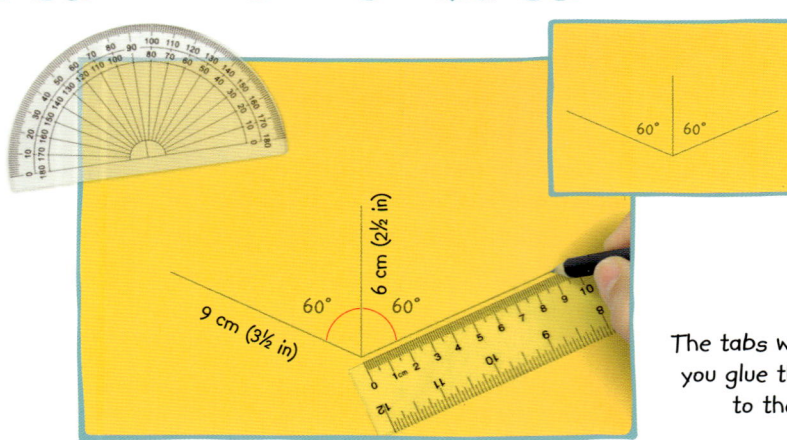

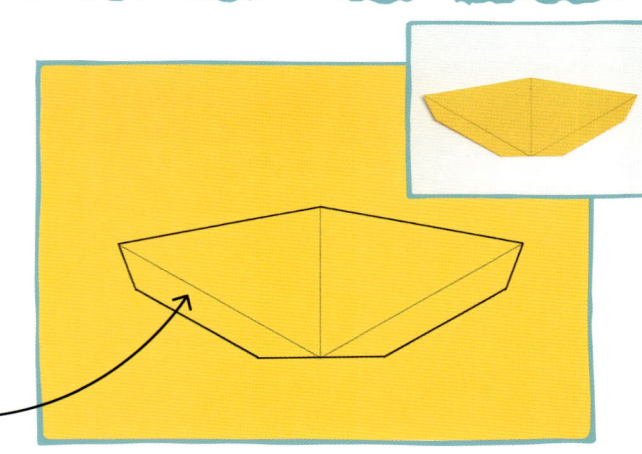

86   SHAPES

9 To make the lion's chin, draw a 6 cm (2½ in) line on another sheet of yellow card. At the bottom of this line, measure two 60° angles, then draw two 9 cm (3½ in) lines along these angles.

The tabs will help you glue the chin to the base.

10 Mark 1 cm (½ in) wide tabs parallel to the two 9 cm (3½ in) lines in pen, then join the ends of these lines with the top of the 6 cm (2½ in) line. Cut along the pen lines, then fold the pencil lines.

Position the muzzle so it crosses the central fold.

11 Turn the muzzle over so the pencil marks are inside, fold the tabs inwards, then stick it down along the top 70° angle you drew in step 3.

12 Take the chin and fold the tabs outwards. Glue the tabs and stick the chin down along the angled pencil lines you drew in step 2.

Cut a folded piece of card to create a symmetrical mane.

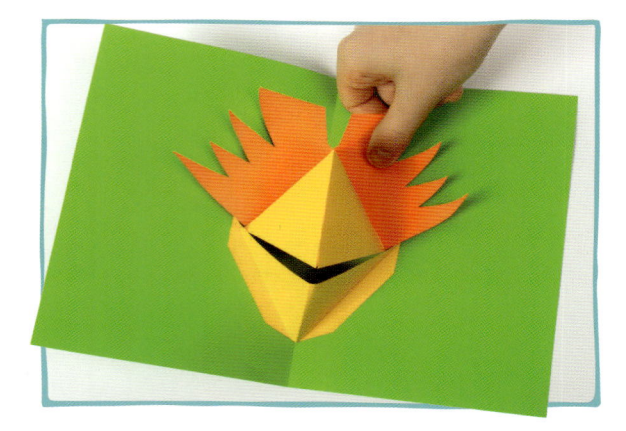

13 Next, make a mane for your lion. Trim some orange card to 6 x 8 cm (2½ x 3 in) and cut triangles into it for the bottom fur. Experiment with other jagged shapes for the top mane.

14 Stick down the top mane around the lion's face. Bend the triangular pieces gently to give the mane a 3D look. Repeat for the bottom mane, too.

POP-UP CARDS   87

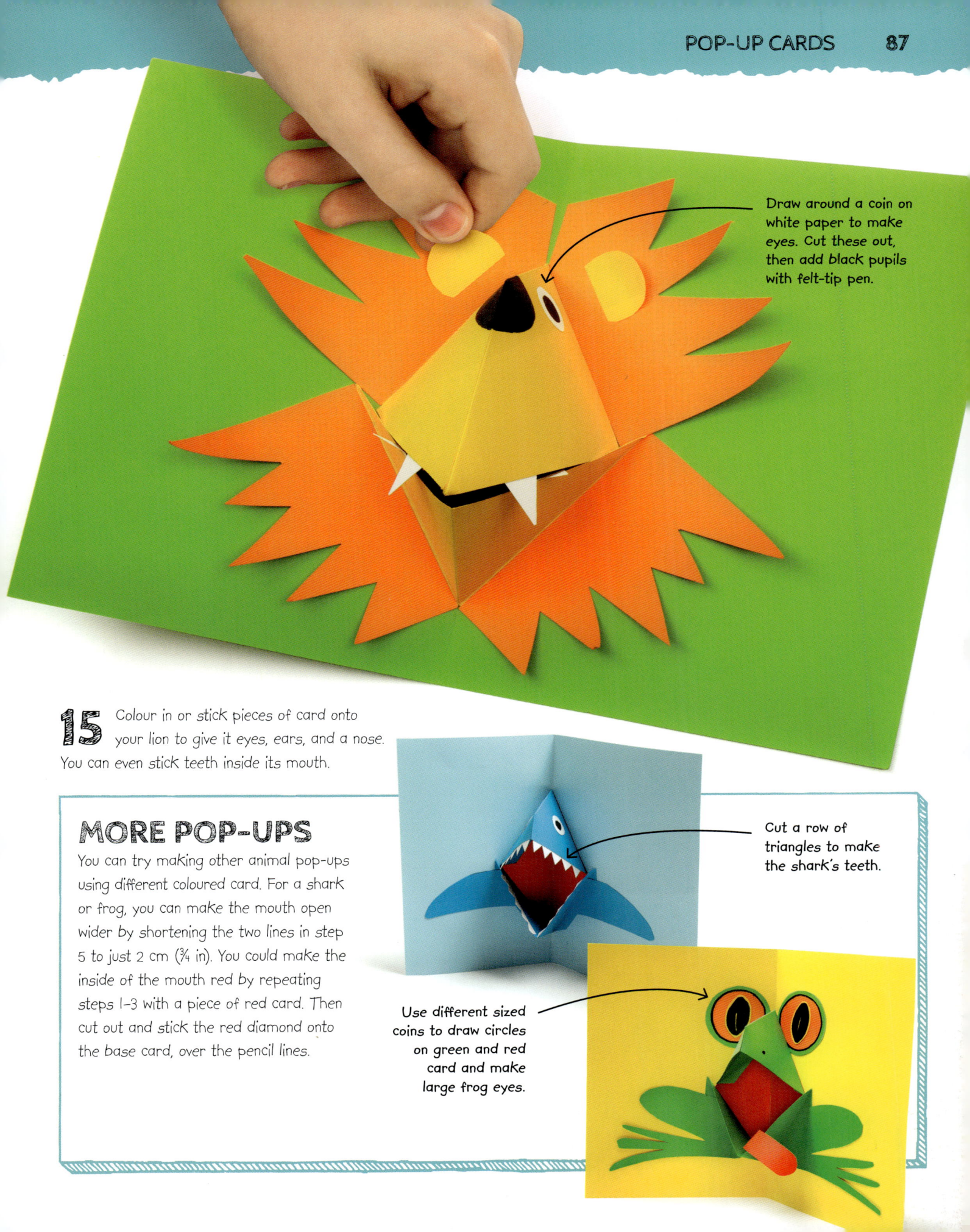

Draw around a coin on white paper to make eyes. Cut these out, then add black pupils with felt-tip pen.

15 Colour in or stick pieces of card onto your lion to give it eyes, ears, and a nose. You can even stick teeth inside its mouth.

MORE POP-UPS

You can try making other animal pop-ups using different coloured card. For a shark or frog, you can make the mouth open wider by shortening the two lines in step 5 to just 2 cm (¾ in). You could make the inside of the mouth red by repeating steps 1–3 with a piece of red card. Then cut out and stick the red diamond onto the base card, over the pencil lines.

Cut a row of triangles to make the shark's teeth.

Use different sized coins to draw circles on green and red card and make large frog eyes.

13

MEASUREMENTS

Whether you're working with weight, height, length, or depth, the projects in this chapter will show you how to master the art of measurements. You'll calculate the speed of a racing car powered by a rubber band, tell the time on a colourful clock, and build a marvellous marble run. You'll learn how to measure the chances of something happening, and you'll even find out how getting the measure of money can help you make a profit at your next school fair.

AWESOME AVERAGES
SPEED TRIALS

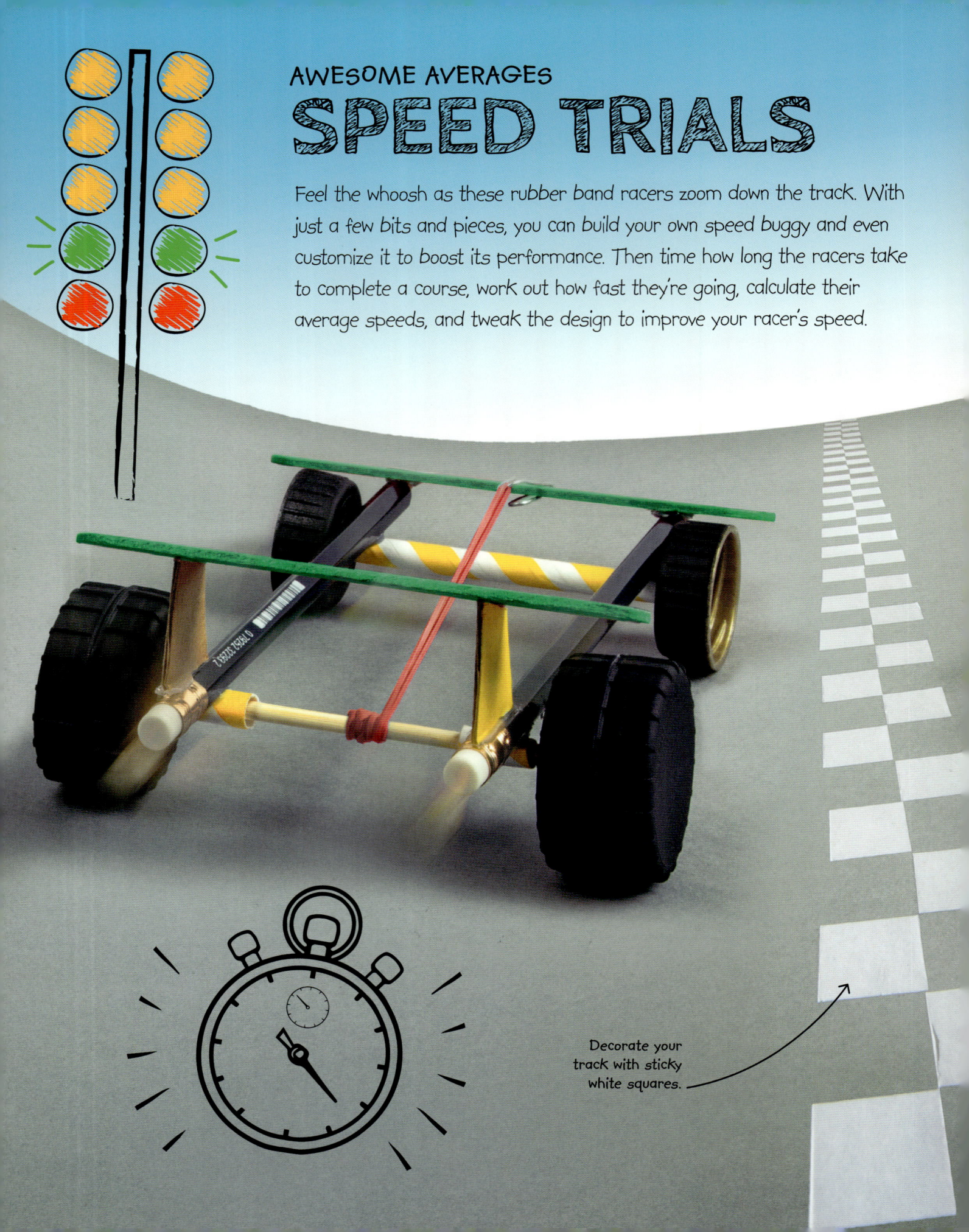

Feel the whoosh as these rubber band racers zoom down the track. With just a few bits and pieces, you can build your own speed buggy and even customize it to boost its performance. Then time how long the racers take to complete a course, work out how fast they're going, calculate their average speeds, and tweak the design to improve your racer's speed.

Decorate your track with sticky white squares.

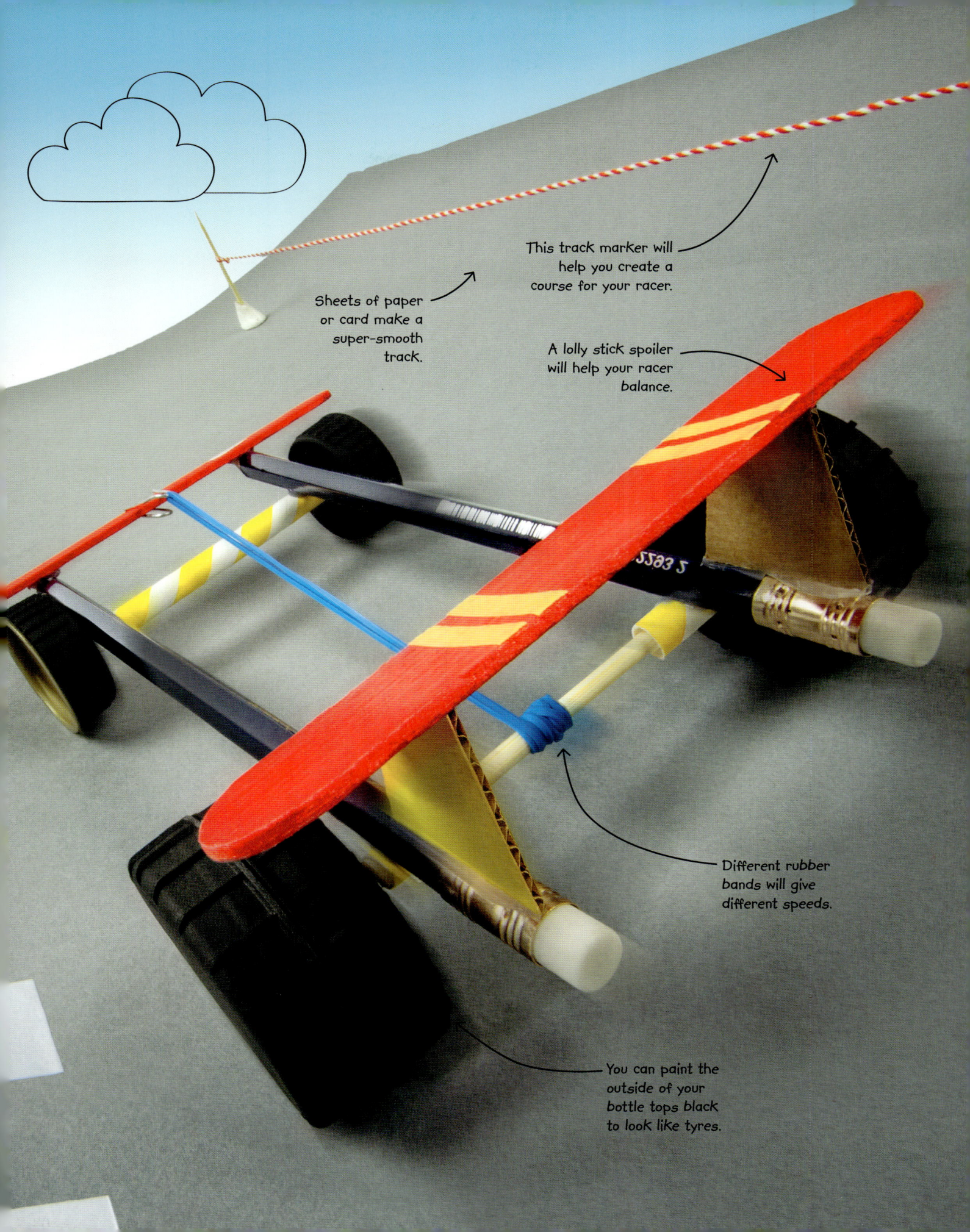

Sheets of paper or card make a super-smooth track.

This track marker will help you create a course for your racer.

A lolly stick spoiler will help your racer balance.

Different rubber bands will give different speeds.

You can paint the outside of your bottle tops black to look like tyres.

HOW TO MAKE A RUBBER BAND RACER

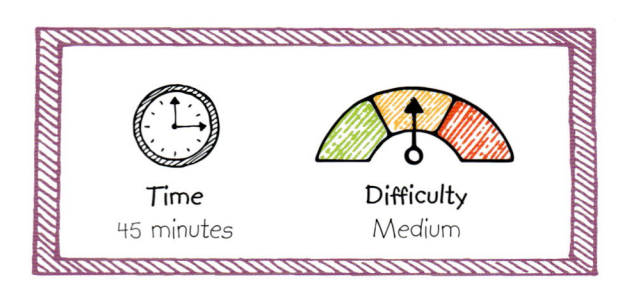

The tension in a twisted rubber band stores energy that, when released, will speed the racer away. By making a track with a set distance, and timing your racer, you can calculate its average speed.

Time 45 minutes
Difficulty Medium

MATHS YOU WILL USE
- QUADRILATERALS to support the spoiler that will help your racer balance.
- TIMING to calculate your racer's speed.
- AVERAGES to get reliable results.

WHAT YOU NEED

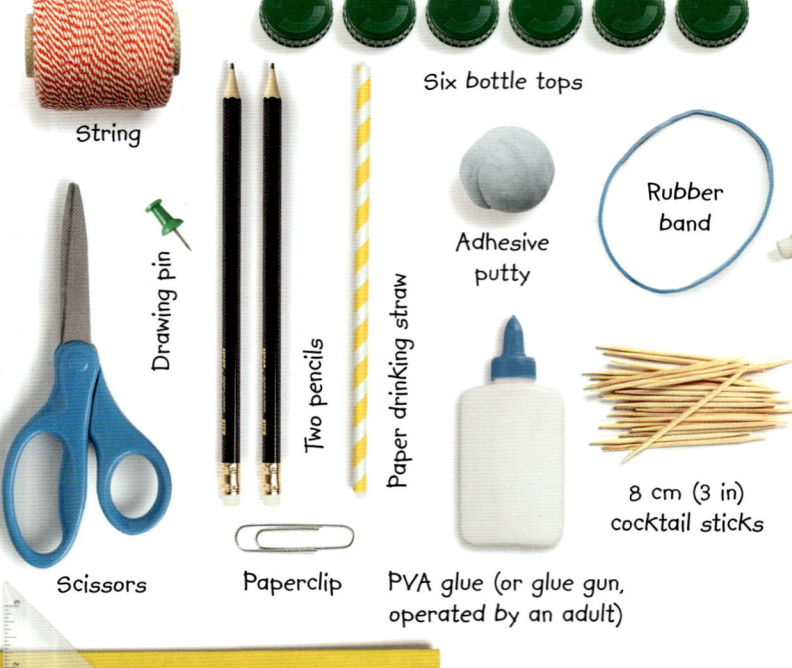

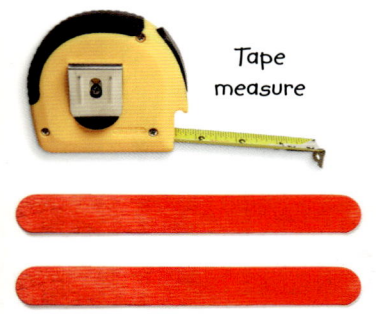

- String
- Six bottle tops
- Drawing pin
- Two pencils
- Paper drinking straw
- Adhesive putty
- Rubber band
- Scissors
- Paperclip
- 8 cm (3 in) cocktail sticks
- PVA glue (or glue gun, operated by an adult)
- Set square
- Stiff card
- Notebook
- Stopwatch or smartphone
- Tape measure
- Two extra wide lolly sticks 11.5 x 1.7 cm (4½ x ⅔ in) (you can use card cut to size)

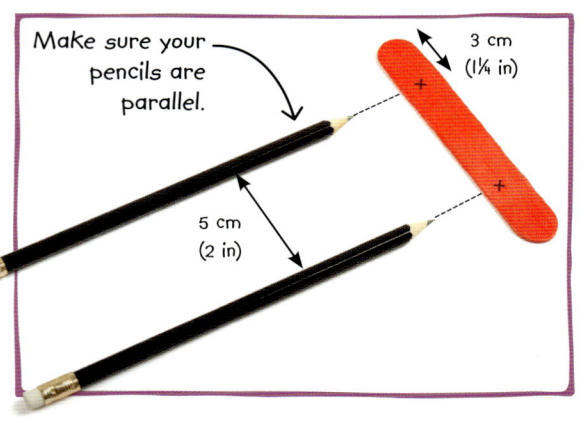

Make sure your pencils are parallel.
3 cm (1¼ in)
5 cm (2 in)

1 Place two pencils 5 cm (2 in) apart. Then place a lolly stick (or stiff card cut to size) at the end of the pencils and make two marks 3 cm (1¼ in) inside each end of the lolly stick.

Hold the pencils in place until the glue sets.
Keep the pencils parallel.

2 Glue the tips of both pencils to the pencil marks. Keep the pencils parallel to each other.

SPEED TRIALS   93

2 cm (¾ in)

You could use a set square to check that the straw is perpendicular (at a right angle) to the pencils.

QUADRILATERALS
A quadrilateral is a four-sided two-dimensional (2D) shape. These shapes are all quadrilaterals.

Square   Kite   Irregular quadrilateral   Rhombus

Parallelogram   Trapezoid   Rectangle

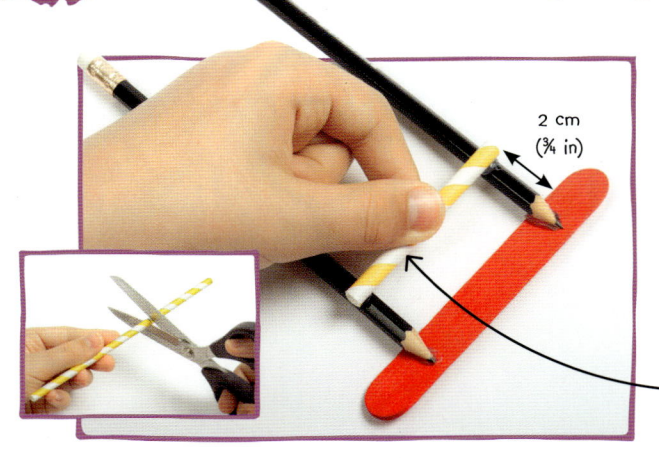

3 Cut a piece of straw to 6.5 cm (2½ in). Glue it to the underside of the pencils, 2 cm (¾ in) from the lolly stick. This will be the front of the racer.

1.5 cm (⅗ in)

2.7 cm (1 in)

2 cm (¾ in)

2.3 cm (⁹⁄₁₀ in)

Don't worry if your measurements aren't precise.

4 To make the spoiler, draw a quadrilateral (a four-sided shape) on a piece of card. The length of the top edge should match the width of the lolly stick.

5 Make a second, identical quadrilateral and then attach one quadrilateral to the end of each pencil. The top of the quadrilateral should slope away from the end of the pencil.

Try to align the lolly stick so there is an equal amount of overhang on both sides.

6 Glue along the top of the two quadrilaterals and attach the second lolly stick to them to form the spoiler that will balance your racer.

The straw will hold a toothpick attached to the wheels.

94 MEASUREMENTS

FIND THE CENTRE OF A CIRCLE
Draw a line across the circle. Halfway along this line, measure a 90° angle and draw another line. The centre is halfway along this second line.

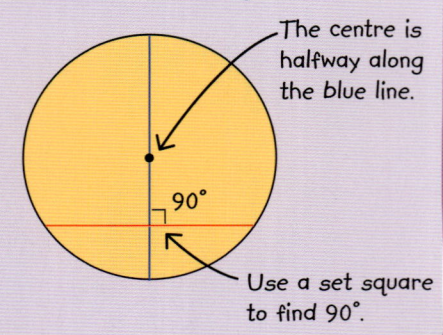

- The centre is halfway along the blue line.
- Use a set square to find 90°.

7 Find and mark the centre of four bottle tops. Press a drawing pin through these caps to create a hole that will fit a toothpick.

- Place a ball of adhesive putty inside the cap to ensure the pin doesn't mark your table when you press it through.

- Use a set square to check your axle is perpendicular, otherwise your wheel may wobble!
- Add some glue to the inside of the bottle top, too, for added strength.

8 Place glue on top of the hole and push in a toothpick so it is perpendicular to the bottle top. Repeat with another toothpick and bottle top.

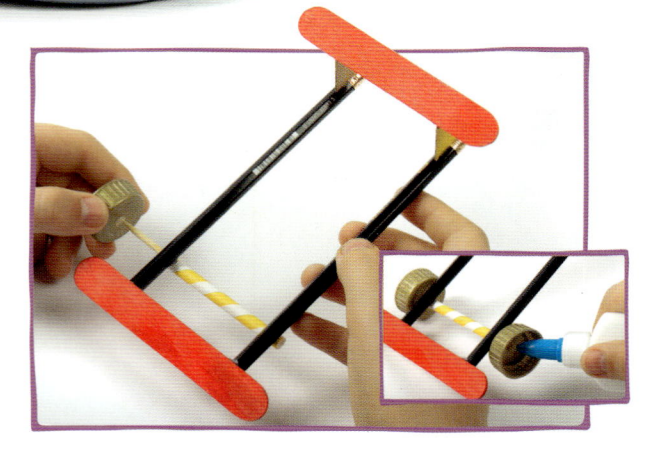

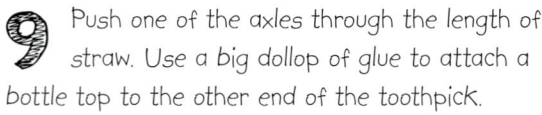

9 Push one of the axles through the length of straw. Use a big dollop of glue to attach a bottle top to the other end of the toothpick.

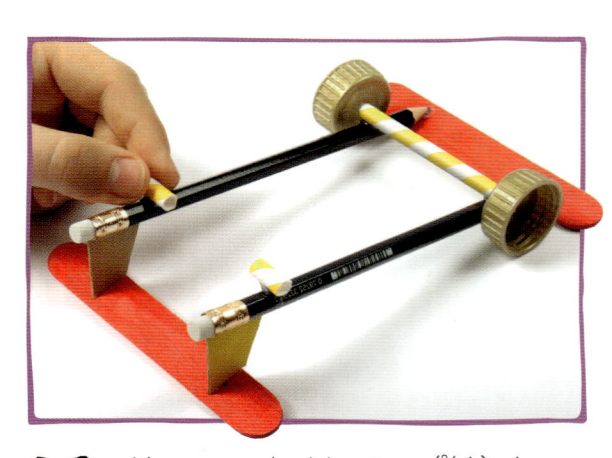

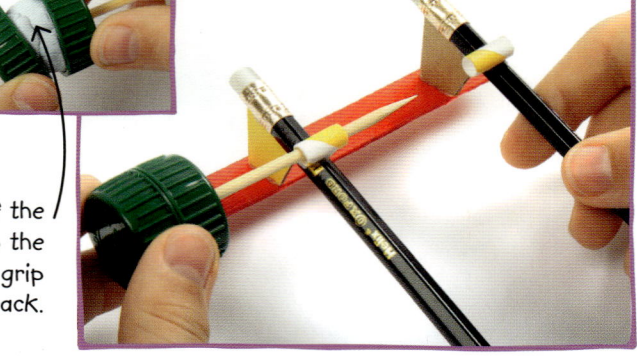

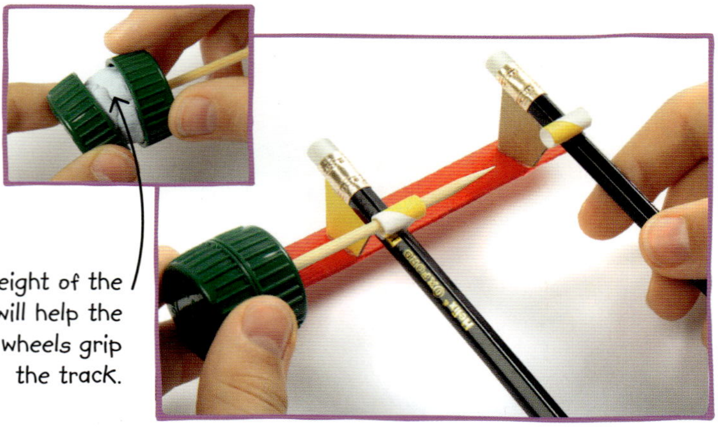

- The weight of the putty will help the rear wheels grip the track.

10 Measure and cut two 2 cm (¾ in) pieces of straw to hold the rear axle. Glue them to the rear of each pencil, in line with each other and parallel to the front axle.

11 Place a large piece of adhesive putty inside one of the bottle tops and press another on top of it so they stick together. Next, thread the toothpick through the two pieces of straw.

SPEED TRIALS   **95**

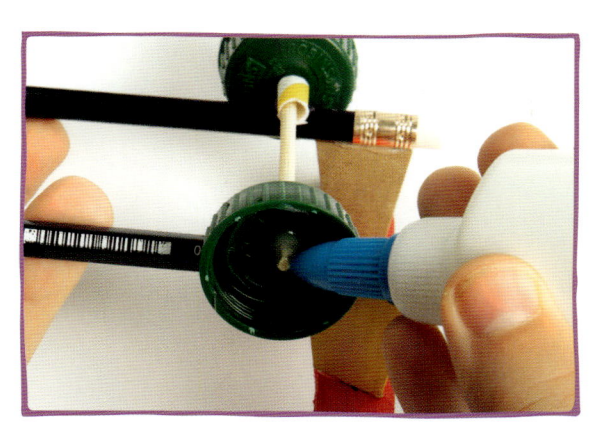

12 Push the second back wheel onto the toothpick and secure well with glue. Fill the cap with adhesive putty and press another top on.

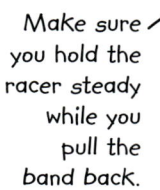

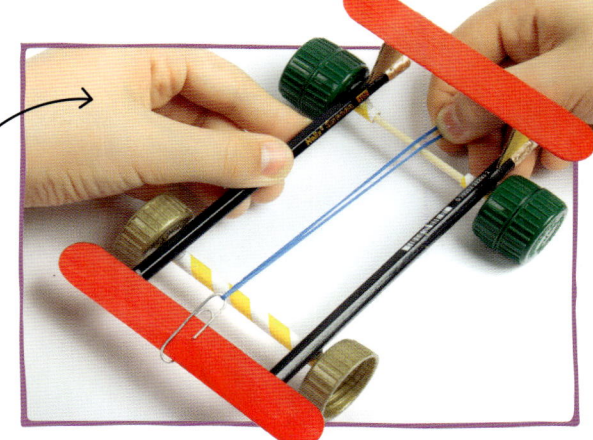

Make sure you hold the racer steady while you pull the band back.

13 Thread a long, thin rubber band onto a paperclip. Attach the paperclip to the front lolly stick, then stretch the rubber band towards the rear axle.

14 Wrap the rubber band over itself multiple times at the rear axle so that it holds itself in place. Don't let go of the wheels as you twist the band!

Decorate your racer with stickers.

You can paint your wheels black to look like rubber.

15 To make your racer go, wind up the rubber band by placing the car on the ground and pulling it backwards. Let go and watch it speed off!

96 MEASUREMENTS

16 To make the track markers, stick a toothpick into a large splodge of adhesive putty. Tie one end of the string to the toothpick.

17 Starting from the toothpick, measure out 1 m (39½ in) of string. Mark it with a pencil or pen, then measure out another 50 cm (20 in), and another. You will use this excess to lengthen the track.

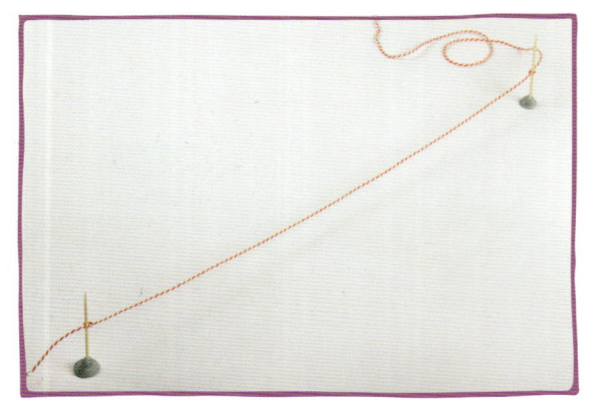

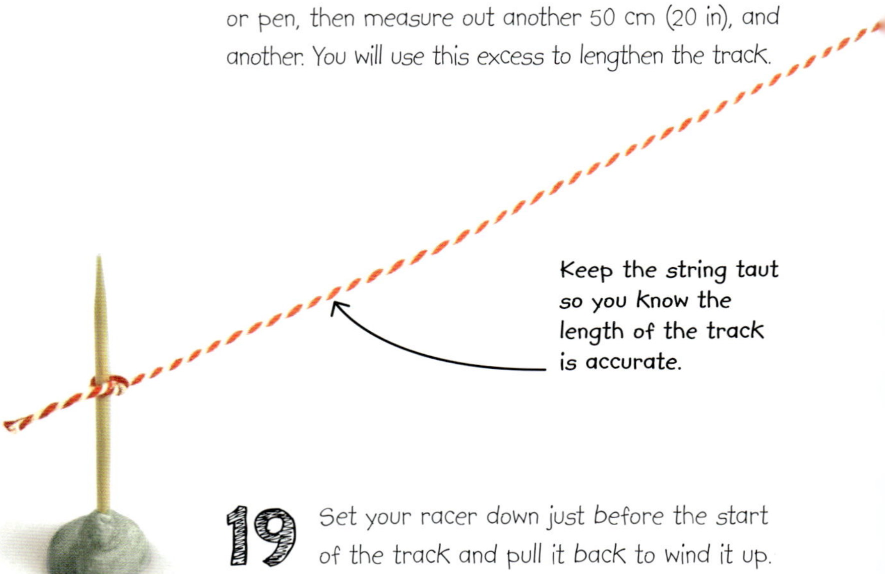

Keep the string taut so you know the length of the track is accurate.

18 Place another toothpick in a blob of adhesive putty and tie the string to it at the first point that you marked. The length of string is your track.

19 Set your racer down just before the start of the track and pull it back to wind it up. Prepare your stopwatch by setting it to zero. You could ask a friend to help by being the timekeeper.

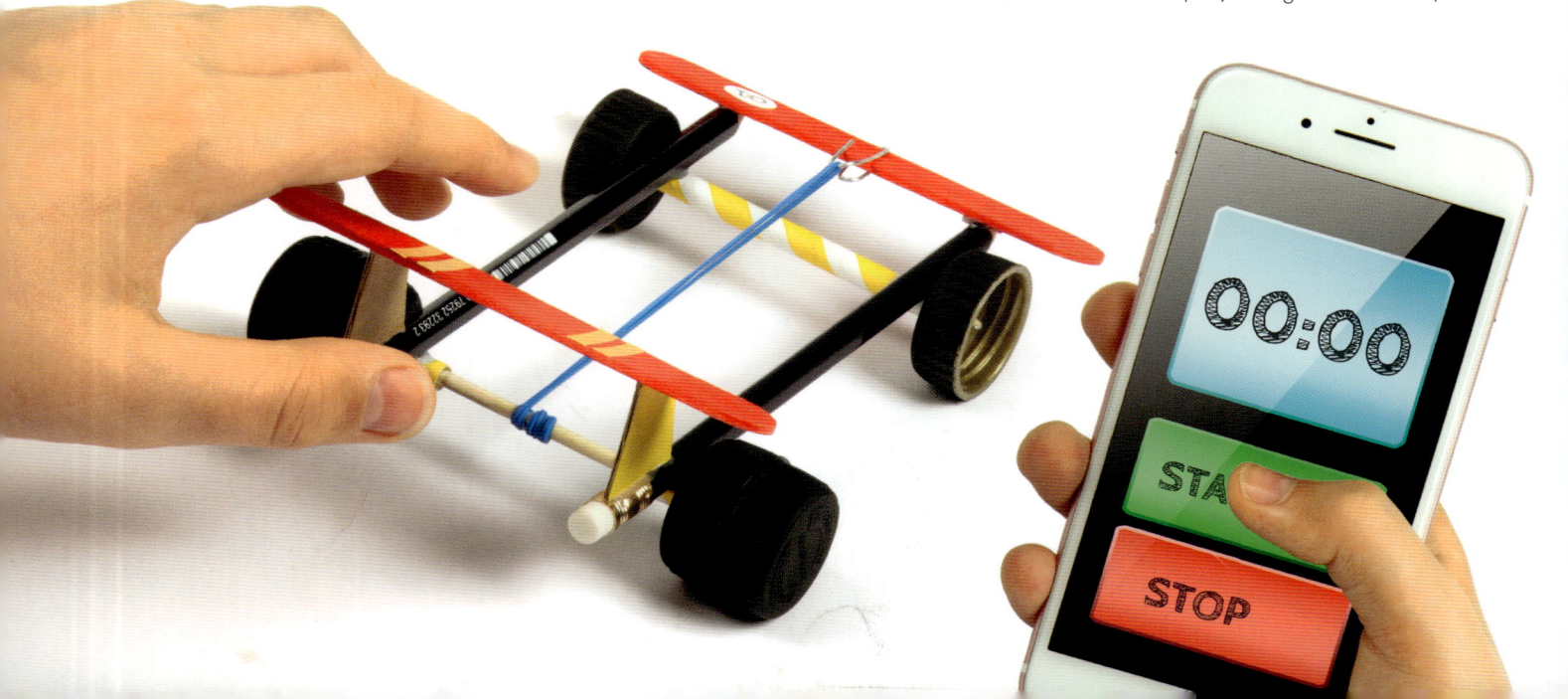

SPEED TRIALS   97

20 Release the racer and at the same moment start the stopwatch. Stop the stopwatch as soon as the racer passes the finish.

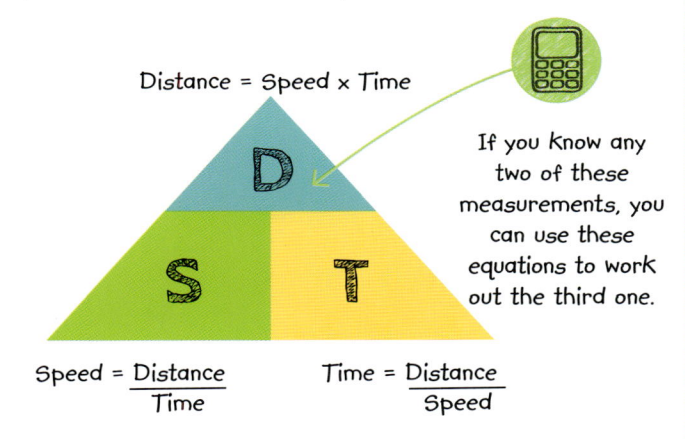

Distance = Speed × Time

D
S   T

Speed = Distance / Time   Time = Distance / Speed

If you know any two of these measurements, you can use these equations to work out the third one.

21 Calculate your racer's speed by dividing the distance it travelled by the time it took to get there. If your racer completes a 60 cm (23⅓ in) course in 3 seconds, it travels at 20 cm per second (8 in/s).

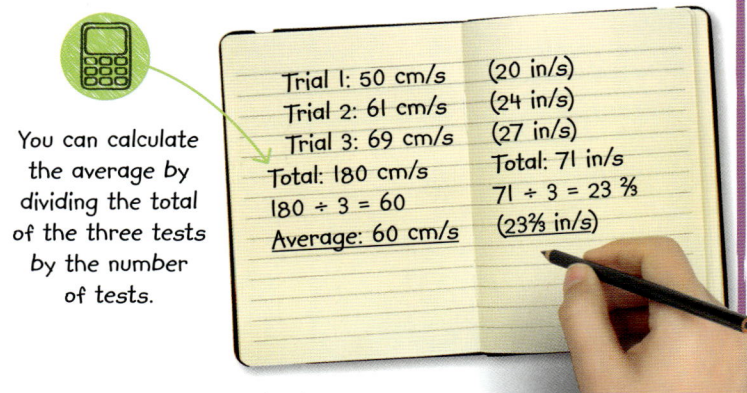

You can calculate the average by dividing the total of the three tests by the number of tests.

Trial 1: 50 cm/s   (20 in/s)
Trial 2: 61 cm/s   (24 in/s)
Trial 3: 69 cm/s   (27 in/s)
Total: 180 cm/s   Total: 71 in/s
180 ÷ 3 = 60   71 ÷ 3 = 23 ⅔
Average: 60 cm/s   (23⅔ in/s)

22 To get a reliable measure of your racer's speed, you need to take an average of several time trials.

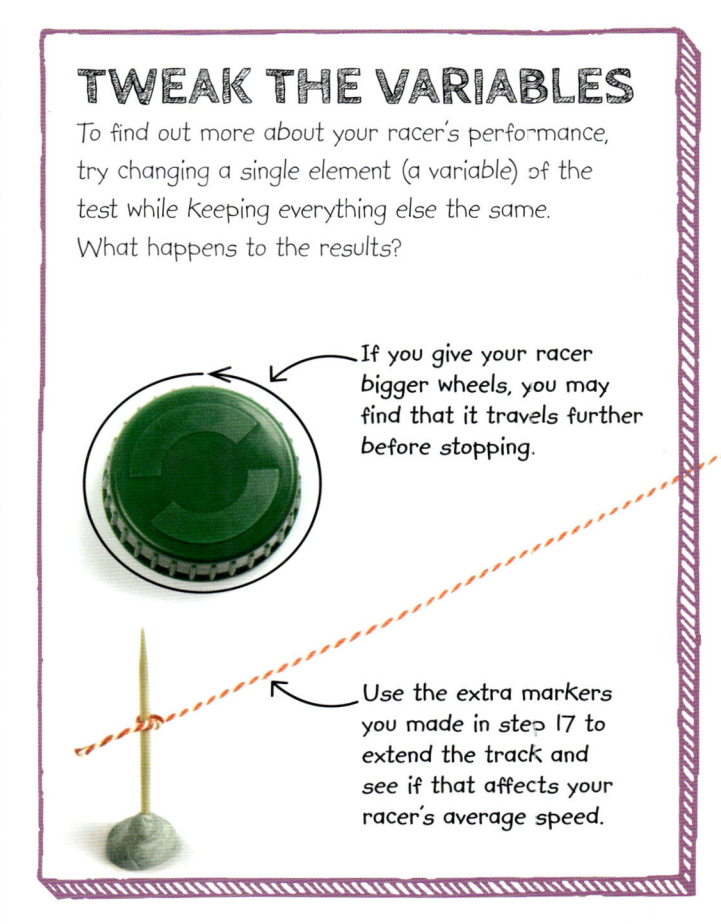

TWEAK THE VARIABLES

To find out more about your racer's performance, try changing a single element (a variable) of the test while keeping everything else the same. What happens to the results?

If you give your racer bigger wheels, you may find that it travels further before stopping.

Use the extra markers you made in step 17 to extend the track and see if that affects your racer's average speed.

REAL WORLD MATHS
USING AVERAGES TO IMPROVE

If you only measure something once, you might get an unexpected or unlikely result. Finding an average means you can be more confident that your measurement is consistent and accurate. Formula One engineers use averages of several time trials to work out how to tweak and improve their team's performance.

Friendship bracelets are meant to be worn until they fall apart.

BRILLIANT BRAIDING
FRIENDSHIP BRACELETS

Show your best friends how much they mean to you by making them a friendship bracelet. You can go for a two-tone or multicoloured bracelet – the choice is yours. To make one, you can either put your maths skills to good use by dividing a cardboard circle into eight equal parts to make a loom, or just weave a pattern freehand. Whatever you choose, your friends will be queuing up wanting more.

Why not make a two-tone bracelet and double its length so the two strands overlap?

Make bracelets for your friends in their favourite colours.

HOW TO MAKE FRIENDSHIP BRACELETS

Have a go at making two different types of friendship bracelet. The first uses a cardboard loom to help you weave your band, while the Candy Stripe bracelet is woven using forward knots. The loom lets you weave different patterns, but the stripe method is simpler.

MATHS YOU WILL USE
- **CIRCUMFERENCE** to work out the minimum length the bracelet needs to be.
- **ANGLES** to divide a circle into equal parts to make a cardboard loom.
- **VERTICAL, HORIZONTAL, AND DIAGONAL LINES** to mark the position of the slits on your loom.
- **PATTERN AND SEQUENCE** to create brilliant bracelets.

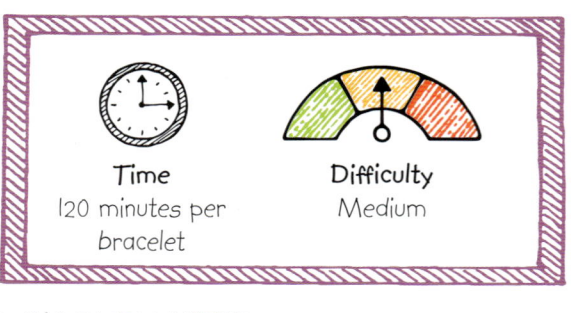

Time 120 minutes per bracelet

Difficulty Medium

WHAT YOU NEED
- Ruler
- Protractor
- Compass and pencil
- Scissors
- Tape measure
- Adhesive putty
- Adhesive tape
- Different-coloured wool or embroidery thread
- Stiff cardboard

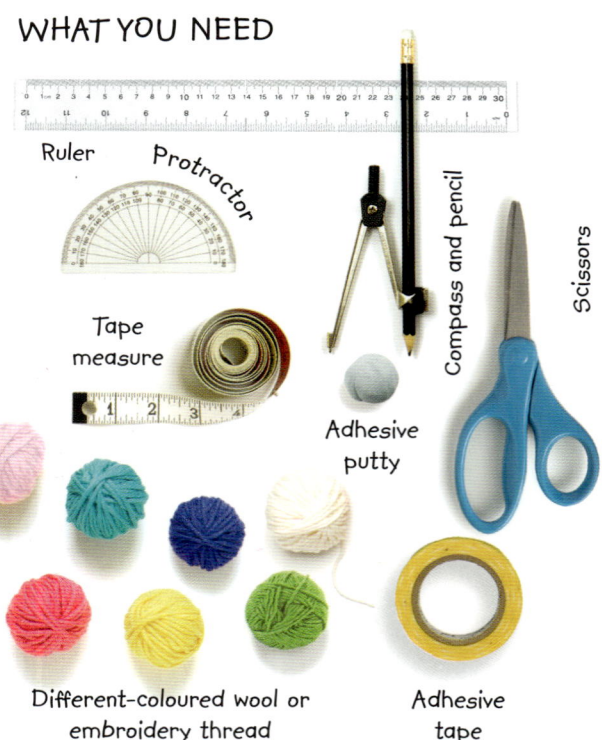

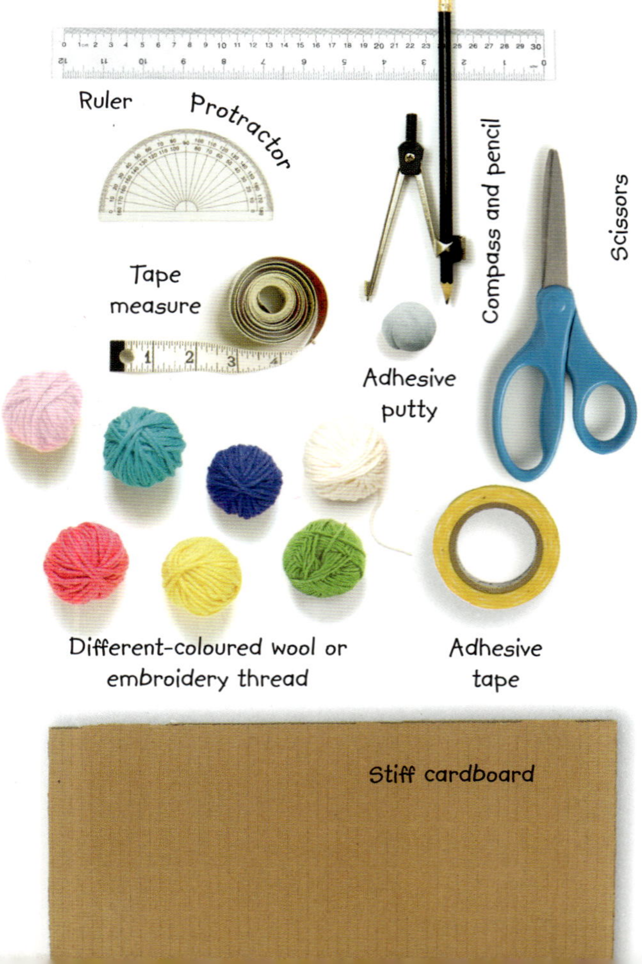

1. USING A CARDBOARD LOOM

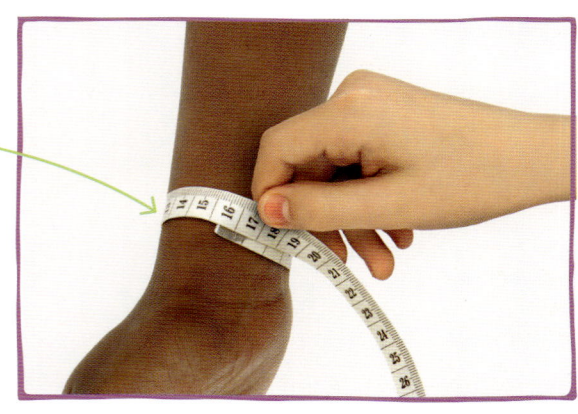

The circumference is the perimeter of a circle or ellipse.

1 Start by measuring the circumference of your friend's wrist with a tape measure. The friendship bracelet will need to be longer than this so you can tie the ends together.

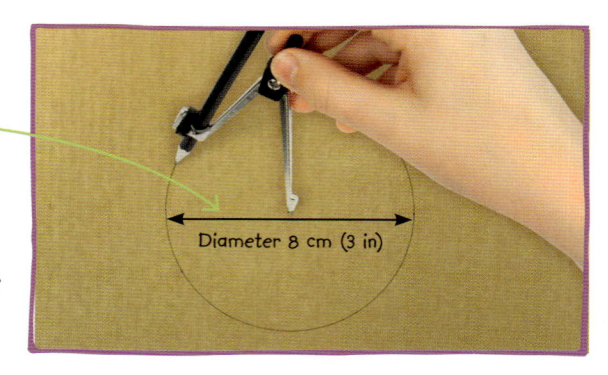

The diameter is a straight line that goes from one side of a circle to the other, passing through the centre.

Diameter 8 cm (3 in)

2 Set your compass to 4 cm (1½ in), insert a pencil, and then draw a circle with a diameter of 8 cm (3 in) on a piece of stiff cardboard.

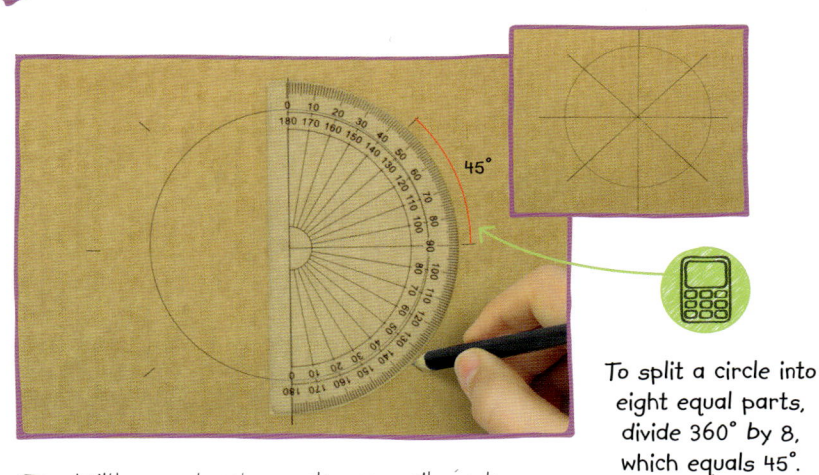

FRIENDSHIP BRACELETS 101

3 With a protractor, make a pencil mark every 45°. Then use a ruler to draw lines from the marks into the centre of the circle. You will now have a circle with eight equal-sized segments.

To split a circle into eight equal parts, divide 360° by 8, which equals 45°.

TYPES OF STRAIGHT LINES
In maths there are different types of straight lines. A vertical line goes straight up and down, while a horizontal line is level and goes from side to side. A diagonal line is a line that slants.

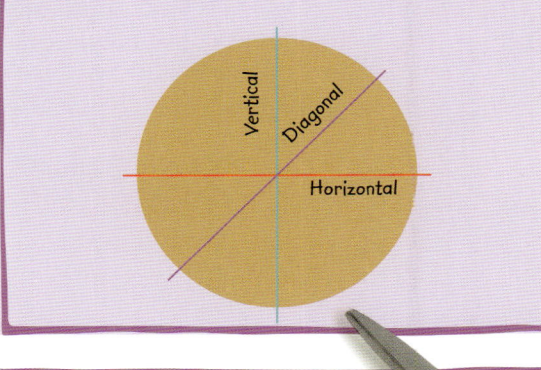

4 Along each vertical, horizontal, and diagonal line, use a ruler to measure 2 cm (¾ in) in from the edge of the circle and mark these points with a pencil.

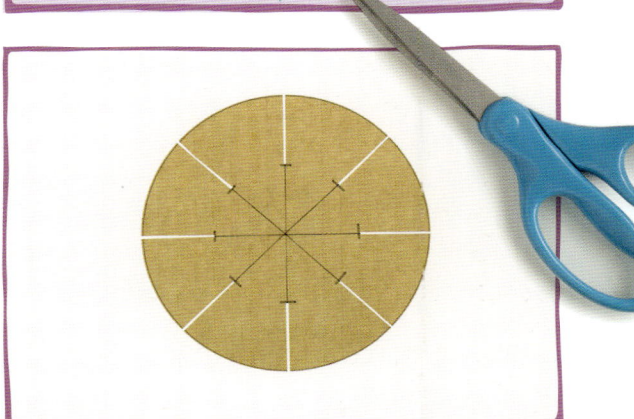

5 Cut out the cardboard circle using scissors. Then carefully cut slits along each line up to the 2 cm (¾ in) mark. This circle will act as your loom.

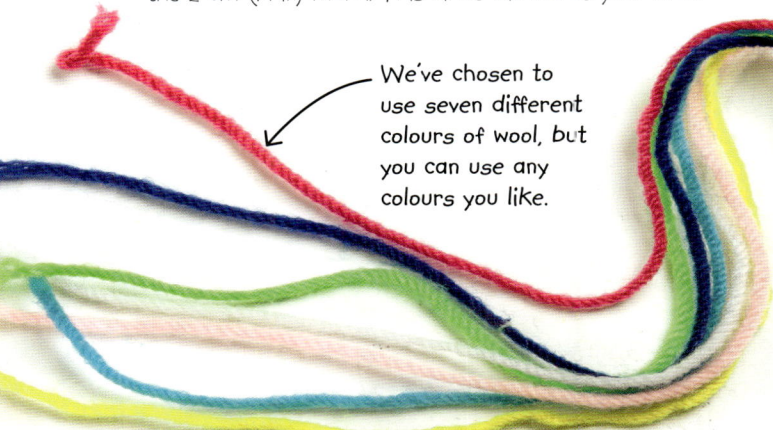

We've chosen to use seven different colours of wool, but you can use any colours you like.

6 Gently punch a hole in the centre of the cardboard loom using the tip of a pencil and adhesive putty. The hole needs to be big enough to feed the wool or embroidery threads through it.

7 Choose the colours of wool or embroidery thread you want to use. Measure seven lengths of thread each approximately 90 cm (35½ in) long using a tape measure and then cut with scissors.

102 MEASUREMENTS

8 Bring all the strands of wool together and tie a knot in one end. Then thread the loose ends through the hole in the middle of the cardboard loom.

Using different coloured wool will help you remember which strand to use next when you start weaving.

The knot will keep the strands from slipping through the hole in the loom.

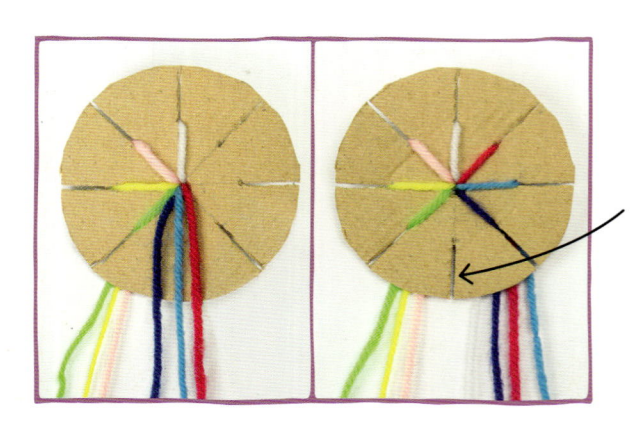

9 Turn the cardboard loom over so the knot is on the underside and then fold one strand of wool over each slit. Leave the bottom slit empty. You are now ready to start weaving your bracelet.

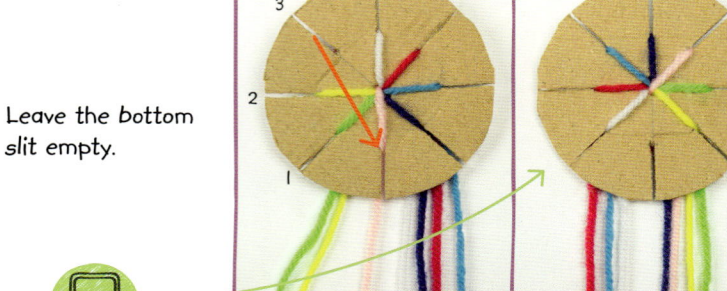

Leave the bottom slit empty.

Rotate the loom anticlockwise by 135°.

10 Count clockwise from the empty slit and take the third strand of wool and pull it across to fill the empty slit. Turn the loom anticlockwise so the new empty slit is at the bottom.

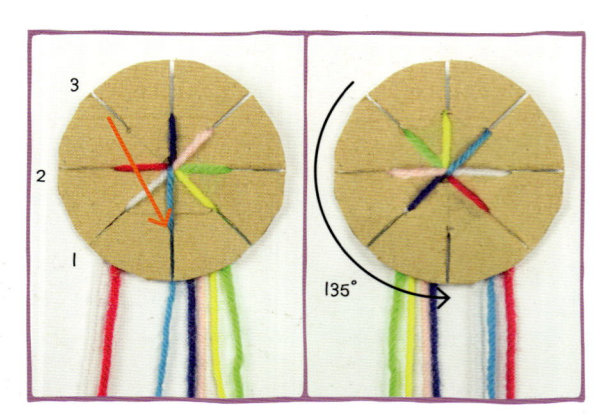

11 Repeat step 10: count three up from the bottom slit and take the wool and thread it over the empty slit. Turn the loom anticlockwise again, so that the new empty slit is pointing downwards.

12 Keep repeating this process, turning the loom anticlockwise each time. You will see the bracelet start to form on the underside of the loom.

FRIENDSHIP BRACELETS   103

13 Keep going until you have a length of woven strands long enough to go around your friend's wrist with about 2 cm (¾ in) of extra length for tying it together.

Leave about 2 cm (¾ in) of wool after the knot to stop the bracelet coming apart.

14 Take the threads off the cardboard loom and pull the bracelet through the hole. Knot the end to stop the weave unravelling and cut off any extra thread, leaving a short tassel after the knot.

15 Tie the finished bracelet around your friend's wrist with a knot as a symbol of your friendship.

PLAYING WITH PATTERN

Once you get good at making a friendship bracelet, why not take your skills further by creating friendship bracelets with geometrical patterns or complex colour sequences? Look for books in your local library, or search online, for instructions on how to make them.

Why not make a bracelet using dark and light tones of the same colour, like this one?

2. CANDY STRIPE BRACELET

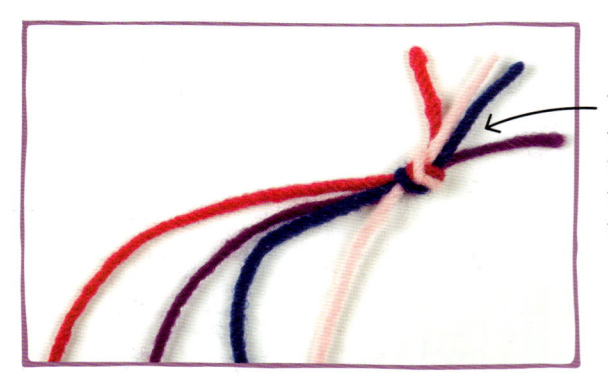

The more threads you use, the wider the bracelet but the longer it will take to make.

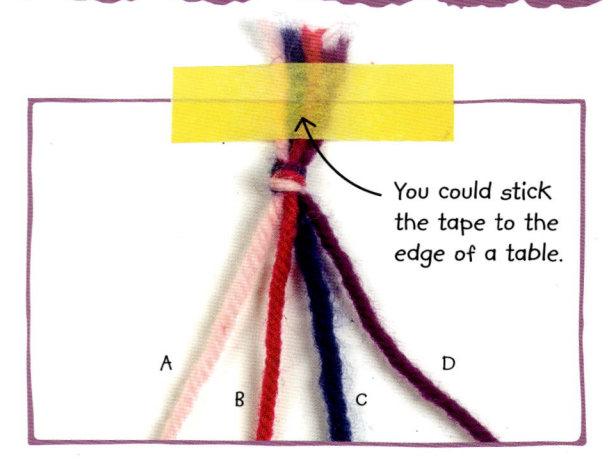

1 Choose the colours and number of threads you want to weave. We have used four threads of different colours. Cut each thread to about 90 cm (35½ in), then line them up and tie the ends together.

You could stick the tape to the edge of a table.

2 Use adhesive tape to attach the threads above the knot to a suitable surface. Separate the strands below the knot and arrange them in the order you'd like the colours to appear in the bracelet.

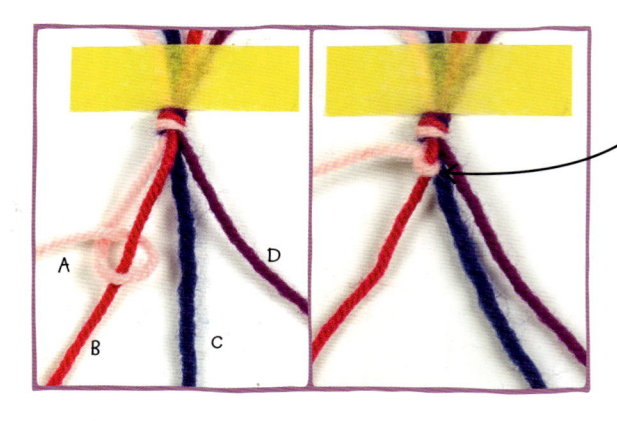

The colour of the first diagonal stripe in the bracelet will be light pink, or strand A.

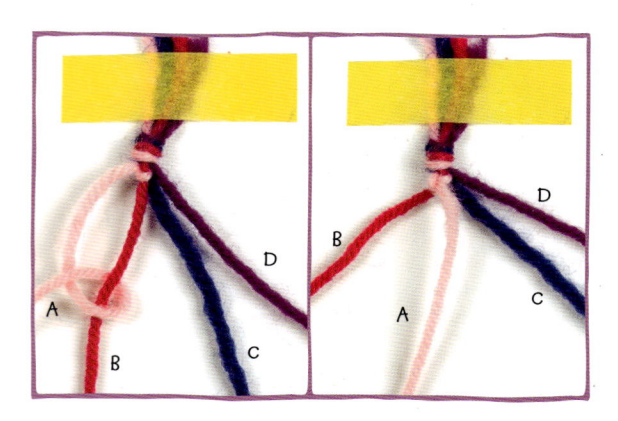

3 Pick up the far left-hand thread (A) and loop it over and under and then through thread B. Holding onto B, push the knot up to the top of the strands and pull it tight.

4 Repeat step 3 using thread A again so you create a double knot. This type of knot is called a forward knot. The action will change the order of threads to B, A, C, D.

TYING A FORWARD KNOT
To tie a forward knot, take thread A and first cross it over and then under thread B. Then loop A through thread B. Hold thread B and pull the knot tight. Repeat to form a double knot.

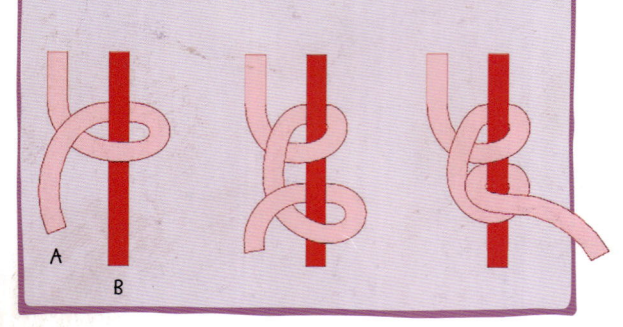

Each time you create a forward knot, the threads will change order.

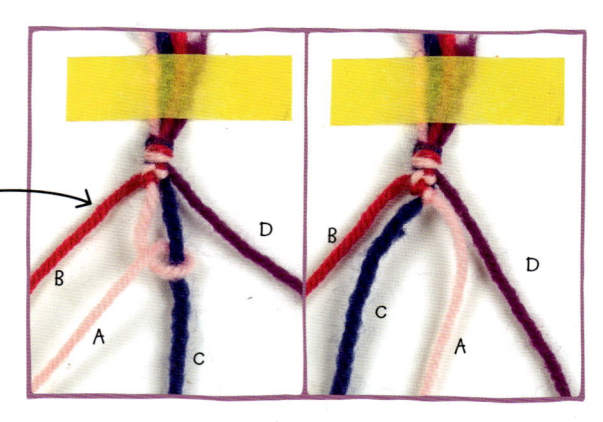

5 Repeat steps 3 and 4, but this time knot thread A twice around thread C. The order of threads will swap to B, C, A, D.

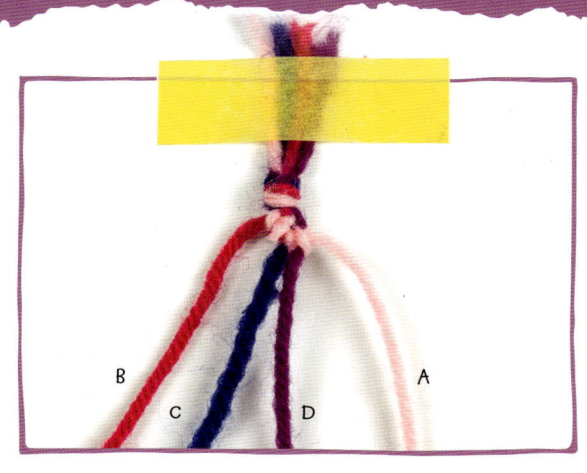

FRIENDSHIP BRACELETS   105

Each time you weave a row of coloured thread, you will create a pattern of diagonal stripes.

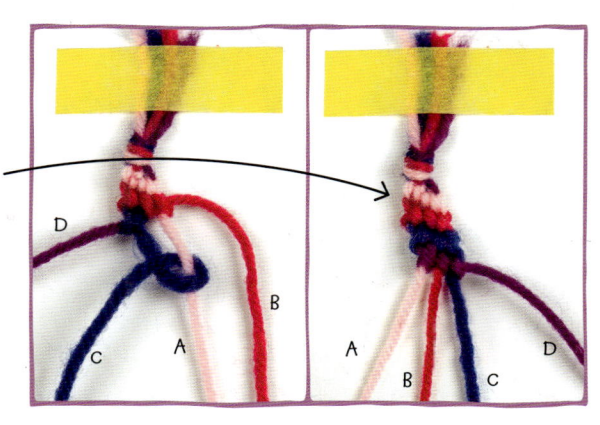

6 Follow steps 3 and 4 again, but this time knot thread A twice around D. The order of threads will then become B, C, D, A and you will have completed one row. Do the process again, starting with thread B.

7 When you have finished weaving a row using thread B, repeat with strand C and then D. Continue braiding until the coloured thread is back to A, B, C, D, which is the order you started with.

8 Repeat steps 3–7, weaving your bracelet row by row. Stop when your bracelet is the right length to fit around your friend's wrist.

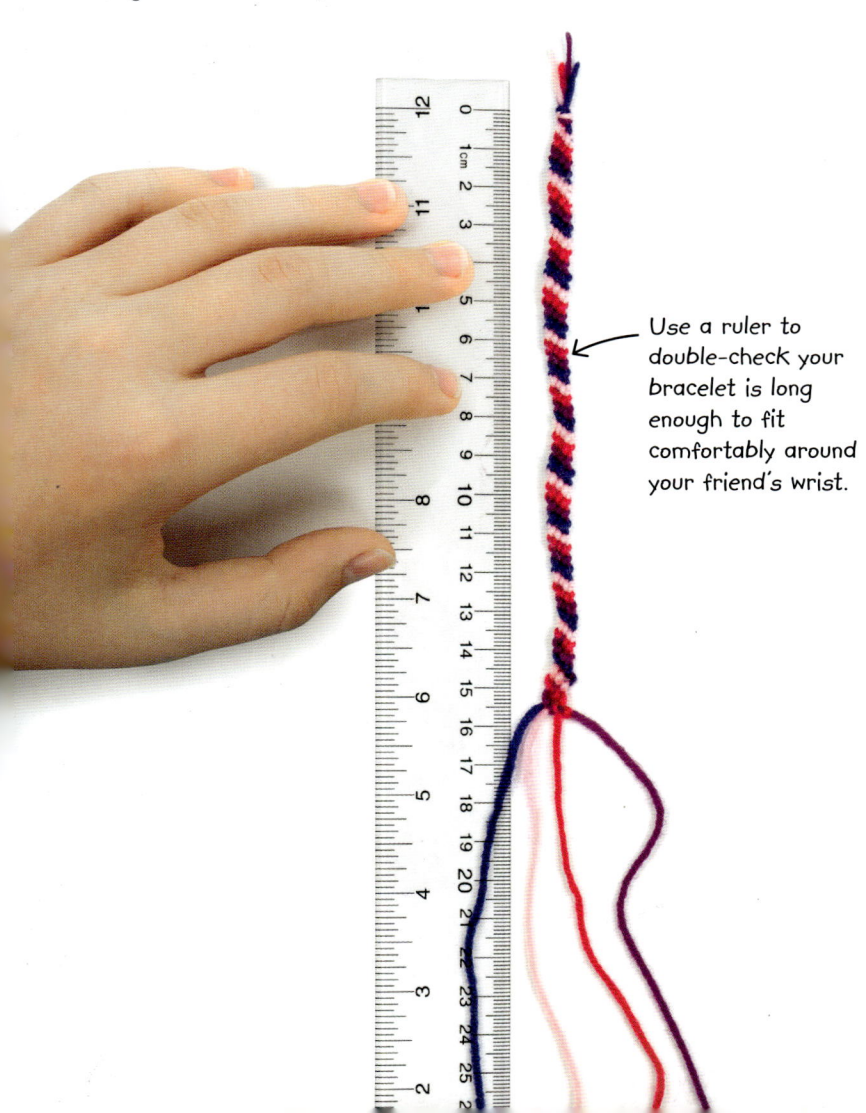

Use a ruler to double-check your bracelet is long enough to fit comfortably around your friend's wrist.

9 Tie the end to stop it coming loose and cut any extra thread, leaving 2 cm (¾ in) of wool after the knot. Then fasten it around your friend's wrist.

REAL WORLD MATHS
WEAVING ON A LOOM

Weaving is a technique in which two sets of thread are interlaced at right angles to make cloth. Looms such as the one pictured here hold hundreds of threads in place, making it possible to weave on a large scale.

RADICAL RATIO
FUN FRUIT DRINKS

If you are having friends over, it's nice to make some delicious drinks. By experimenting with different ingredients, you can create exciting flavours and even give your drink a unique layered look! The key to these recipes is the relative amounts of the different ingredients that you use, known as the ratio.

A slice of fruit makes a colourful garnish.

You can serve your fruit drinks in old jam jars for a cool look.

Make sure you get permission to use fancy glasses.

MATHS YOU WILL USE
- RATIO to get the perfect colour and flavour.
- MEASURING of the ingredients.
- CALCULATION to work how much you need.
- DENSITY to create a layered drink.

HOW TO MAKE FUN FRUIT DRINKS

The recipes here are for two different types of drinks – first a sweet raspberry and peach juice, then a layered smoothie. For the layering, we have used strawberries, peaches, and kiwis. You can replace any of those ingredients with other fruit but the colours may not be so vivid.

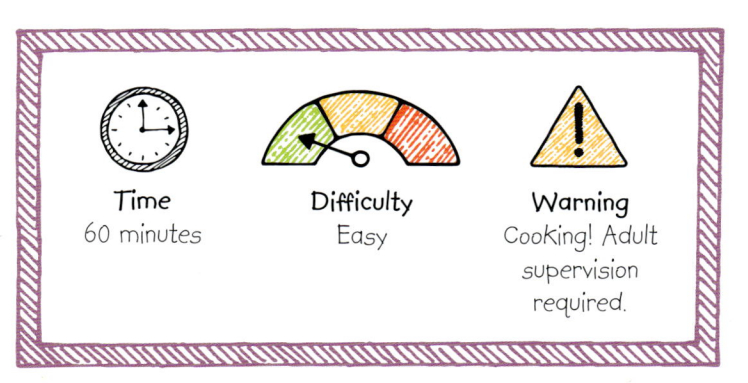

Time: 60 minutes
Difficulty: Easy
Warning: Cooking! Adult supervision required.

WHAT YOU NEED

- Blender
- Pitcher
- Ice cubes
- Measuring jug
- 250 g (0.55 lb) sugar
- 500 g (1.1 lb) Kiwis, peeled
- 500 g (1.1 lb) raspberries
- 500 g (1.1 lb) strawberries
- 1 kg (2.2 lb) drained tinned peaches
- Saucepan
- Weighing scales
- 3 lemons
- Fancy glasses or jam jars
- Fork
- Spatula

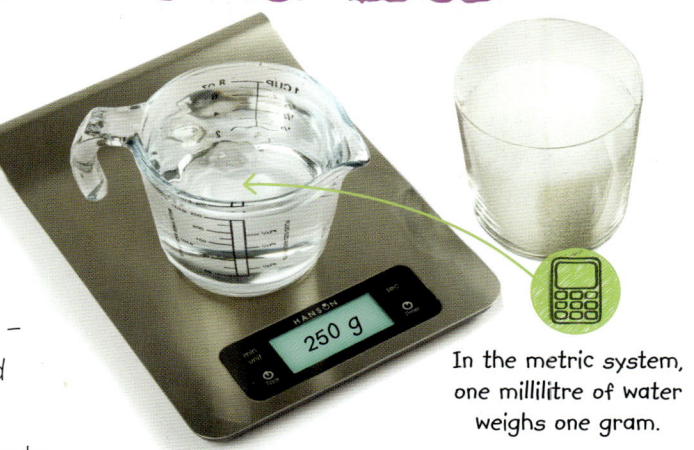

In the metric system, one millilitre of water weighs one gram.

1 Mix 250 g (0.55 lb) of sugar with 250 ml (8.5 fl oz) of water. Sugar is solid so it is measured in weight, while liquid water is measured in volume.

2 Pour the water and sugar into a saucepan and heat gently. Ask an adult to help with this. Once the sugar has dissolved to form a syrup, set the pan aside until the liquid has cooled.

3 Weigh out 500 g (1.1 lb) of raspberries and mash with a fork to form a purée. Do the same with the peaches.

MEASUREMENTS

4 Squeeze the lemons into a pitcher with the water and ice cubes, then stir in the peach and raspberry purée and sugar syrup. Serve in a fancy glass (ask permission) and garnish with fruit.

How does changing the ratio of ingredients affect the taste? What happens if you add more sugar or lemon juice?

Don't add ice to the Kiwi fruit.

De-stalk the strawberries before blending.

5 To make the second fruit drink, use separate bowls to weigh out 500 g (1.1 lb) each of strawberries, kiwis, and peaches.

6 Ask an adult to help you purée each fruit in the blender separately, adding 50 g (0.1 lb) of ice to the strawberries and to the peaches as you blend.

Calculate the density of each purée:

$$\text{Density} = \frac{\text{Weight}}{\text{Volume}}$$

The volume of the strawberry purée is greater than the volume of the Kiwi purée.

7 Pour each of the puréed fruits into a measuring jug and check the volume of the purées. You will see that each one has a different volume.

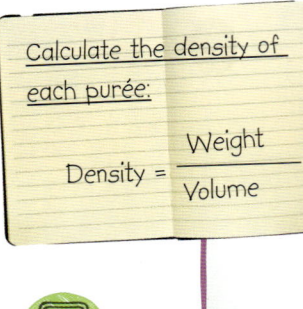

8 Place each purée on the scales in turn to find their weights. Then calculate each one's density by dividing the weight of the purée by its volume. Make a note of which purée is densest.

FUN FRUIT DRINKS 109

9 Pour 75 ml (1.7 fl oz) of the densest mixture into your glass followed by 50 ml (2.5 fl oz) of the second densest. Lastly pour 25 ml (0.8 fl oz) of the least dense mixture.

Subtract the volume you need to pour from the total volume in the measuring jug and keep pouring until that much remains in the jug.

The peach purée is less dense than the kiwi so it will settle on top.

The kiwi purée is the densest liquid so it should be poured first.

The ratio of strawberry to peach and kiwi is 1:2:3. There is three times as much kiwi as strawberry.

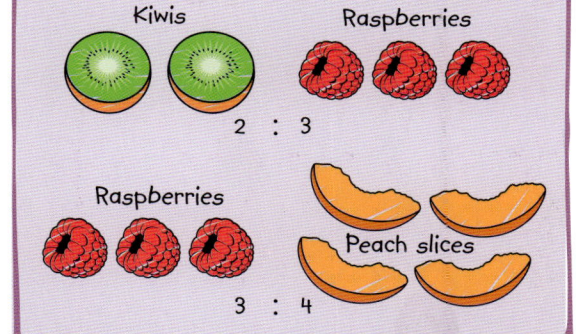

One part strawberry purée

Two parts peach purée

Three parts kiwi purée

10 You will instantly see the ratio of the ingredients in your fruit drink by how the layers settle in the glass or jam jar. Enjoy!

RATIO
We can use ratios to compare the size or amount of two or more different things. Ratio is written as a series of numbers with two dots on top of each other in between them.

Kiwis   Raspberries
2 : 3

Raspberries   Peach slices
3 : 4

CATERING FOR A PARTY
No one should go without treats at a party, so anyone organizing an event has to make sure that they provide enough to keep everyone happy. One way to do this is by multiplying the amount of ingredients needed for each drink by the number of guests who are expected to come to the party.

POWERFUL PERCENTAGES
CHOCOLATE TRUFFLES

This project is a real test, not of your maths skills but of your power to resist temptation! These delicious truffles are sure to be a hit, but if you find them a little too sweet or bitter for your taste, you can tweak the percentages of milk or dark chocolate to get the flavour just right.

Don't leave your truffles lying around unattended!

Use a potato peeler to create chocolate swirls.

HOW TO MAKE CHOCOLATE TRUFFLES

These delicious treats are easy to make, but you might get messy hands along the way! You will need to melt the chocolate gently on the stove, so make sure you get adult help. Then have fun experimenting with different flavours and coatings for your truffles.

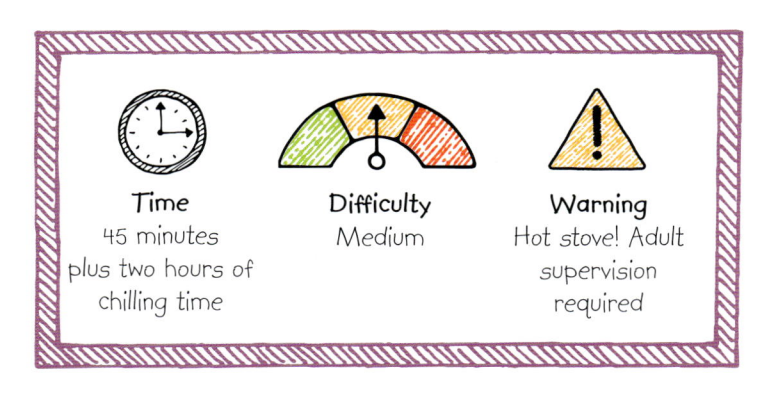

MATHS YOU WILL USE
- MEASURING as you weigh out your ingredients.
- PERCENTAGES to find your ideal balance of sweetness to bitterness.

Time
45 minutes plus two hours of chilling time

Difficulty
Medium

Warning
Hot stove! Adult supervision required

FOR 25 TRUFFLES, YOU NEED

- 200 g (7 oz) dark or milk chocolate, plus extra squares for making chocolate swirls
- 25 g (¾ oz) unsalted butter 
- 150 ml (5 fl oz) double cream and measuring jug 
- Chopped pistachios
- Cocoa powder 
- Desiccated coconut

(or other sprinkles of your choice)

- Vanilla essence or other flavourings such as peppermint or orange
- Saucepan
- Weighing scales 
- Heatproof bowl
- Potato peeler
- Teaspoon
- Spatula

You can use either all dark or all milk chocolate, or 50% (100 g (3.5 oz)) of each, depending on how sweet you want your truffles.

1 Weigh the chocolate and butter on your scales and carefully pour 150 ml (5 fl oz) of cream into a measuring jug.

2 Break the chocolate into tiny pieces and place in a heatproof bowl. The pieces need to be small so they melt quickly.

MEASUREMENTS

3 Pour the cream and butter into a saucepan and heat gently until the butter melts into the cream and the mixture starts to come to the boil.

⚠ Ask an adult to help you with this step.

4 Pour the hot cream and butter mixture into the bowl with the chocolate pieces. With a spatula, mix until all the chocolate has melted.

5 If you want to add flavour to your truffles, add a few drops of peppermint, orange, or vanilla extract. Place the mixture in the fridge to cool down.

Dust your hands with cocoa powder to make shaping the truffles easier.

6 After about two hours, take the mixture out of the fridge. Using a teaspoon, scoop out 25 bite-sized pieces of chocolate and roll each one into a ball. To be really precise, you could weigh each ball.

Five truffles with a pistachio coating means 20% of your batch will be green.

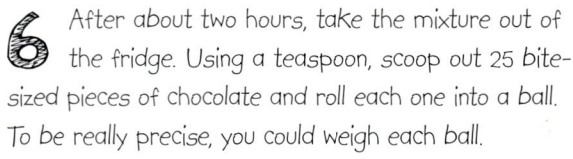

7 Decide how many truffles you want to coat in coconut, chocolate powder, or nuts. Spread the topping on your worksurface and roll the truffles in it. Reserve some truffles to coat in chocolate swirls.

CHOLATE TRUFFLES 113

Your chocolate will be easier to shave if you chill it in the fridge first.

8 To make chocolate swirls, cut shavings from a chocolate bar with a potato peeler.

9 Roll the remaining truffles in the chocolate swirls to create a flaky outer coating. Keep the truffles in the fridge until it's time to eat them. If you want to give your truffles as a gift, see pages 114-17 for how to make a chocolate box.

SWEET OR DARK?

You can make your truffles sweeter by adding a higher percentage of milk chocolate, while a lower percentage of milk chocolate will make them taste more bitter. Percentages are a useful way of comparing and measuring amounts by representing them as parts of 100. To work out what percentage one number is of another number, divide the lower number by the higher number and multiply the result by 100.

TOTAL CHOCOLATE NEEDED FOR RECIPE = 20 squares

DARK = 8 squares

MILK = 12 squares

Amount to find as a percentage.

100% = 20 squares

The whole amount of anything.

Our whole amount is 20 squares.

$\dfrac{8}{20}$ = 0.4 × 100 = **40%**

Total amount of chocolate.

Percentage of dark chocolate.

$\dfrac{12}{20}$ = 0.6 × 100 = **60%**

Percentage of milk chocolate.

THREE-DIMENSIONAL FUN
CHOCOLATE BOX

If you've managed not to eat them all, the delicious chocolate truffles from pages 110–13 make a great gift for family or friends. For a perfect present, make a personalized chocolate box to store them in. To build one, you'll need to start with a net, which is a 2D outline of a 3D shape.

Why not stick two pieces of card together to give the box a different colour on the inside.

MATHS YOU WILL USE
- NETS to convert 2D shapes to 3D shapes.
- DIAMETER to find the width of a circle.
- AREA to find the size of a shape.
- DIVISION to work out the shape of your box.

CHOCOLATE BOX 115

HOW TO MAKE A CHOCOLATE BOX

The starting point for making this box is measuring the size of the treats you want to store inside it. Then you'll need to plan how you want to display them. The instructions here are for a pattern of two layers of truffles in a simple grid.

Time 45 minutes
Difficulty Medium

WHAT YOU NEED

- Scissors
- Paper glue
- Ribbon
- Pencil
- Marker pen
- Sweets to put in your box (we used the truffles on pages 110–13)
- A3 coloured card (we stuck two pieces of card together to give the box different colours inside and out)
- Set square
- Ruler

3D SHAPES AND NETS

Imagine a 3D shape being unfolded into a flat area. This is called a net and it shows how 3D objects can be made out of 2D shapes.

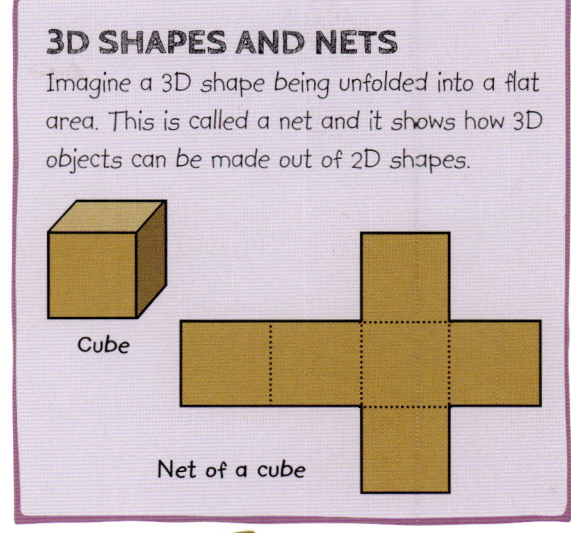

Cube

Net of a cube

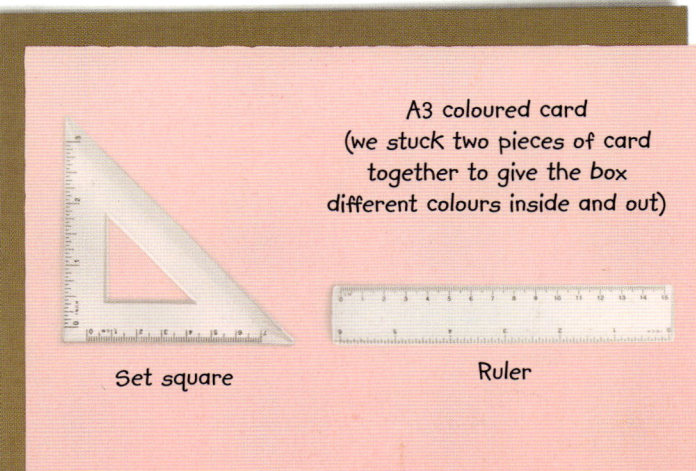

1 First work out how big your box and the dividers inside it need to be. To do this, measure the width of your biggest sweet. We are using the truffles from pages 110–13, which are 3 cm (1¼ in) wide.

2 Decide on a pattern for displaying your sweets. Here we have chosen a 2 x 4 grid of eight sweets. Inside the box there will be 16 chocolate truffles in two layers.

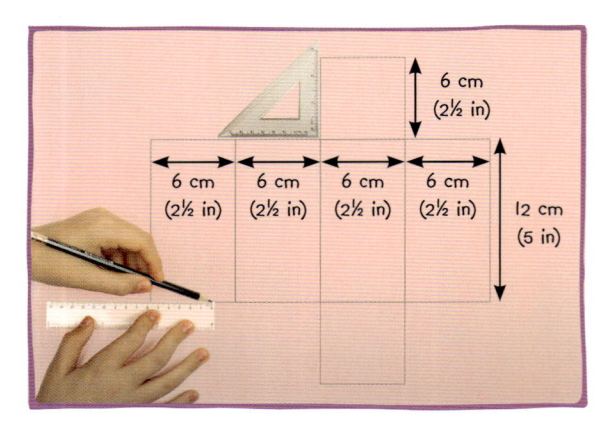

3 Use a pencil, ruler, and set square to measure and draw your box's net on a piece of card. Our shape is a rectangle with long sides that are double the length of the short sides.

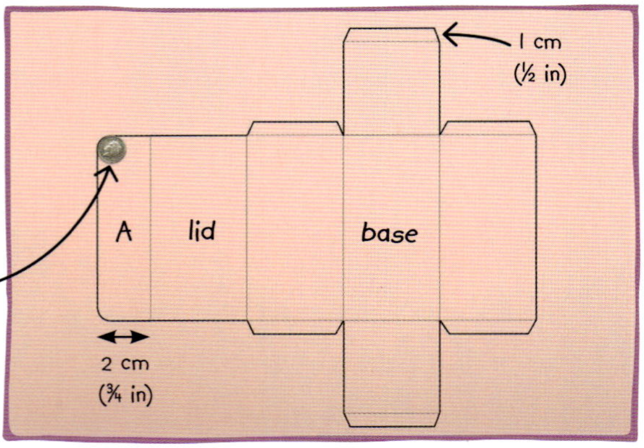

4 Add tabs to your net to allow you to stick the faces together, and a large flap (A) to the front of the lid. Draw around the shape in pen. This will be your cut line. Pencil lines will be the fold lines.

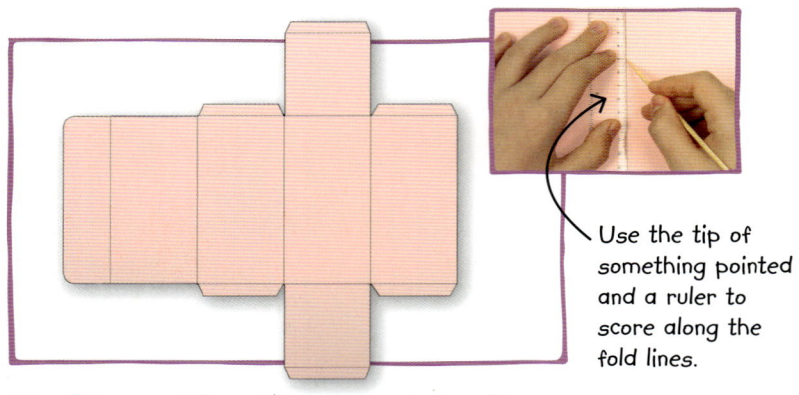

Use the tip of something pointed and a ruler to score along the fold lines.

5 Cut around the outline of your shape with scissors so you are left with the net. Score along the pencil lines using something pointed (but not sharp) and a ruler.

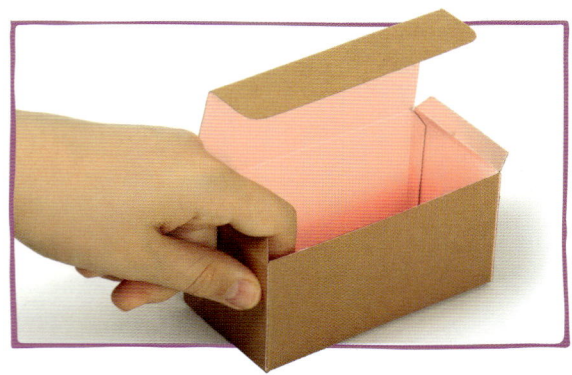

6 Fold along the scored lines, then add glue to the four side tabs that form the body of the box. Don't glue the other three tabs. Fold up the sides of the box and press on the tabs.

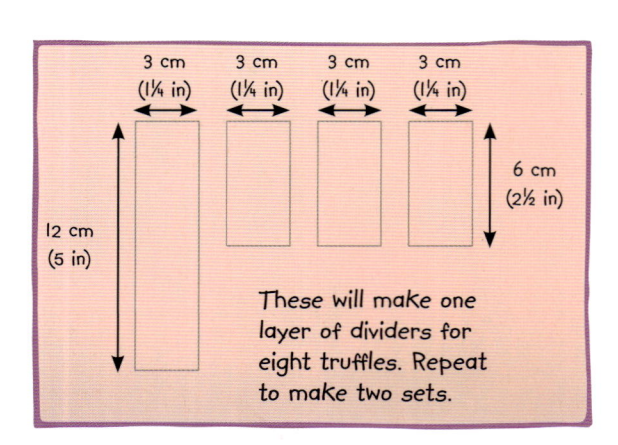

These will make one layer of dividers for eight truffles. Repeat to make two sets.

To space out your slits evenly, divide the length of the long divider by four and use a ruler to measure where they should go.

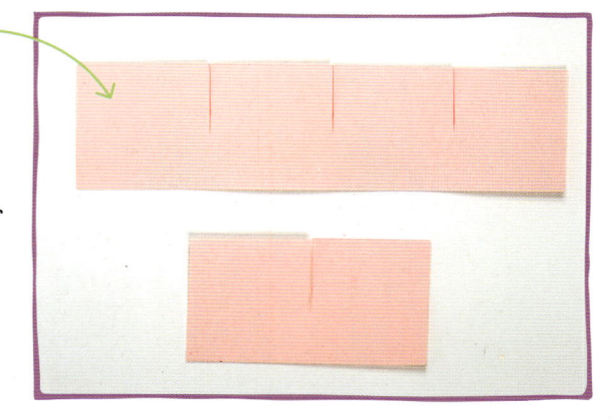

7 To make dividers for eight truffles per layer, use the length and half the height of your box to draw a long divider. Repeat this to make three short dividers, but using the box width.

8 With scissors, cut out your dividers. Cut a slit halfway down the middle of each of the short dividers. Cut three equally spaced-out slits in the long divider.

CHOCOLATE BOX   117

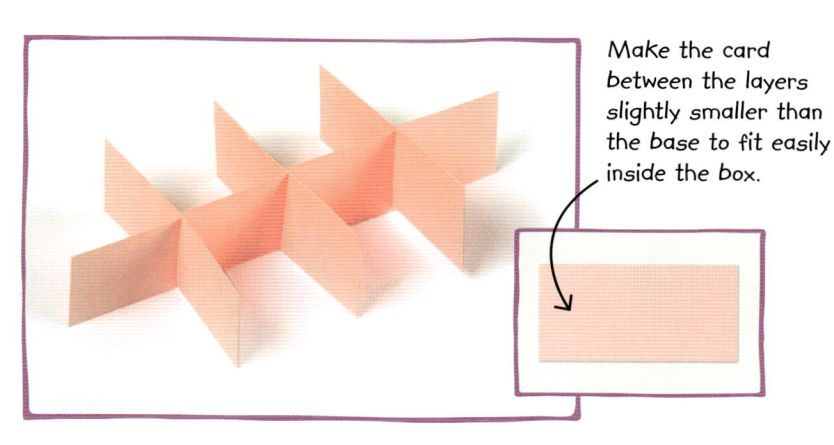

Make the card between the layers slightly smaller than the base to fit easily inside the box.

9 Slot the four pieces of card together at right angles. Cut a piece of card the same shape as the base of your box to separate the layers.

10 The two sets of dividers and separator card should look like this when assembled and will fit snuggly inside the chocolate box.

Each compartment should hold one truffle.

11 Place the lower divider in your box and fill with truffles before adding the separator card and then the top layer.

Don't glue your lid tab down – the ribbon will hold it in place.

12 Tie a colourful piece of ribbon around your box to secure it. You can decorate the outside with stickers if you like.

PERFECTLY PRICED
POPCORN SALE TRAY

If you have a playground charity sale or school fair coming up, why not make a sale tray bursting with yummy popcorn cones to raise money? Or turn a movie night with friends into a cinema experience by bringing out some popcorn cones. Whatever you decide, this fun project will show you how to design a 3D tray, create cones, and calculate how to price your popcorn to make a tasty profit!

MATHS YOU WILL USE
- **RADIUS AND DIAMETER** to draw the correct-sized holes for the popcorn cones.
- **CALCULATION** to work out the cost of making each cone and the price they need to be to make a profit.

Fill each cone with delicious buttery, salty, or sugary popcorn. What will you chose?

The ribbon around your neck will keep your hands free for serving customers.

ORN

70P
EACH

120 MEASUREMENTS

HOW TO MAKE A POPCORN SALE TRAY

The key to this project is to make the cones before you begin work on the tray. You don't want the cones to be too big to fit inside! The size of the sale tray we have made here allows space for 12 popcorn cones.

Time 3 hours

Difficulty Hard

WHAT YOU NEED

- Ruler
- Rubber
- Large bowl of popcorn
- Compass and pencil
- Felt-tip pen
- Adhesive putty
- Scissors
- PVA glue
- Adhesive tape
- A2 thick card (420 x 594 mm, 16½ x 23⅖ in)
- A4 coloured or plain white paper
- 200 cm (80 in) of red ribbon

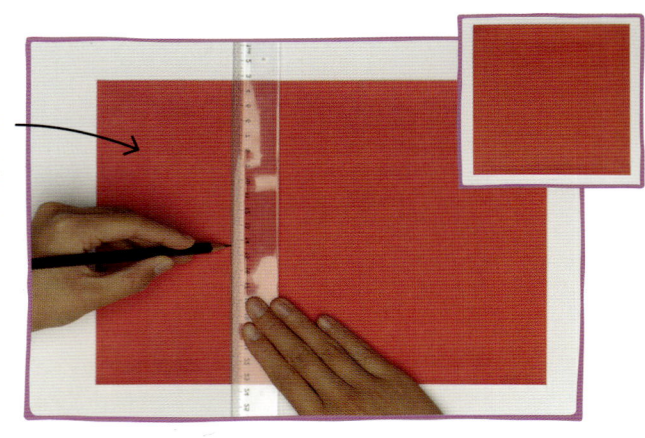

Why not make cones of different colours? We used eight red and four white squares.

1 To make each cone, take a sheet of paper and use a pencil and ruler to measure a square 21 x 21 cm (8 x 8 in). Cut out the square and repeat another 11 times to make 12 squares in total.

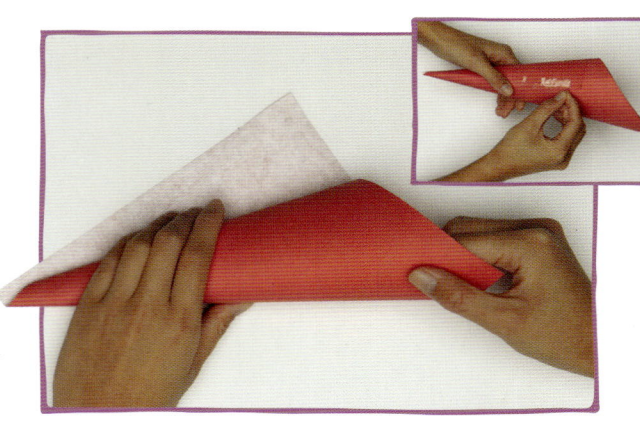

2 Rotate the paper square by 45° so it looks like a diamond and then roll it up into a cone with a point at one end. Stick tape where the edges meet so the paper does not unravel. Repeat to make 12 cones.

A cone is wide at one end and narrows to a point at the other end.

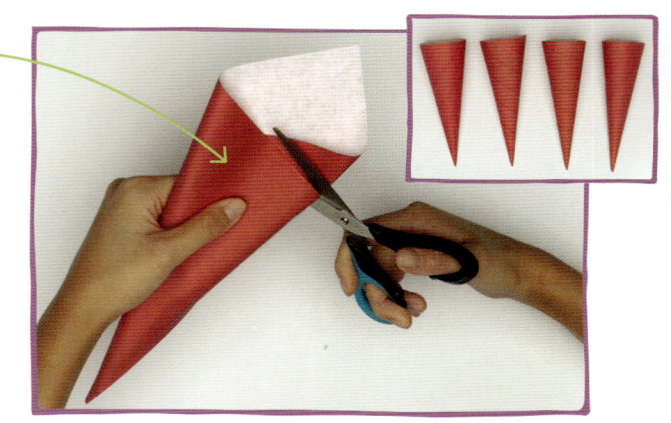

3 With a pair of scissors, carefully cut the pointy tops off all 12 cones. The open end should be level all the way around the circumference.

POPCORN SALE TRAY   121

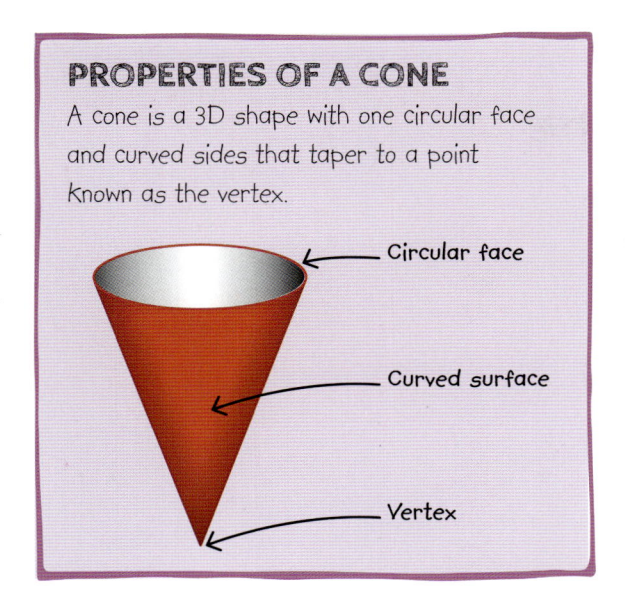

PROPERTIES OF A CONE
A cone is a 3D shape with one circular face and curved sides that taper to a point known as the vertex.

- Circular face
- Curved surface
- Vertex

The diameter of a cone is at its widest at the opening and becomes narrower the closer it is to the vertex.

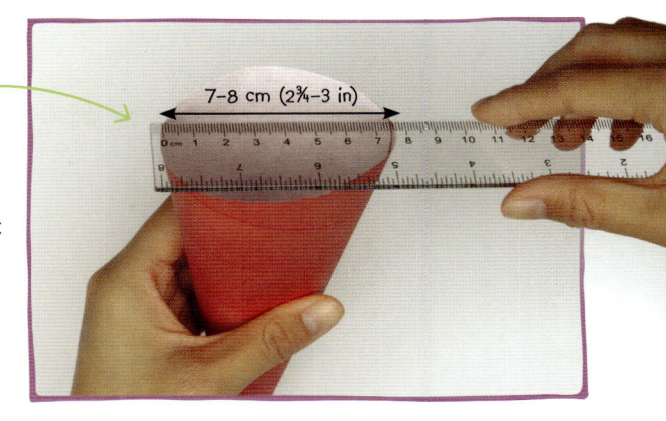

7–8 cm (2¾–3 in)

4. Check all 12 cones have roughly the same diameter of 7–8 cm (2¾–3 in) at the opening. This ensures each one will hold the same amount of popcorn when filled. Place your cones to one side.

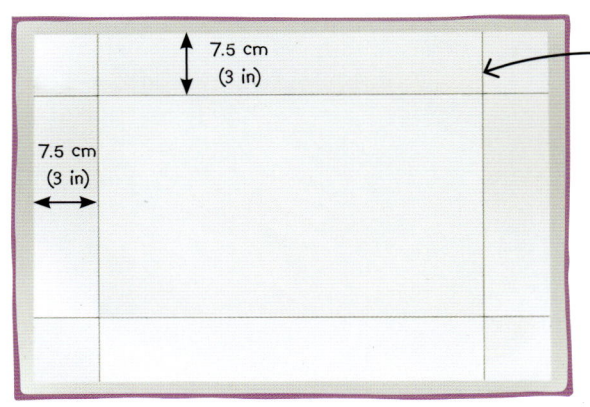

7.5 cm (3 in)

7.5 cm (3 in)

These lines will be your fold lines when you assemble the tray.

13 cm (5 in)

24 cm (9½ in)

Draw the vertical lines in between the top and bottom horizontal lines.

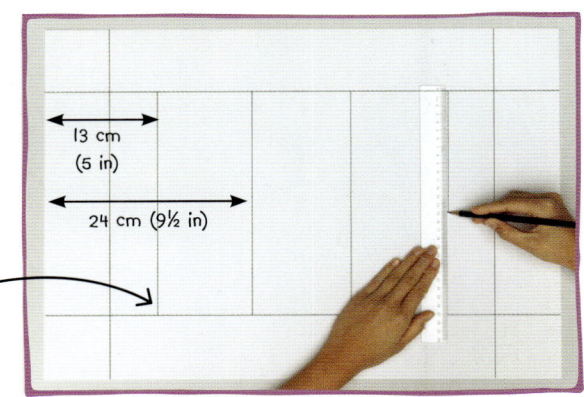

5. To make the tray, turn your piece of thick A2 card and draw a line 7.5 cm (3 in) in from each of the four sides of the card.

6. Then draw two vertical lines, 13 cm (5 in) and 24 cm (9½ in) in from the left side. Repeat on the right-hand side, so you end up with four new lines.

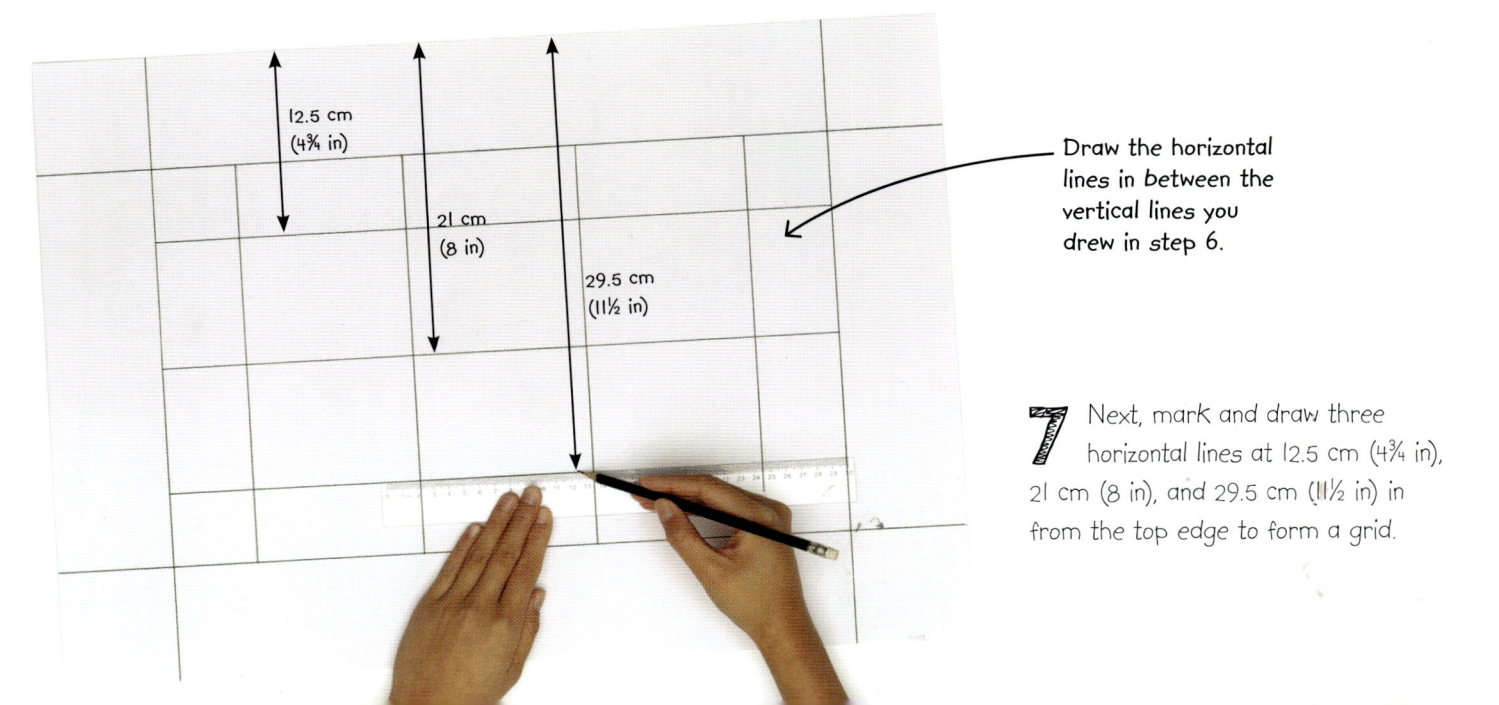

12.5 cm (4¾ in)

21 cm (8 in)

29.5 cm (11½ in)

Draw the horizontal lines in between the vertical lines you drew in step 6.

7. Next, mark and draw three horizontal lines at 12.5 cm (4¾ in), 21 cm (8 in), and 29.5 cm (11½ in) in from the top edge to form a grid.

122 MEASUREMENTS

8 In the top corners, make a pencil mark along the side 1 cm (½ in) above the horizontal line. Then draw a diagonal line connecting this point to where the horizontal and vertical lines meet. Repeat for the bottom corners, but make the mark below the horizontal line. These will be your glue tabs.

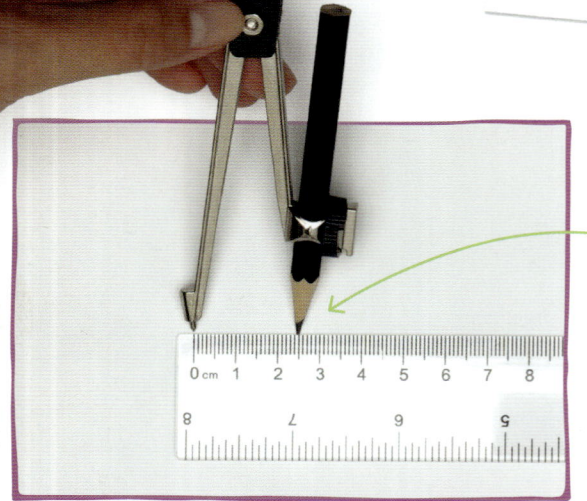

1 cm (½ in)

Glue tab / Glue tab / Glue tab / Glue tab

9 To make holes for the cones, set your compass to a radius of 2.5 cm (1 in). The diameter of the widest part of your cone is 8 cm (3 in), so don't make the holes too big or your cones will fall through them!

A circle with a radius of 2.5 cm (1 in) will have a diameter of 5 cm (2 in).

10 Place your compass point where one of the horizontal and vertical lines intersect to form a cross, then draw a circle. Repeat for each cross until you have drawn 12 circles of equal size.

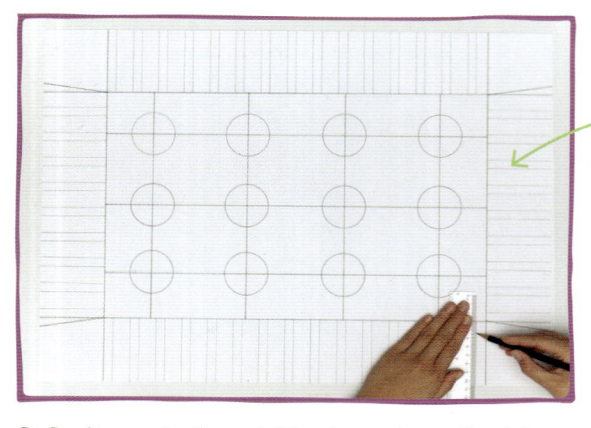

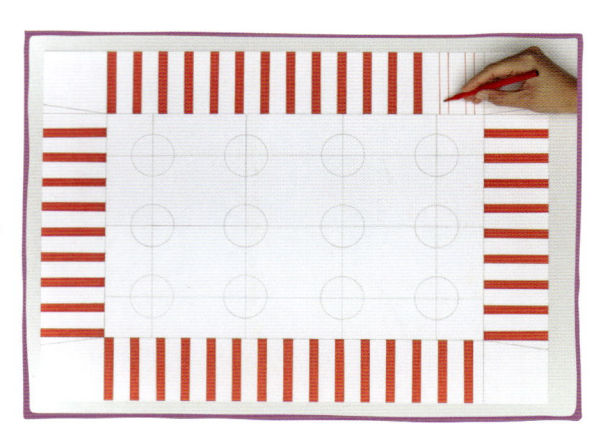

11 Decorate the outside of your box with stripes. Use a ruler and pencil to draw 1 cm- (½ in-) wide vertical lines with 2 cm (¾ in) in between.

When the net of the tray is folded to make a 3D shape, the stripes will be on the outside.

12 Carefully colour in your stripes using a bright red felt-tip pen or a colour of your choice.

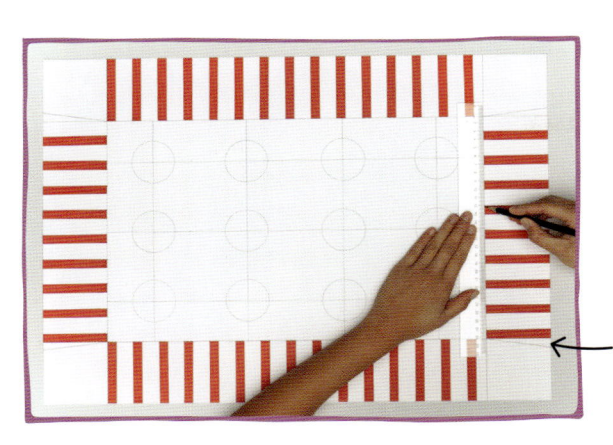

POPCORN SALE TRAY 123

Cut out all four triangles to make the glue tabs.

13 Score along the four fold lines using a ruler and pencil. Then use scissors to cut out the small triangle glue tabs in each corner.

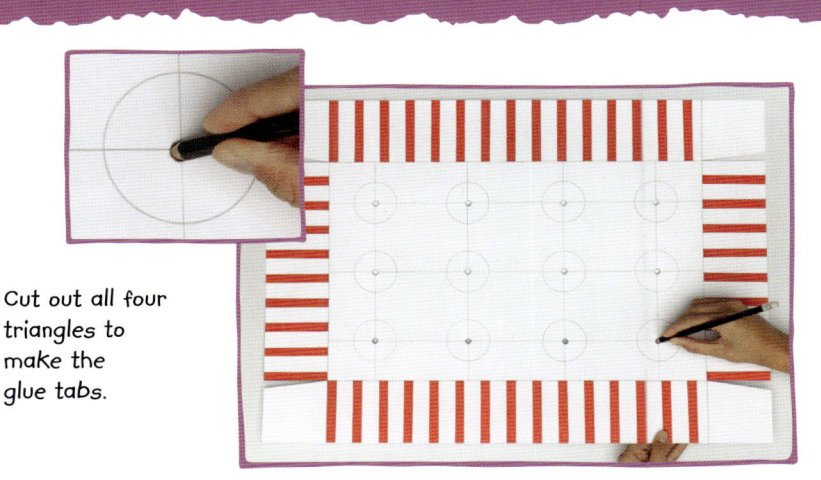

14 One by one, punch a hole in the centre of each circle by pressing a pencil into some adhesive putty on the underside.

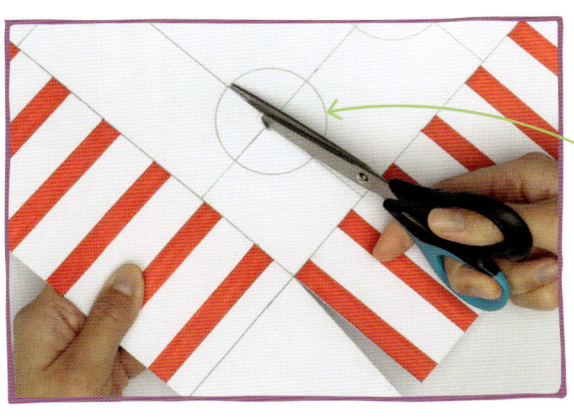

Make sure the glue tabs are on the inside.

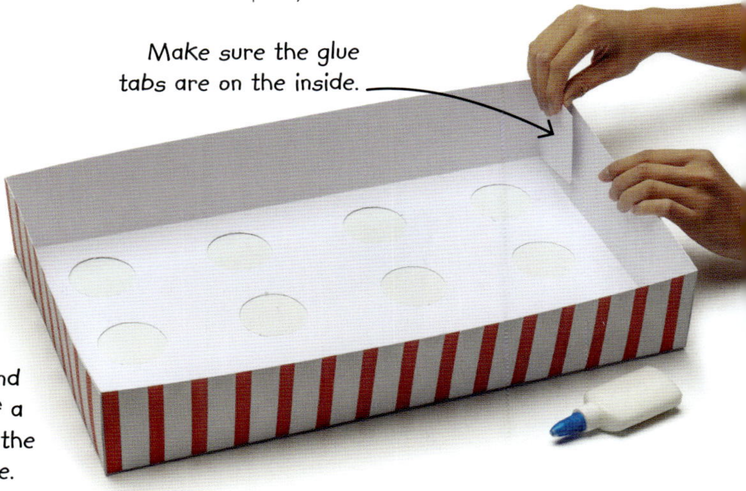

The line around the outside of a circle is called the circumference.

15 Place scissors inside one of the pierced holes and snip along the lines inside the circle. Then cut around the circle's circumference. Repeat until all the circles have been cut out. Rub out the pencil marks.

16 Turn your card over and fold the four sides upwards. Bend the tabs in at the corners so they are on the inside of the tray. Dab PVA glue on each tab and stick the sides together firmly.

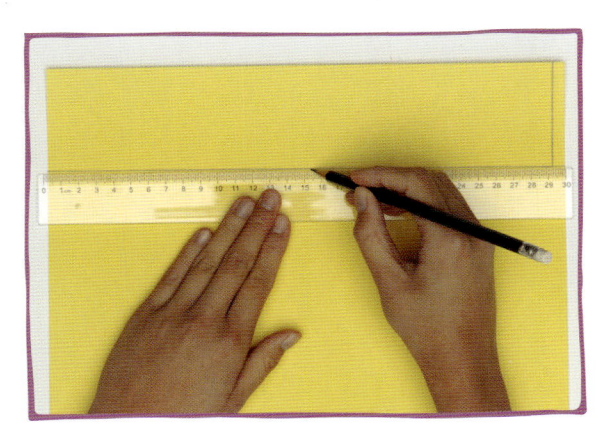

18 Flip over the tray so the holes are at the top, then add glue to the back of your sign and stick it in the centre of one of the longer sides. Press down and allow to dry.

17 Now make a sign for your tray. Draw a rectangle 6 x 29 cm (2¼ x 11½ in) on a piece of card. Write "Popcorn" and cut out the sign.

124 MEASUREMENTS

19 Cut two 100 cm (40 in) lengths of ribbon. Turn your tray over, and measure and mark on the inside 13.5 cm (5¼ in) from the front along both sides. Tape one end of each ribbon to the sides where you made the marks.

20 Turn the tray over again and hold it in front of you. Ask someone to tie the two ribbons together around your neck. Now place the 12 empty cones into the holes in the tray. Fill a bowl with popcorn and then carefully spoon it into each cone until they are all full. You're now ready to sell your popcorn!

You could add a price tag here.

REAL WORLD MATHS
SHOP PRICES

The price of food in shops is calculated to cover not only the cost of the food and its packaging, but also the expense of transporting it, staff wages, and the rental of the shop. If the price is too high, no one will buy the food, so it must be worked out very carefully.

HOW TO PRICE YOUR POPCORN

If you want to sell your popcorn, you will need to work out what you should charge for each cone, based on the cost of the popcorn, and the price of making your cones and tray. You will need to cover your costs, but not make the price so expensive that you put people off. Add a little bit extra on top of the overall cost to make a profit from your sale. When you have decided on the price to charge, make a tag with the cost and glue it to the tray.

ITEM	COST	NUMBER	TOTAL COST
Popcorn	£1.52	1	£1.52
Cone	£0.10	12	£1.20
Tray	£4.00	1	£4.00
		OVERALL COST	£6.72
		COST PER CONE (OVERALL COST DIVIDED BY 12)	£0.56

1 List the cost of the popcorn, the paper for one cone, and materials for making the tray. Add up the total (multiply the cone paper cost by 12) to work out your overall spending. Divide this by the number of cones to work out the cost of one cone. You now know the minimum price you need to charge for each cone to make back what you spent.

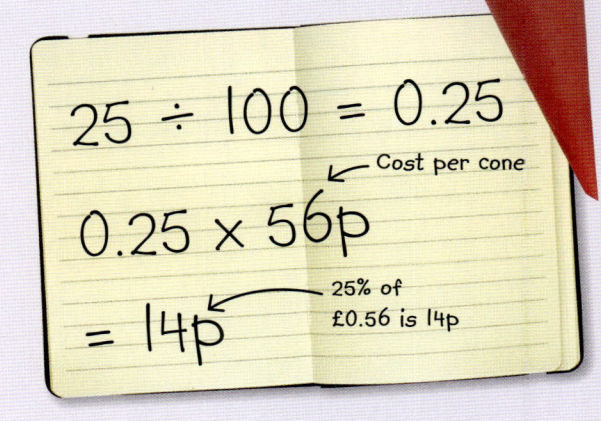

$$25 \div 100 = 0.25$$

$$0.25 \times 56p$$ ← Cost per cone

$$= 14p$$ ← 25% of £0.56 is 14p

2 To make a profit, you will have to charge a bit more for each cone. To work out how to make 25 per cent profit, divide 25 by 100 and multiply by the cost per cone. A 25 per cent profit on one cone is £0.14. To increase the profit, you would need to use a higher percentage.

25% PROFIT PER CONE	£0.14	TOTAL INCOME	£8.40
COST PER CONE	£0.56	TOTAL COST	£6.72
PRICE PER CONE (COST PLUS PROFIT)	£0.70	TOTAL PROFIT (INCOME MINUS COST)	£1.68

3 If each cone costs £0.56 and you add a profit of £0.14, you can charge £0.70 per cone. If you sell 12 cones at £0.70, your income will be £8.40. To work out the profit, subtract your total spend of £6.72 from this figure, which will give you a profit of £1.68.

4 Once you have worked out what to charge for your popcorn, make a circular badge with a diameter of 8 cm (3¼ in) out of card. Use a felt-tip pen to write out the price per cone so it stands out, then glue the price tag to the front of your sale tray.

Use sweet wrappers to add a pop of colour to your shadows.

DISTANCE AND DEFINITION
SHADOW PUPPETS

What stories would you tell if you had your very own puppet theatre? With just some card, paper fasteners, bamboo skewers, and a light source, you can turn your bare walls into a stage set for drama. And by playing with the distance between your puppets and the light, you can make your card actors huge or teeny-weeny.

SHADOW PUPPETS 127

HOW TO MAKE A SHADOW PUPPET

One of the best things about shadow puppet theatre is that you can perform it practically anywhere. All you need is a bare wall and a bit of light. Don't worry if you find drawing your puppet tricky – you can always copy a template. There are lots available online.

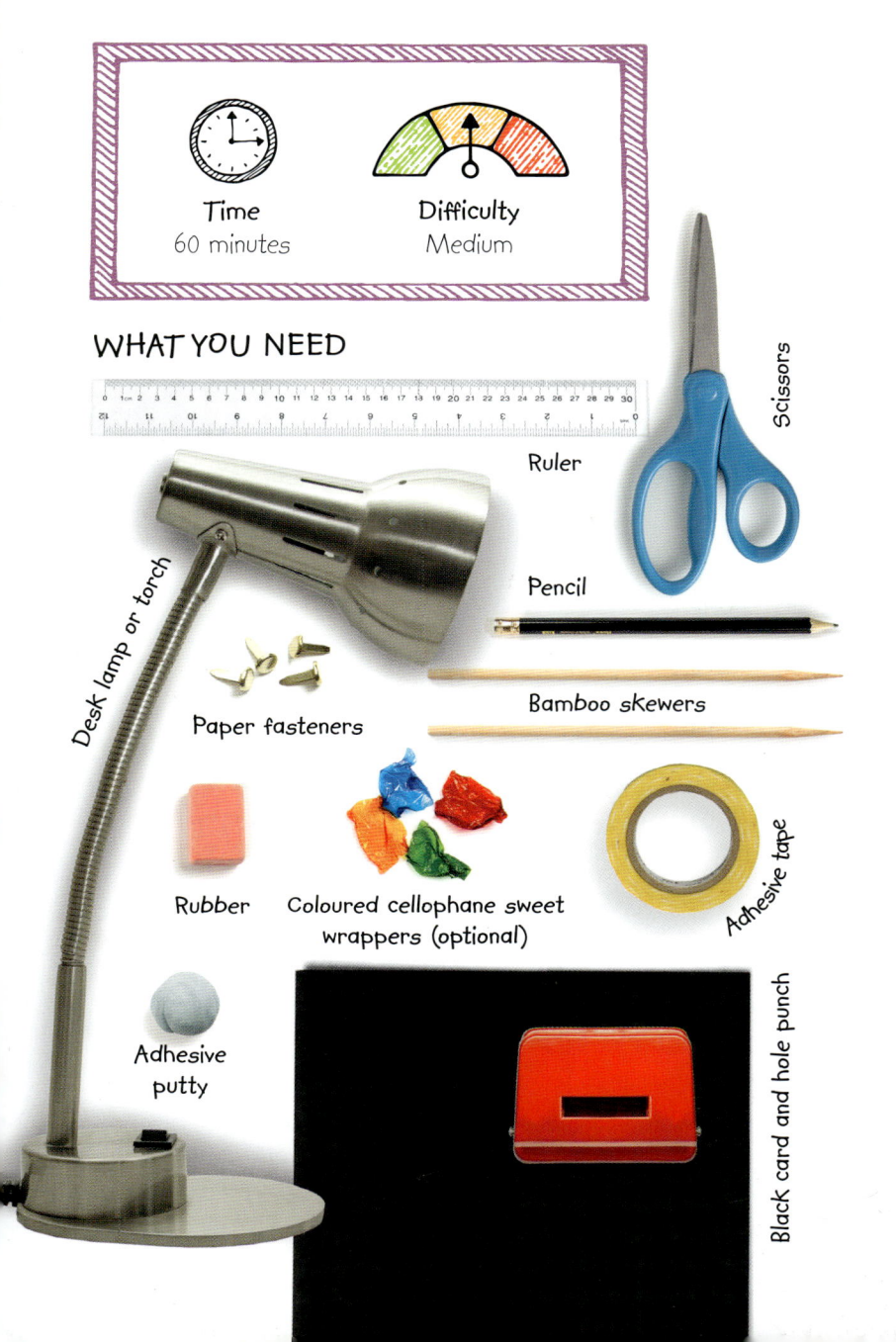

MATHS YOU WILL USE
- MEASURING to shape the perfect template.
- DOUBLING AND HALVING to shrink or strengthen your puppet's shadow.

If you don't get your drawing right first time, just rub it out and try again. Or you could photograph this image and use it as a template.

Time 60 minutes
Difficulty Medium

WHAT YOU NEED

- Ruler
- Scissors
- Pencil
- Desk lamp or torch
- Paper fasteners
- Bamboo skewers
- Rubber
- Coloured cellophane sweet wrappers (optional)
- Adhesive tape
- Adhesive putty
- Black card and hole punch

1 Draw your puppet design onto a piece of black card using a pencil. If you're following our dragon design, make sure you draw the wings separately from the body.

2 Once you've drawn your outline, use scissors to carefully cut out the main body template and any separate pieces such as the wings.

128   MEASUREMENTS

Use a hole punch to create neat circles for eyes.

3 Decide where you want to add movable joints, and mark the spots on the main body and wings with a pencil. Place a piece of adhesive putty under the card and use a pencil to punch a hole.

4 Line up the holes in the wings with the ones you've made on the puppet's body and thread a paper fastener through to fix them in place.

Cut a flame shape out of a red sweet wrapper and stick to the back of the puppet. You could also add colour detail to the wings.

5 Attach two bamboo skewers to the back of the puppet's wings and body with tape, leaving enough of the sticks showing so you can hold onto them. Your shadow puppet is now ready to perform.

6 Direct a lamp towards a clear section of a wall (or a large white bedsheet or piece of card). Turn on your light and hold your puppet between the light source and the wall.

A lamp will cast a wide shadow, but if you want a more focused beam you could use a torch.

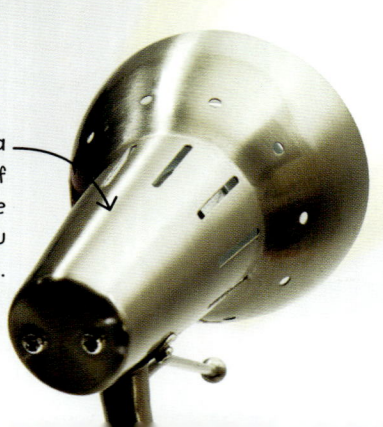

When you move the sticks up and down, the puppet's wings will move.

SHADOW PUPPETS 129

GO LARGE

It's fun to play around with the size of your shadow puppets. Measure the distance of the puppet from the light source at various intervals, starting near the lamp, then moving further away. Record your findings and see if you can work out how much bigger your shadow is than the size of the puppet? What's the biggest shadow you can make? Can you see how the focus changes, the smaller the shadow? Try experimenting with more intricate shadow puppets and look at the patterns they create.

1 Lengthen the distance between the lamp and the puppet (A). What effect does this have on the shadow's height (B)? What about its sharpness?

2 Now shorten the distance between the lamp and the puppet. How does this affect the height of the shadow (B)? Does it make the shadow stronger or sharper?

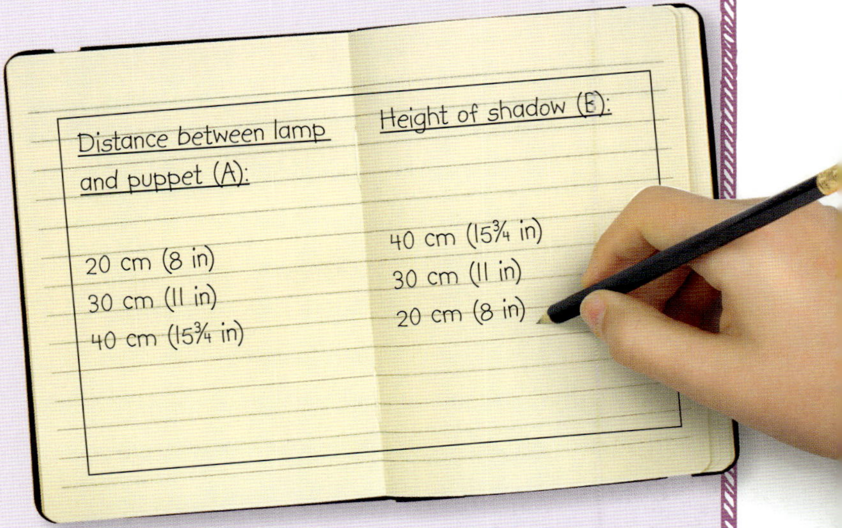

Distance between lamp and puppet (A):	Height of shadow (B):
20 cm (8 in)	40 cm (15¾ in)
30 cm (11 in)	30 cm (11 in)
40 cm (15¾ in)	20 cm (8 in)

3 Record your findings in a chart. What can you see about the relationship between the size of the shadow and the distance from the lamp? Do they grow and shrink in equal proportion?

REAL WORLD MATHS
INDONESIAN SHADOW PUPPETS

Shadow puppetry has been an art form in the country of Indonesia for more than a thousand years. Puppet shows are often used to celebrate special occasions, such as birthdays or weddings. Indonesian puppeteers control their creations with great skill, varying the lengths of the puppets' rods to create huge shadows and dramatic effects.

MATHS YOU WILL USE

- **PROBABILITY** to work out your chances of winning a jelly bean.
- **ESTIMATION** to find out how many jelly beans are in the jar.
- **FRACTIONS, DECIMALS, AND PERCENTAGES** to present probabilities.

FEELING FORTUNATE?
LUCKY DIP

Are you feeling lucky? You'll need to be to win this game! Pick a jelly bean at random from a jar and spin your brand-new spinner. If the colour on the spinner matches the colour of the bean, you get to eat the chewy treat. You can work out the likelihood that something might happen by using a maths technique called probability.

If the spinner picks the same colour you picked, you get to eat the bean. What are the chances of that happening?

HOW TO PLAY
LUCKY DIP

This project is pretty simple to do, but once you've made it you will have a game you can play again and again with friends. Make sure that you don't have too many different colours of jelly bean as you'll need to be able to colour your spinner to match the beans. We have used six colours.

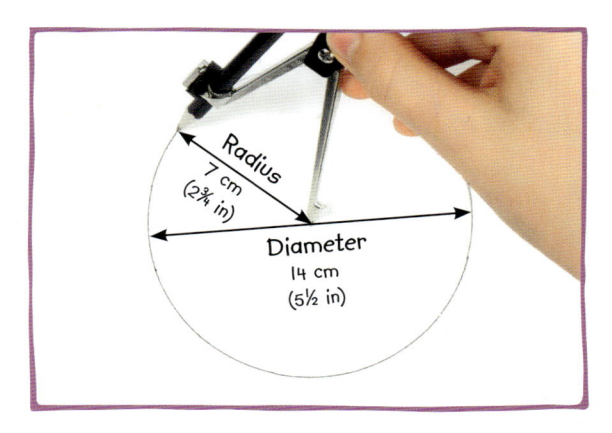

Time 30 minutes

Difficulty Easy

WHAT YOU NEED

Ruler, Protractor, Lots of jelly beans, Compass and pencil, Adhesive putty, Paper glue, Short pencil, Scissors, Paint brush, Empty jar, Paints or coloured pencils, Weighing scales, Calculator, Stiff card, White paper

1 Set your compass to a width of 7 cm (2¾ in) and draw a circle with a 14 cm (5½ in) diameter on white paper. Note the centre of the circle.

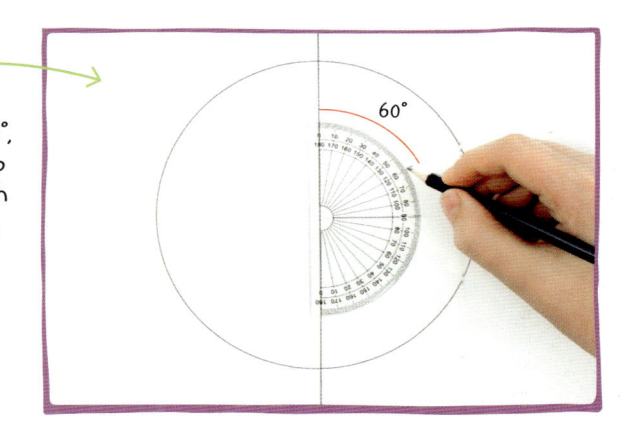

A full circle is 360°, so to divide it into six segments each one must be 60°.

2 You now need to divide your circle so you have one segment for each bean colour. Draw a line through the circle, then place the protractor over the centre and use it to measure each segment.

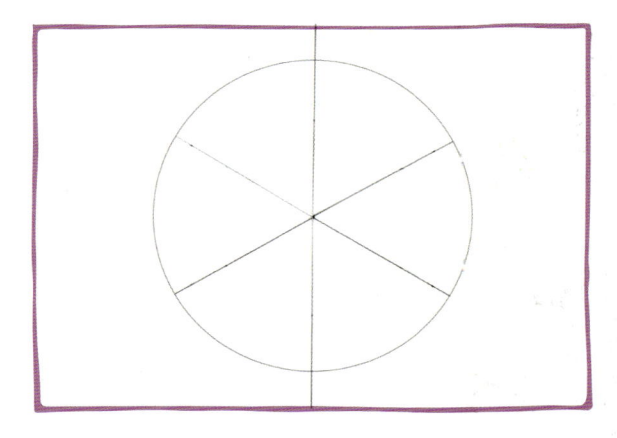

3 Use a ruler to draw lines from the angles you marked to the centre of the circle. This will give you a "pie" of six equal parts.

132 MEASUREMENTS

4. Glue the paper with the circle onto a piece of stiff card and then carefully cut around the outline of the circle.

5. Colour each of the six segments to match the six colours of your jelly beans. You can use paints, pencils, or felt-tip pens.

6. Place a piece of adhesive putty under the centre of the circle, then push a short pencil through the circle to create a hole.

Try not to eat all of the jelly beans before you pour them into the jar.

PROBABILITY
You can use probability to measure how likely something is to happen. Probability is usually shown as a fraction.

Here, the probability of getting green is one in six, or 1/6.

Here, the probability of getting green is just one in two, or 1/2.

7. Pick a jelly bean from the jar and spin the spinner. If it matches the colour lying on the table when the spinner stops, you get to eat the jelly bean! If it doesn't match, return it to the jar.

The probability of the spinner landing on orange is 1/6.

LUCKY DIP   133

PRESENTING PROBABILITY

If there were no green beans in a jar, the chance of picking one would have a probability of zero, while if there were only green beans, drawing one would have a probability of one. If there were some green beans, the likelihood of picking one would have a probability of between zero and one. You can use fractions, decimals, and percentages to represent probability.

DECIMALS

$$1/5 = 1 \div 5 = 0.2$$

If you were picking one of these five beans at random, you'd have a one in five chance of getting a red bean, that's a probability of 1/5. To turn this into a decimal, divide the top number of the fraction by the bottom number.

PERCENTAGES

$$2/5 = 2 \div 5 = 0.4$$
$$\times 100 = 40\%$$

In this example, you'd have a two in five chance of picking a red bean. To change the fraction to a percentage, you first work it out as a decimal and then multiply it by 100.

HOW MANY JELLY BEANS ARE IN THE JAR?

Why not challenge your friends to guess how many jelly beans are in the jar? Using some clever maths you'll be able to reveal how close their guess is. You can work out the number of jelly beans by finding the weight of a single one and dividing that by the weight of all the jelly beans that you can fit inside the jar.

2 Place your jar on the scales and set them to zero. Fill the jar with jelly beans and note the weight. Guess how many jelly beans are in the jar.

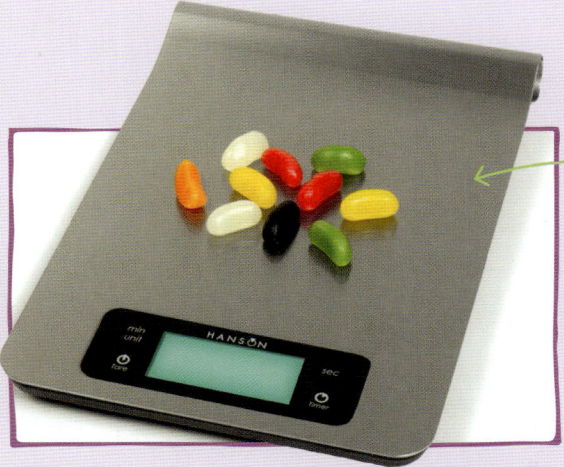

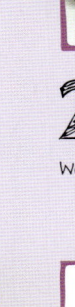

To make it easier to find the weight, assume that each of these 10 jelly beans weighs the same amount.

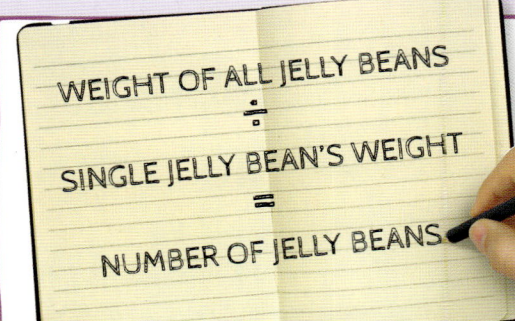

WEIGHT OF ALL JELLY BEANS
÷
SINGLE JELLY BEAN'S WEIGHT
=
NUMBER OF JELLY BEANS

1 Take 10 jelly beans and weigh them on the scales. Divide the weight by 10 to give you an accurate estimate of the weight of one jelly bean.

3 Divide the weight of all the jelly beans by the weight of one jelly bean to work out how many jelly beans are in the jar. How close were you?

Silver paint makes the runners look like shiny steel.

These towers have been painted to look like rusty old pipes.

SUPER CHUTES
MARBLE RUN

Budding engineers will love the thrill of this challenge. With just a few cardboard tubes, PVA glue, and a little bit of patience you can build your own marble race track. Use angles to add a few twists and turns, then watch as the marbles whizz down the run at top speed!

The steeper the slope, the faster the marble will zoom down the track.

MATHS YOU WILL USE
- ANGLES to allow the marble to run freely down the track.
- 3D SHAPES to construct your run.
- MEASUREMENT to work out the height of the towers, the length of the runners, and the time your marbles take to compete the run.

136 MEASUREMENTS

HOW TO MAKE A
MARBLE RUN

The secret to making this marble run is to take your time: plan out your design first, then work on the construction, just like an engineer would. The more securely you slot the cardboard tubes together, the sturdier the marble run and the better the end result.

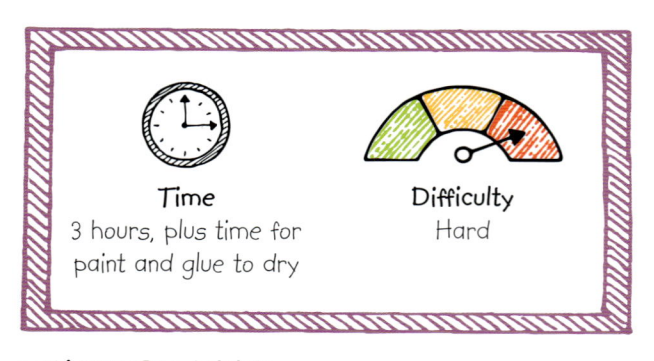

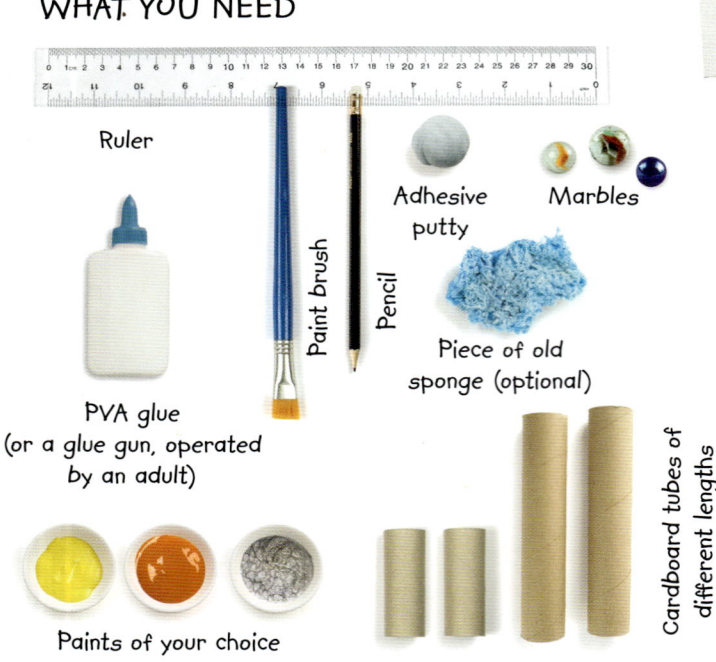

Our marble run has five towers, but you can use more if you like.

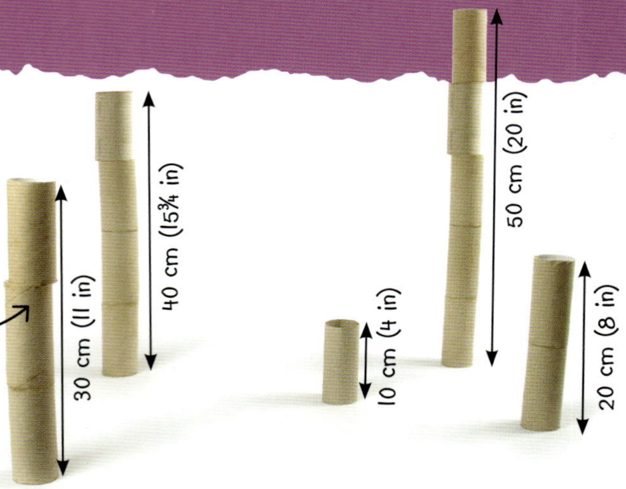

30 cm (11 in)
40 cm (15¾ in)
10 cm (4 in)
50 cm (20 in)
20 cm (8 in)

Time
3 hours, plus time for paint and glue to dry

Difficulty
Hard

WHAT YOU NEED

Ruler
PVA glue (or a glue gun, operated by an adult)
Paint brush
Pencil
Adhesive putty
Marbles
Piece of old sponge (optional)
Paints of your choice
Cardboard tubes of different lengths
White paper
Large piece of flat, stiff card
Scissors

1 Plan your marble run by stacking cardboard tubes on top of each other to create towers of different heights. Then position the towers in decreasing height order, with varying distances between them to create a set of angled slopes.

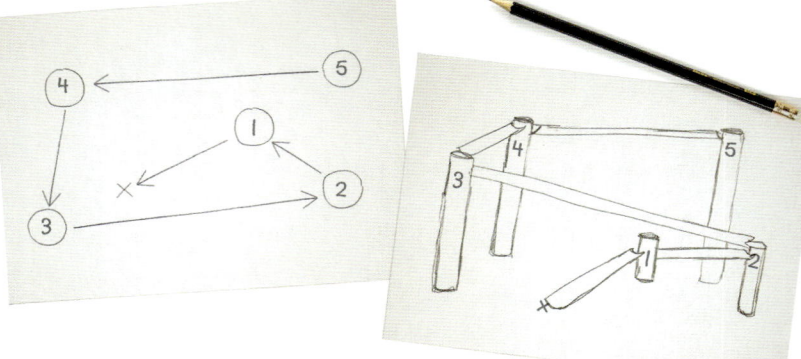

2 Sketch out the design from a bird's-eye and side-on view, remembering to mark with a cross where you would like the marble run to finish. Number each tower from 5 to 1, with 5 being the tallest tower.

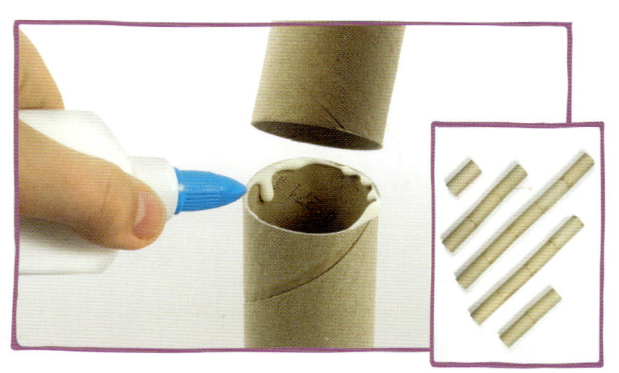

3 Use PVA glue to stick the cardboard tubes together to form towers. Leave them to dry overnight standing upright so they don't separate. You should now have five towers of different heights.

MARBLE RUN   137

4 Paint the towers and leave them to dry. You could add stripes or other details. We painted ours yellow, then dabbed rust-coloured paint using a sponge to make them look like rusty old pillars.

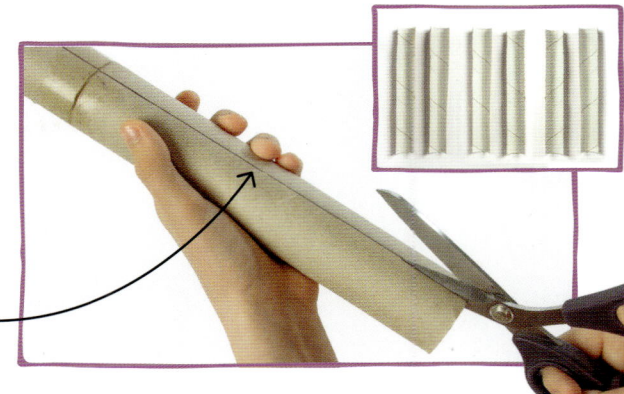

Draw a line with a ruler first to guide you with the cut.

5 To make the runners, glue two long kitchen roll tubes together to create an extra long one. Repeat twice. Leave upright to dry overnight, then cut them lengthways to create six long runners.

6 Trim 1 cm (½ in) off the width of each runner to make them slightly narrower. Paint all six and leave to dry. We used silver paint to make them look like steel, but you can use any colour you like.

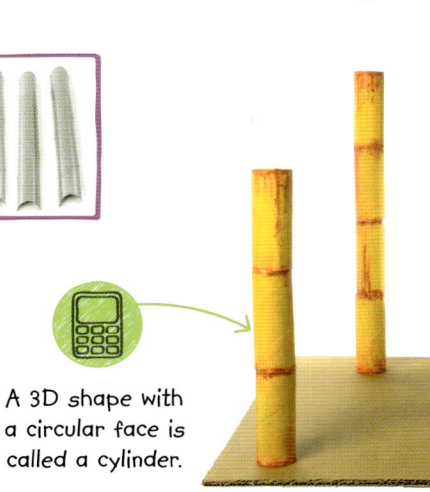

A 3D shape with a circular face is called a cylinder.

7 Refer back to your sketch and place the painted towers vertically on a large piece of flat cardboard in the positions according to your plan. Draw a circle around the base of each tower.

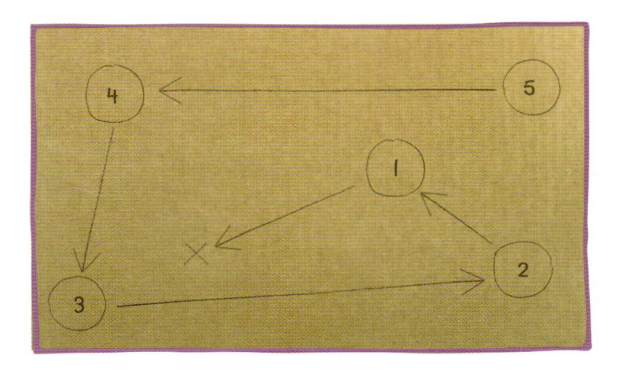

8 Number the circles as you did in your plan. Mark where the end of the marble run will be with a cross. In pencil, lightly draw arrows so you remember where the runners will be placed.

The distance between towers might be more than one ruler length. You'll need to add together the two measurements.

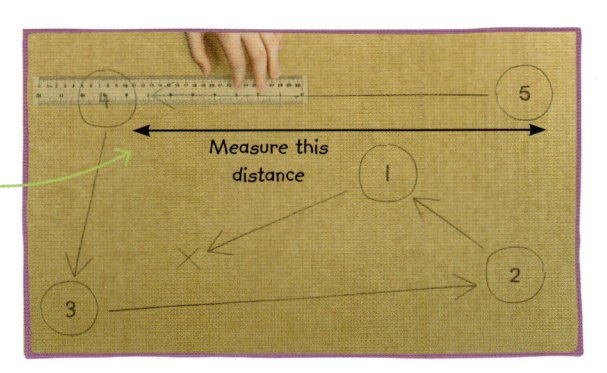

9 Measure and note the distance between the furthest edge of circle 5 and the nearest edge of circle 4. Repeat this to work out the length of each runner in the marble run.

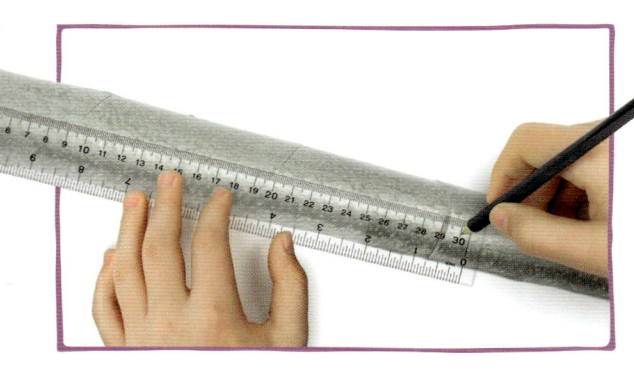

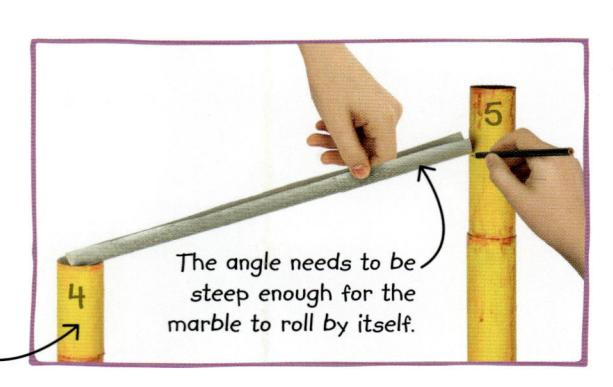

138 MEASUREMENTS

10 With a ruler and pencil, measure out the equivalent lengths on your painted runners and cut them to length. Number each section so you remember which runner will link which two towers.

Fix the towers to the base temporarily with adhesive putty to keep them in place.

The angle needs to be steep enough for the marble to roll by itself.

11 With towers 5 and 4 on the cardboard base, rest one end of runner 5 on top of tower 4 and adjust its angle so that it reaches near the top of tower 5. Mark the meeting point on tower 5 in pencil.

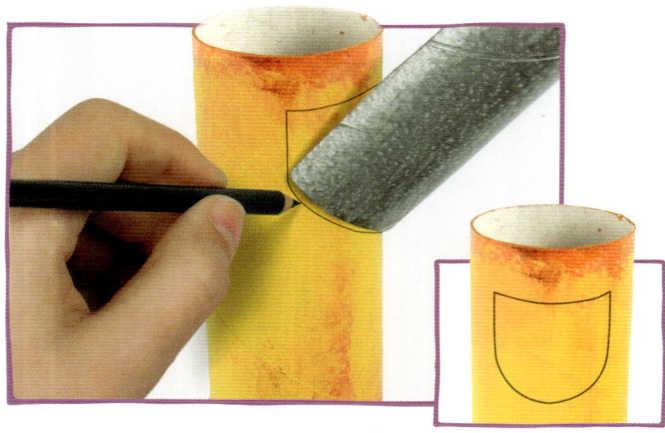

12 Use the runner as a template to draw a curve on the side of tower 5, above the mark you made. Draw two vertical lines at each end and a horizontal one joining them to make a "shield" shape.

13 To make it easier to cut out the "shield", press the tip of a pencil through the card to make a hole, then use scissors. Use the offcut as a template in the next step.

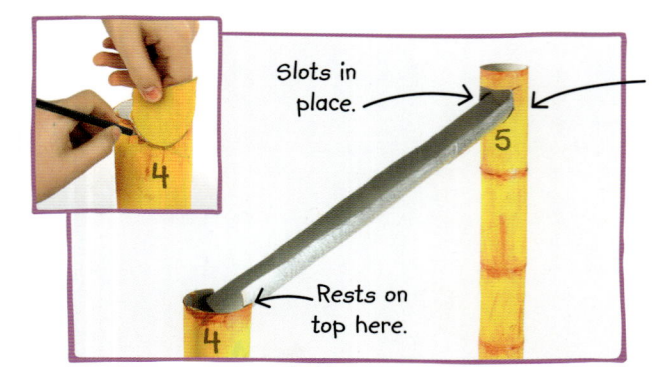

Slots in place.

Make sure the runner fits snugly inside tower 5 so that the marbles don't drop down inside.

Rests on top here.

14 Use the template to draw a curve at the top of tower 4, and cut it out with scissors. Insert the first runner between towers 5 and 4, but don't glue it in place just yet.

The vertical towers are connected by diagonal runners.

15 Repeat steps 11 to 14 until all the towers are connected. Make sure the slots and runner cuts are made on the correct side of each tower so they follow the direction of travel.

MARBLE RUN   139

16 When you are happy with your construction, test the run with a marble and adjust the lengths of the runners if needed. Then secure the marble run. Glue the bottom of each tower to the base first, then put the runners in place and glue securely.

A marble is a solid 3D circle, also known as a sphere.

17 Once the glue has dried, drop a marble into your run and watch it speed down the track. Have fun!

HOW FAR WILL THEY GO?

Can you guess how far a marble will roll once it reaches the end of the track? Test it out and record your results. Measure the distance with a ruler – did you guess correctly? You can also have fun predicting how long it will take different-sized marbles to whizz down the track and come to a stop. Use a stopwatch to time the marbles and then measure the distance they travel. The length and angle of the runners will impact on the marble's speed. The shorter the distance between the towers, the steeper the angle and the faster the marble will roll. Does the size of the marble change your results?

How far will your marble travel before stopping?

MAGICAL MASTERPIECES
OPTICAL ILLUSIONS

Grab some pencils, paper, and your maths kit, and get ready to create some optical art! These clever pictures use colour, light, and patterns to trick our brains into seeing something that isn't really there. So although you are making flat drawings, mathematical magic makes the lines pop off the page so that the shapes look three-dimensional.

Don't worry if your lines aren't perfect. It'll still look 3D.

Be bold with your shading. This is what gives your artwork the 3D look.

OPTICAL ILLUSIONS   141

HOW TO CREATE OPTICAL ILLUSIONS

Try your hand at two optical artworks. The first uses clashing colours and curved lines so that the shape bends off the page, while in the second, shading and cut-outs combine to make a cuboid float away! In both cases, shadow helps to create depth.

MATHS YOU WILL USE
- ANGLES to shape the structure of your drawing.
- CONCENTRIC CIRCLES to create the outline of your optical illusion.
- CONVEX AND CONCAVE LINES to make your drawing look like it's bending.

Time 60 minutes
Difficulty Easy

WHAT YOU NEED
- Ruler
- Protractor
- Compass and pencil
- Black pen
- Scissors
- Contrasting coloured pencils (darker and lighter shades)
- White paper
- Rubber
- Smartphone

PROJECT 1 - CIRCLE ILLUSION

Marking the halfway point of all four edges will ensure that you find the exact centre.

1 Find the centre of your piece of paper by measuring its length and width and dividing each measurement by two. Draw a straight line across the paper from each of the halfway points.

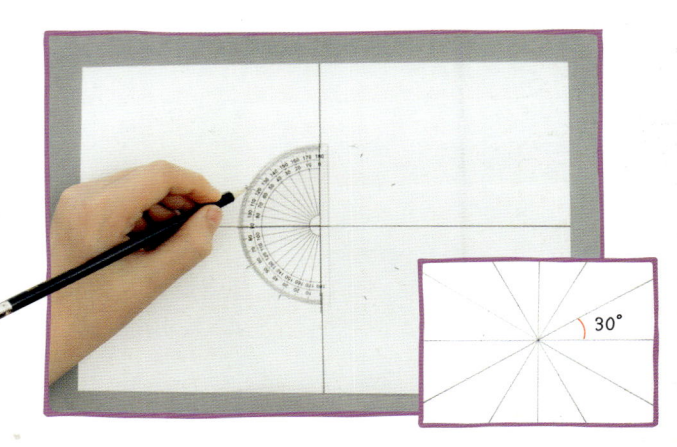

2 With the middle of a protractor over the centre, mark out sections of 30°. Draw lines from the centre to the edge of the paper at 30° increments to create a "pie" of 12 equal slices.

30°

142 MEASUREMENTS

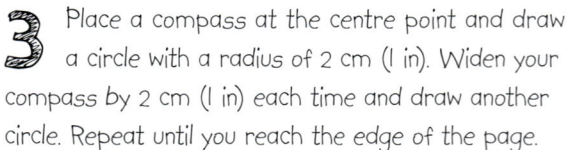

3 Place a compass at the centre point and draw a circle with a radius of 2 cm (1 in). Widen your compass by 2 cm (1 in) each time and draw another circle. Repeat until you reach the edge of the page.

Lines like this are convex, which means they curve outwards, while concave lines curve inwards.

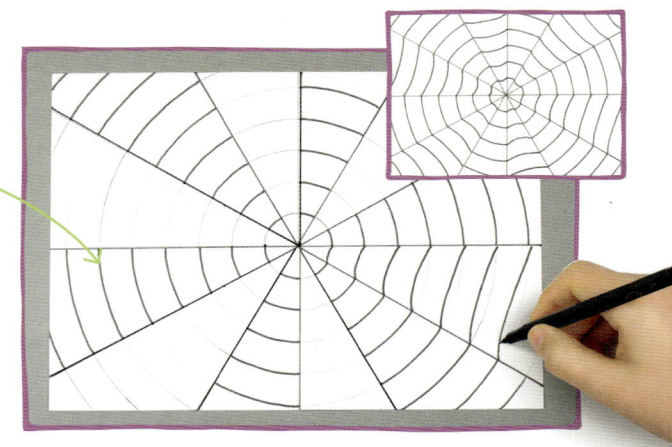

4 With a black pen, draw over the straight lines. Go over the curved lines inside every alternate "slice". Finally, join the curves with concave lines that bend towards the centre of the circle.

5 Take one colour and mark out every other "slice", and then every alternate section within each slice, to avoid mistakes once you start colouring in.

Alternating contrasting colours with white will make your drawing even more mind-bending.

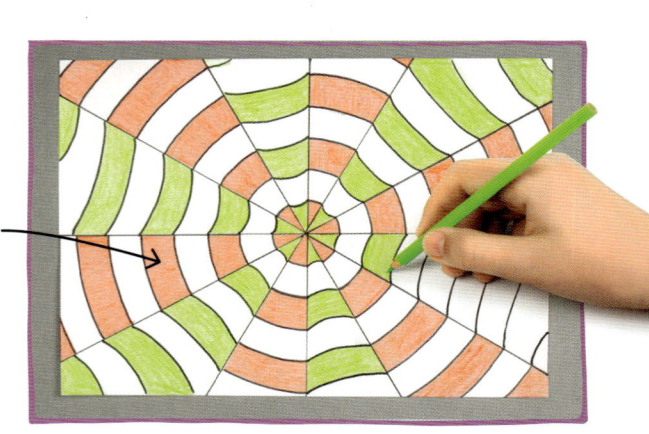

6 Repeat step 5, but this time use your second, contrasting colour.

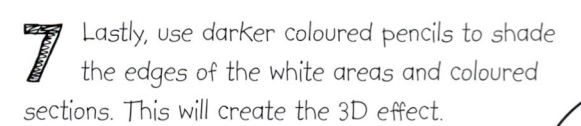

7 Lastly, use darker coloured pencils to shade the edges of the white areas and coloured sections. This will create the 3D effect.

Make your shading darker at the edges and lighter in the middle to make your illusion look 3D.

REAL WORLD MATHS
CONCENTRIC CIRCLES

Circles of different sizes that lie within each other but all share the same midpoint are called concentric circles. You can find them on an archery target. Can you think of any other examples?

OPTICAL ILLUSIONS   143

PROJECT 2 - FLOATING CUBE

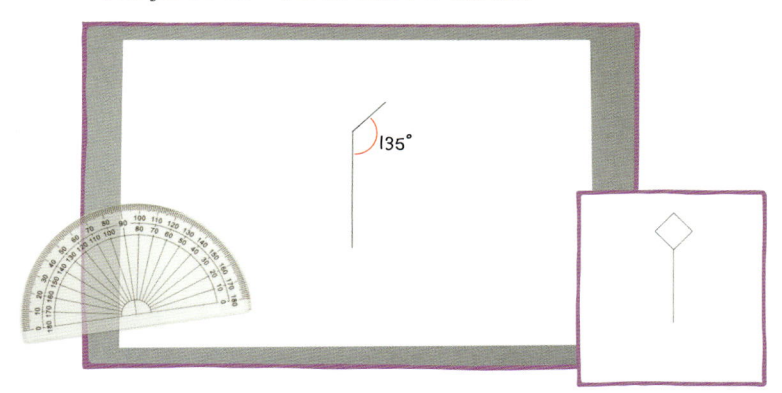

1 Draw a vertical line that is 9 cm (3½ in) long. Use a set square and a protractor to draw a 4 cm (1½ in) diagonal line at its top, at an angle of 135°. Add three 4 cm (1½ in) lines to form a tilted square.

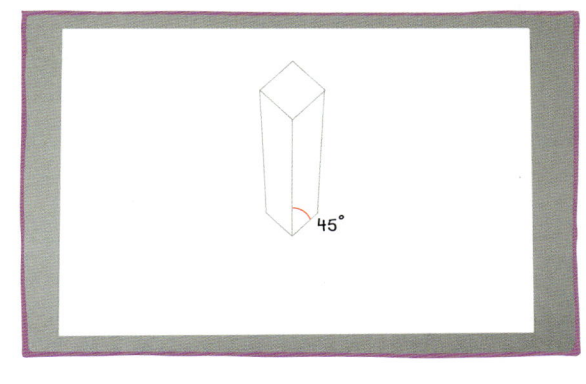

2 At the bottom of the vertical line, draw a 3 cm (1¼ in) line at an angle of 45°, then repeat on the other side. Connect these lines to those at the top to form a cuboid.

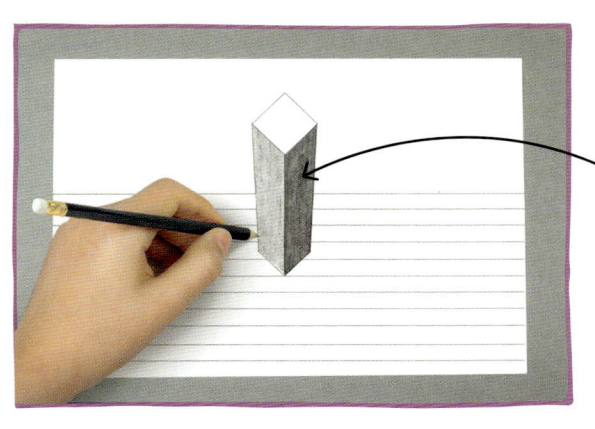

Shading one side of the cuboid darker than the other creates the illusion of depth.

3 Halfway down the page, draw horizontal lines on either side of the cuboid at 1 cm (½ in) intervals. Shade the two long sides of the cuboid.

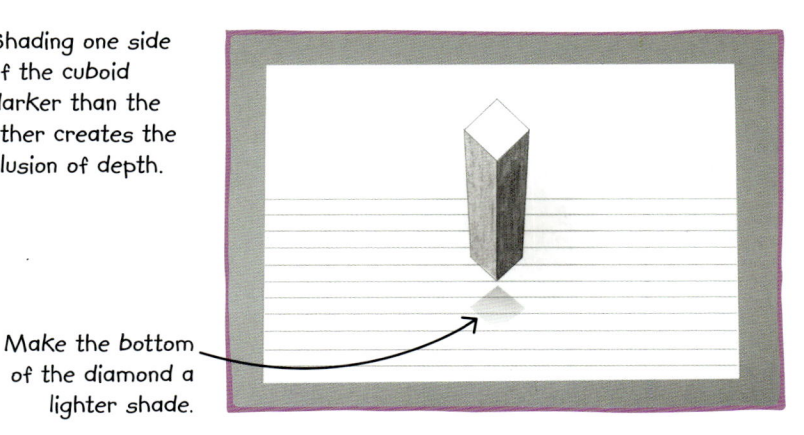

Make the bottom of the diamond a lighter shade.

4 Create a shadow effect by shading a diamond shape directly underneath the cuboid. It should look like it's hovering!

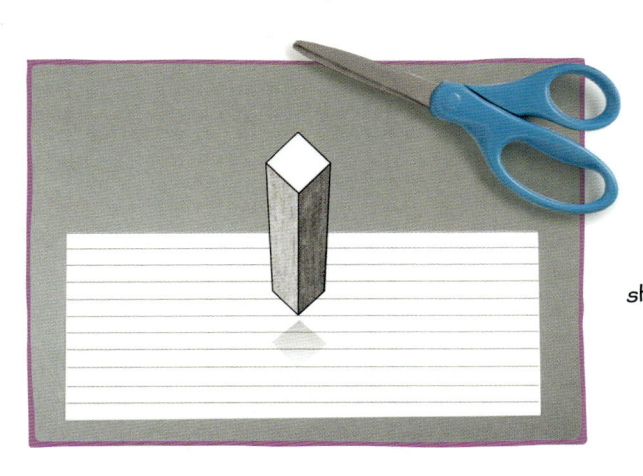

5 Draw around the outside of the cuboid with a black pen, then cut out the top and along the highest horizontal line. This makes the cuboid appear to jump off the page, giving the illusion that it is 3D.

Try using the phone to film a shape-shifting video for your friends!

6 Look at your drawing through the camera of a smartphone, moving the phone's angle to watch what happens. The 2D drawing will appear to change size and shape!

TERRIFIC TIMING
MAKE YOUR OWN CLOCK

What better way to keep your day on track than by making your own clock? You'll need a working clock mechanism for this activity (you can find these in craft shops and online), along with some modelling clay and colourful paints to decorate your timepiece just the way you like it. Painting the clock face is also the perfect chance to practise your fractions, as it's divided into 12 equal sections. Ready? It's time to start!

MATHS YOU WILL USE
- DIVISION to divide your clock into 12 sections.
- ANGLES to measure the lines marking the hours.
- TELLING TIME so you can add your schedule to the finished clock.

Each time the short hand passes one of these marks, a new hour begins.

TIDDLES

We have decorated our clock with coloured wedges, but you can use any pattern you like.

Use a black marker pen to draw the numbers clearly on your clock.

LUNCHTIME

HELP TIDY THE KITCHEN

DO SOME HOMEWORK

BEDTIME

DINNER

FEED TIDDLES

Stick reminders on the different hours so you remember when to do things!

HOW TO MAKE YOUR OWN CLOCK

The clock mechanism will make your finished product tick, but it's important to measure the sections of the clock carefully to make sure the numbers are in the right place. Once the clay is set, decorate the clock by copying our painted pattern or make up your own.

Time
45 minutes plus 24 hours of drying time

Difficulty
Medium

WHAT YOU NEED

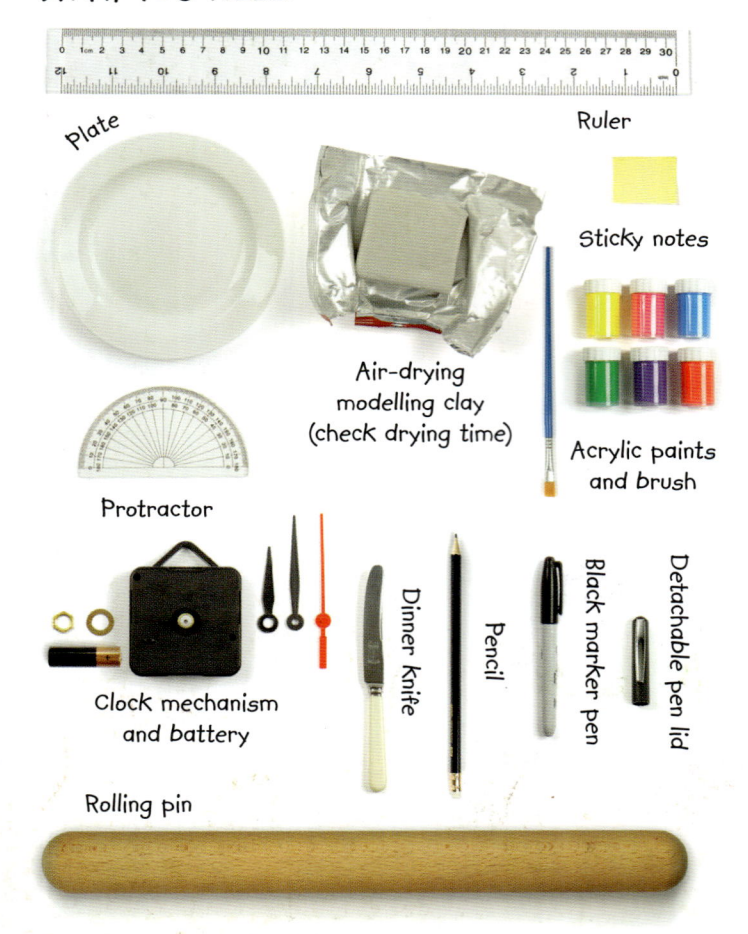

- Plate
- Ruler
- Air-drying modelling clay (check drying time)
- Sticky notes
- Acrylic paints and brush
- Protractor
- Clock mechanism and battery
- Dinner knife
- Pencil
- Black marker pen
- Detachable pen lid
- Rolling pin

1 Roll your clay out into a rough circle that is larger than your plate and approximately 0.5 cm (¼ in) thick. Try to make it nice and flat.

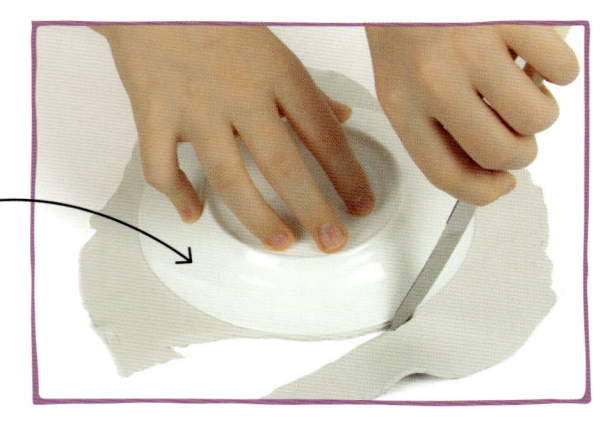

The plate you choose will determine the size of your finished clock face.

2 Place your plate on top of the clay and cut around it with a dinner knife to make a circle shape. Gently lift the plate off the clay.

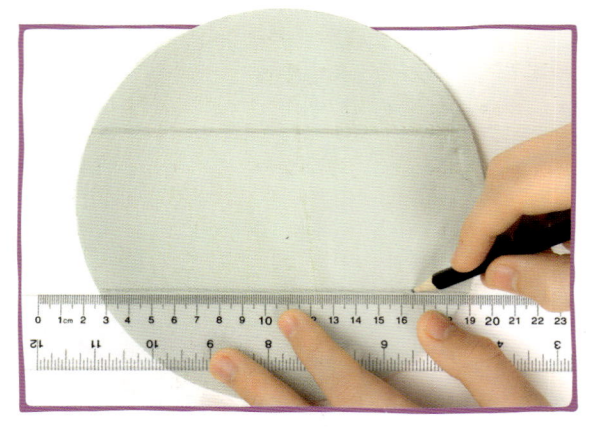

3 To find the centre of the clay circle, use a pencil to lightly draw two parallel lines across it. Make sure that the lines are equal in length.

MAKE YOUR OWN CLOCK   147

Check that your pen lid is wider than the shaft at the front of the clock mechanism.

4. Draw two diagonal lines joining the two opposite corners of the parallel lines. The point where they meet is the centre of the circle.

5. Push the pen lid through the centre point of the circle to make a hole. Leave the clay to dry on a flat surface. It may take a few days.

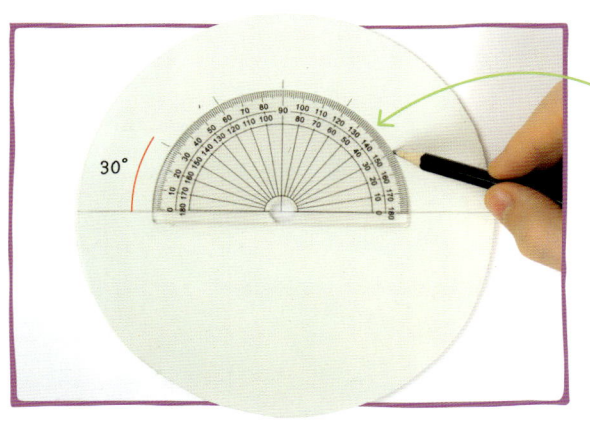

A circle is 360°, and 360 divided by 12 (for each hour of a 12-hour clock) is 30°.

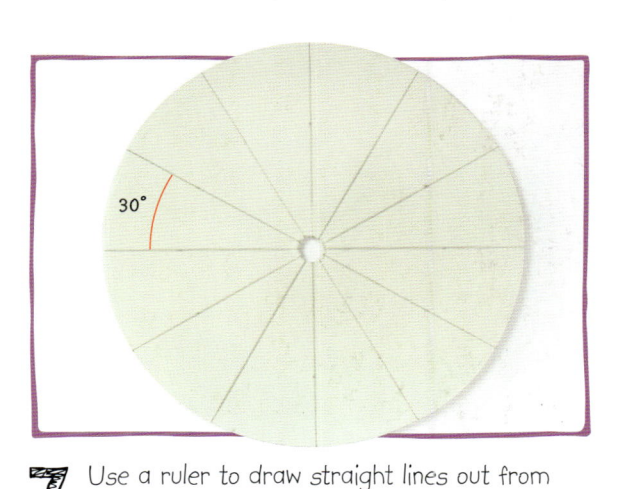

6. Once it has fully dried, flip your clay circle over. Draw a line across the middle of the circle and place a protractor over the hole. Mark with a pencil every 30°. Rotate your protractor 180° and repeat on the other half.

7. Use a ruler to draw straight lines out from the centre of the circle to create 12 segments. Each of these will represent one hour.

8. Paint the clock in different colours with your acrylic paints, using any pattern you like. Allow the paint to fully dry – this could take up to two hours.

Will you paint your clock in bold shades or pretty pastels?

MEASUREMENTS

9 Using a pencil, draw numbers from 1 – 12 around the clock face. Then go over the numbers with a black marker pen to make them stand out.

10 Push the base of your clock kit through the hole in the centre of the face. Make sure the hook for hanging up the clock is aligned with number 12.

11 Place the circular brass washer onto the clock shaft and then tighten the hexagonal nut on top of it. Don't over-tighten the nut in case you crack the clay.

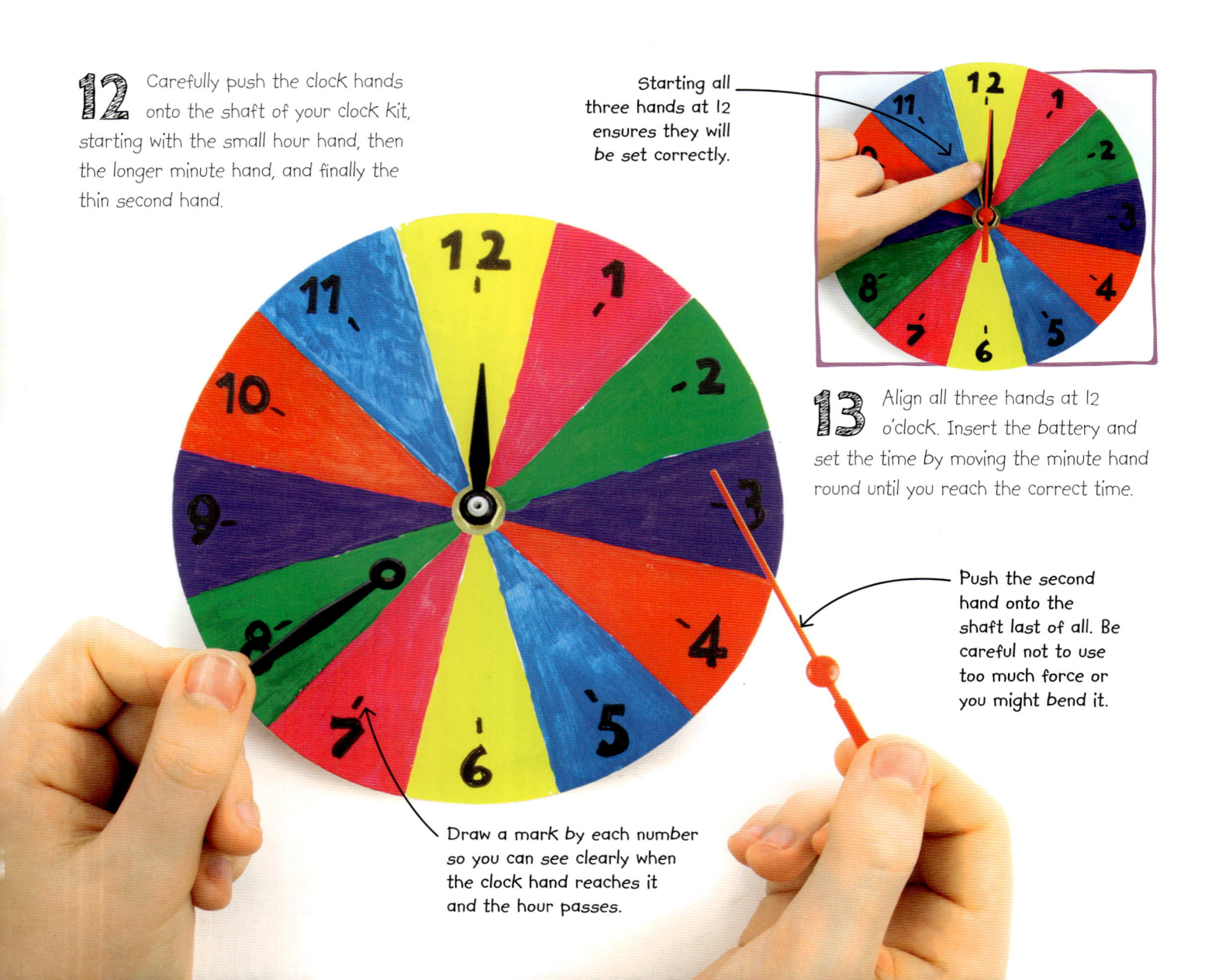

12 Carefully push the clock hands onto the shaft of your clock kit, starting with the small hour hand, then the longer minute hand, and finally the thin second hand.

Starting all three hands at 12 ensures they will be set correctly.

13 Align all three hands at 12 o'clock. Insert the battery and set the time by moving the minute hand round until you reach the correct time.

Push the second hand onto the shaft last of all. Be careful not to use too much force or you might bend it.

Draw a mark by each number so you can see clearly when the clock hand reaches it and the hour passes.

MAKE YOUR OWN CLOCK 149

14 To help remind you of the things you need to do at certain times, you can write them on sticky notes and put them on the clock face. You can move these around depending or what you are up to each day. Trim the notes to size if they are too large.

LUNCHTIME
HELP TIDY THE KITCHEN
DO SOME HOMEWORK
FEED TIDD

TELLING THE TIME

There are two types of clock, analogue – like the one you've just made – or digital, which displays the 24 hours in a full day and night on a digital screen. All of the clocks here show the same time – 5 minutes to midnight – but in different ways. To convert a 24-hour time to a 12-hour format, simply subtract 12 from the hours. So 23.00 would be 11.00, because 23 - 12 = 11.

On this analogue clock, Roman numerals mark the hours.

On a digital 24-hour clock, midnight is 00.00. The first two figures show the hour, the next two the minutes, followed by the seconds.

The numbers on this analogue clock mark the hour, while the small dashes represent the minutes past the hour.

Hang your feeder in your garden using a piece of string looped under the roof.

You can use coloured lolly sticks or you can paint plain ones with environmentally-friendly paint.

Different foods will attract different species. Robins love mealworms!

DELIGHTFUL DATA
LOLLY STICK BIRD FEEDER

How would you like to have a garden busy with birds swooping in for a visit? This colourful feeder will quickly become the new hotspot for local birds. To put it together, you'll need to master the use of angles to make a strong structure that can hold the bird food. Once you've built the feeder, you can create a graph to help you work out what food your birds like best.

Birds will come to visit your feeder, but you must be patient. They may take a few days to find it.

Some birds like perches, others don't.

HOW TO MAKE A LOLLY STICK BIRD FEEDER

This project might look a little complicated, but it is surprisingly simple and you will quickly find yourself with a brand new bird feeder. You may need to be a little patient with the birds while they find you, but once they do you can keep a tally of their visits to work out what kind of food they like best.

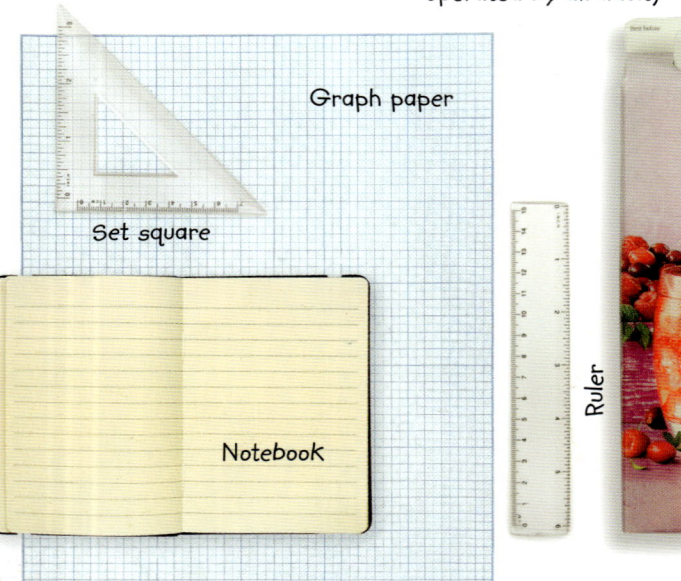

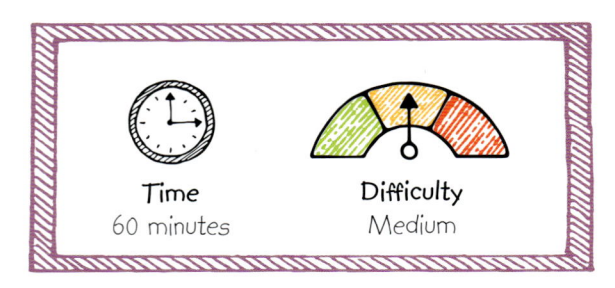

Time 60 minutes
Difficulty Medium

MATHS YOU WILL USE
- ANGLES to get the perfect roof pitch.
- HALVES to make the perches.
- PARALLEL LINES to form a strong base.
- GRAPHS to find the best food for the birds.

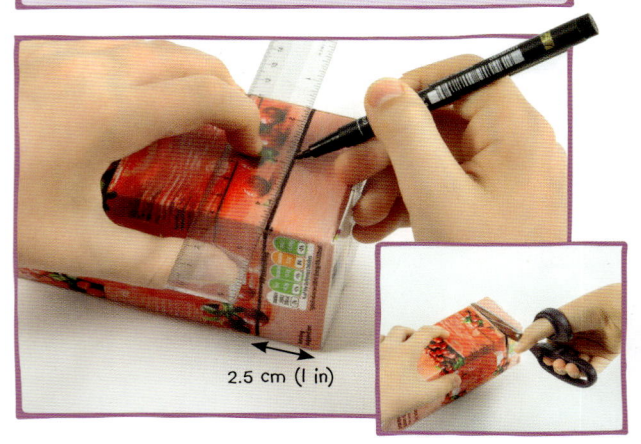

WHAT YOU NEED

- Adhesive tape
- String
- Scissors
- Coloured pencils
- Marker pen
- 73 lolly sticks
- Bird food
- PVA glue (or a glue gun, operated by an adult)
- Set square
- Graph paper
- Notebook
- Ruler
- Empty drinks carton

1 Start by making the bird feeder tray out of a drinks carton with a base 7 × 7 cm (2¾ × 2¾ in). Draw a straight line 2.5 cm (1 in) from the bottom of the carton and then cut along the line.

2 Place 12 lolly sticks next to each other and then put the bird feeder tray on top, making sure that you have two sticks on either side of the tray.

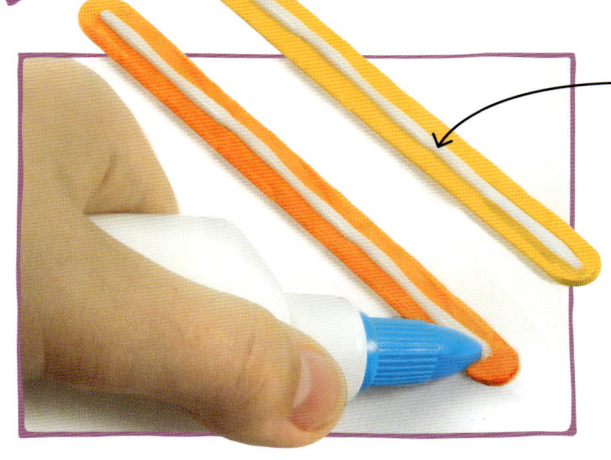

LOLLY STICK BIRD FEEDER 153

3 Glue two lolly sticks from end to end. These two sticks will hold the 12 sticks on the bottom of the feeder's base together.

Make sure you glue along the whole length of the lolly stick.

Use a set square to draw a right angle on paper as a guide for placing the sticks.

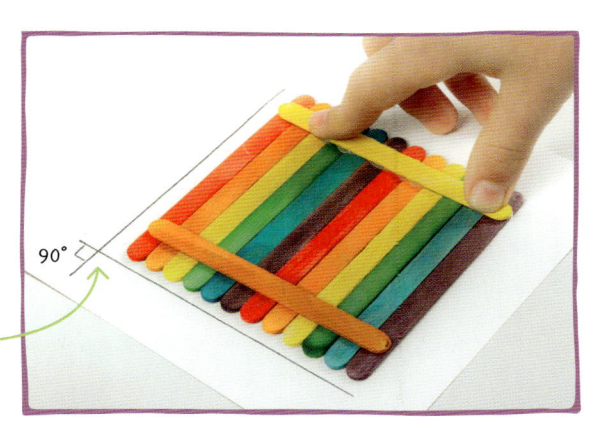

4 Place the glued sticks 1 cm (½ in) from the edge of the feeder. The two sticks should be at right angles to the sticks that form the base.

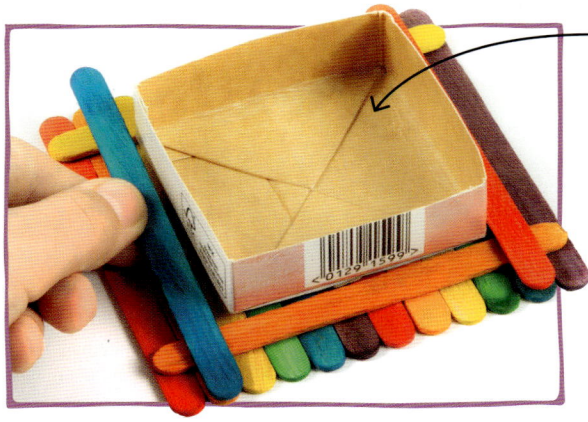

5 Repeat step 4, but this time only dab glue onto the ends of each lolly stick about 1 cm (½ in) in from the edge. Place the sticks so they form right angles with the two sticks you have just glued.

Make sure the tray can fit on the base before building up the layers of sticks, but don't stick it down.

6 Repeat steps 4 and 5 to build up walls of sticks that can hold the bird feeder tray in place. Stop when you have three layers on two sides and two layers on the other two.

Divide the length of the whole lolly stick by two to work out how long the shortened one should be.

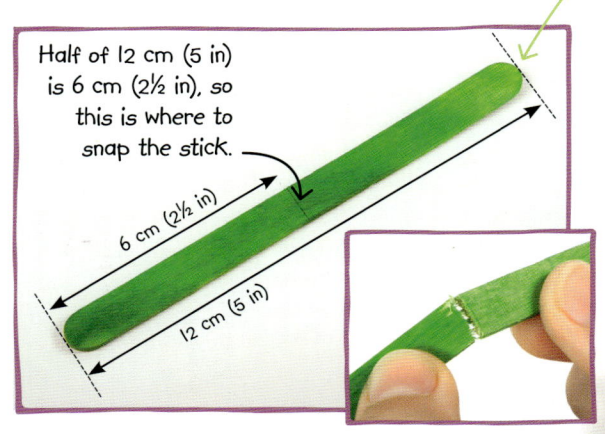

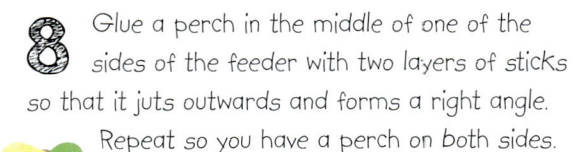

Half of 12 cm (5 in) is 6 cm (2½ in), so this is where to snap the stick.

6 cm (2½ in)

12 cm (5 in)

7 To make the perches, measure halfway along the stick and draw a line. Snap the stick in half neatly. Ask an adult to help if this is tricky.

8 Glue a perch in the middle of one of the sides of the feeder with two layers of sticks so that it juts outwards and forms a right angle. Repeat so you have a perch on both sides.

154 MEASUREMENTS

9 Continue to build up the layers of lolly sticks on each side of the feeder until the lower sides come up to the same height as the tray.

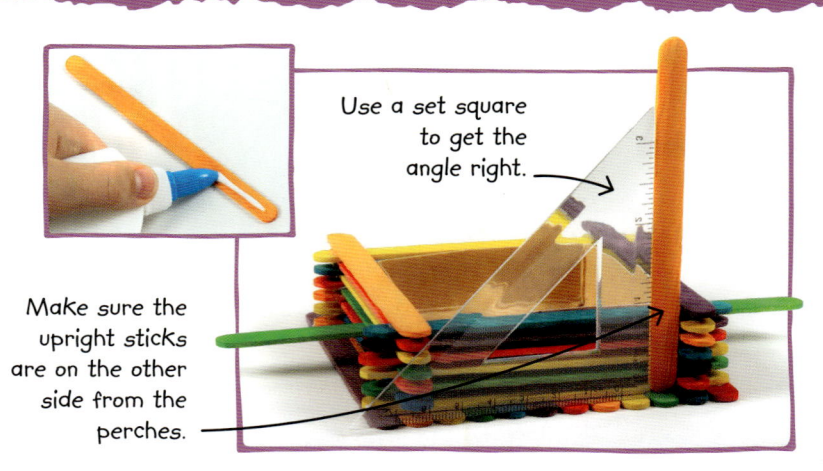

Use a set square to get the angle right.

Make sure the upright sticks are on the other side from the perches.

10 Glue one end of a stick and place it on an outside corner of the bird feeder so that it sticks up at a right angle to the base.

11 Repeat step 10 so that there are four vertical sticks – one at each corner of the tray.

These horizontal sticks should be parallel to each other.

12 Dab glue 2 cm (¾ in) from both ends of a stick and place it horizontally across the vertical sticks. Repeat on the opposite side.

13 To make the roof, place two columns of 12 lolly sticks next to one another and then join them together down the middle with adhesive tape.

The width of the roof should measure the length of one lolly stick.

LOLLY STICK BIRD FEEDER   155

14 Glue another lolly stick, place it along the adhesive tape and press firmly. Repeat so there is a lolly stick either side of the adhesive tape.

15 Glue the length of another lolly stick and place it 0.5 cm (¼ in) in from the edge of the roof. Repeat on the other side.

This angle is less wide than a right angle. This is known as an acute angle.

16 Flip the roof over and gently fold it so that it forms a triangle with the adhesive tape on the inside.

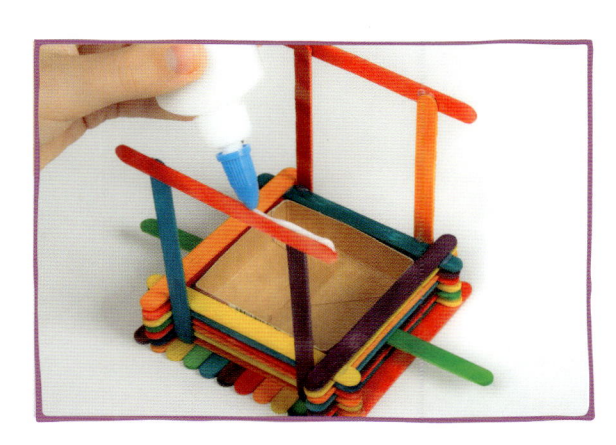

17 Dab glue along the top edge of the horizontal sticks.

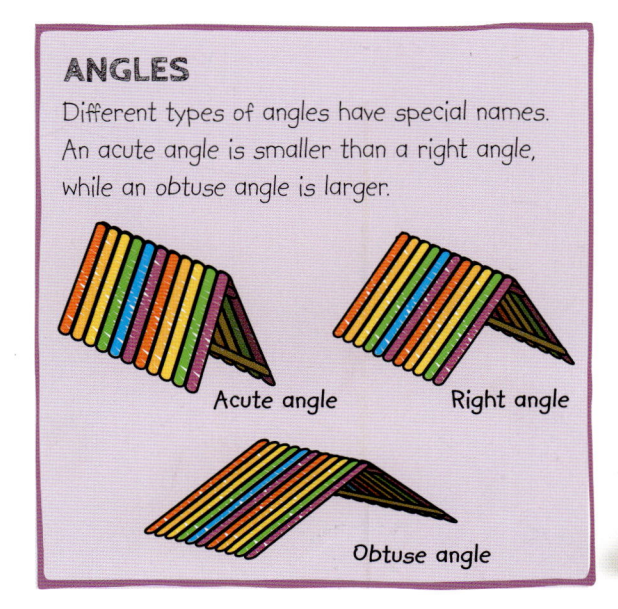

ANGLES
Different types of angles have special names. An acute angle is smaller than a right angle, while an obtuse angle is larger.

Acute angle

Right angle

Obtuse angle

18 Place the roof on top of the sticks and firmly hold in place. Leave until the glue is dry.

MEASUREMENTS

19 Glue along the top of the roof where the two sides meet. Place a lolly stick across the top of the roof and hold firmly until set. Your bird feeder box is now ready to attract birds!

20 Hang your bird feeder in the garden and fill the tray with tasty treats.

Make sure your nuts are chopped. Birds can choke on whole nuts!

Place food in the tray and put the tray in the feeder.

TRACK YOUR BIRDS

To work out what food the birds in your garden like best, try a few different sorts to see how many birds come to visit. You can use a tally chart to record the visits, and once you've gathered the data, you can turn your tally into a graph. Use the graph to help you analyse what you've discovered and pick the food that your garden's birds prefer. For the most accurate results, make your observations at the same time each day.

Mealworms

Mixed bird seed

Chopped nuts

1 You will have to try different foods over a few weeks to work out what the birds in your garden like to eat. We started with chopped nuts the first week, and then tried seeds and mealworms.

Use a ruler to draw a line between the points on your graph.

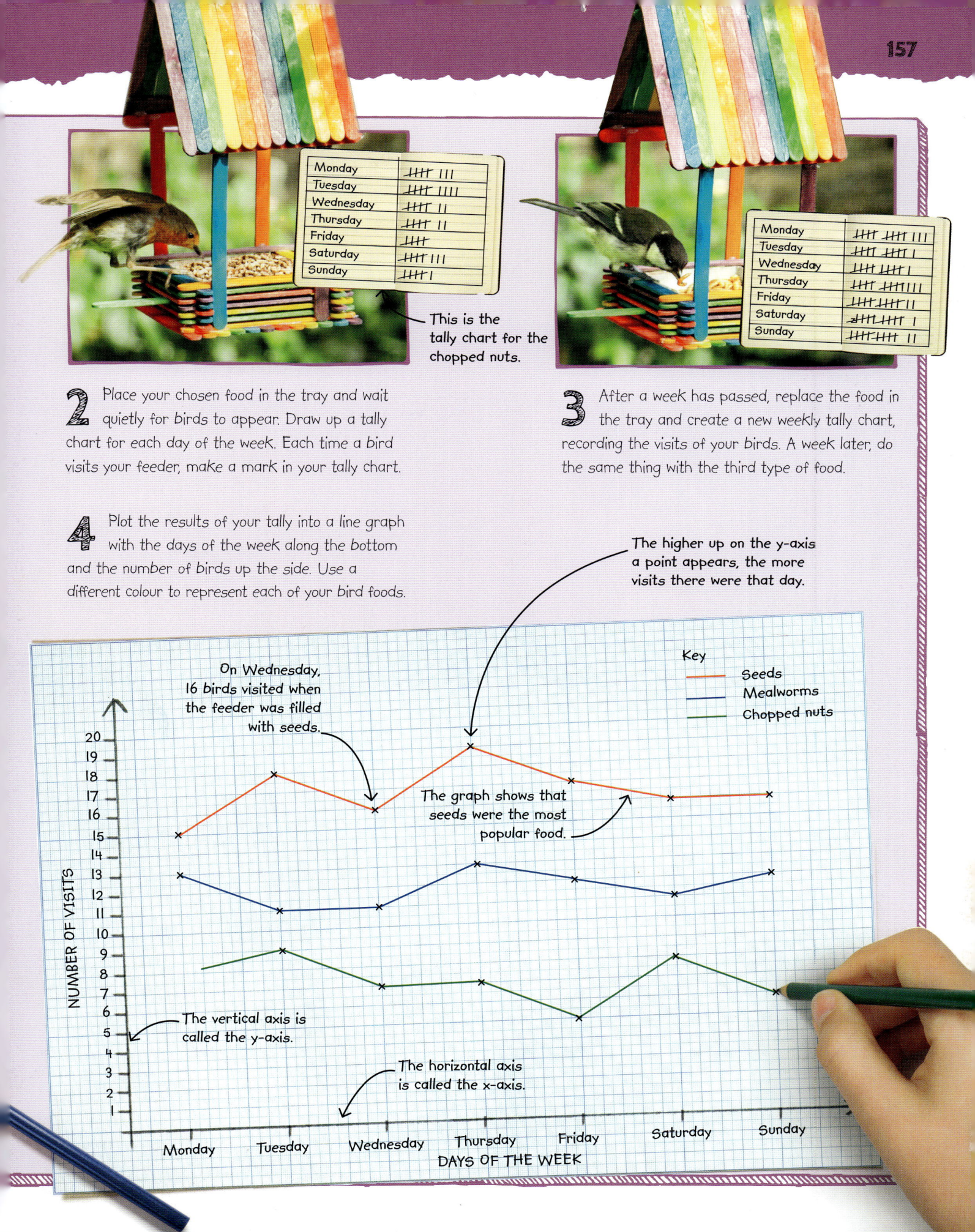

Monday	|||| |||
Tuesday	|||| ||||
Wednesday	|||| ||
Thursday	|||| ||
Friday	||||
Saturday	|||| |||
Sunday	||||	

This is the tally chart for the chopped nuts.

Monday	|||| |||| |||
Tuesday	|||| ||||	
Wednesday	|||| ||||	
Thursday	|||| |||| ||||
Friday	|||| |||| ||
Saturday	|||| ||||	
Sunday	|||| |||| ||

2 Place your chosen food in the tray and wait quietly for birds to appear. Draw up a tally chart for each day of the week. Each time a bird visits your feeder, make a mark in your tally chart.

3 After a week has passed, replace the food in the tray and create a new weekly tally chart, recording the visits of your birds. A week later, do the same thing with the third type of food.

4 Plot the results of your tally into a line graph with the days of the week along the bottom and the number of birds up the side. Use a different colour to represent each of your bird foods.

The higher up on the y-axis a point appears, the more visits there were that day.

On Wednesday, 16 birds visited when the feeder was filled with seeds.

The graph shows that seeds were the most popular food.

Key
- Seeds
- Mealworms
- Chopped nuts

NUMBER OF VISITS

The vertical axis is called the y-axis.

The horizontal axis is called the x-axis.

DAYS OF THE WEEK

GLOSSARY

ALGEBRA
The use of letters or other symbols to stand for unknown numbers when making calculations.

ANGLE
A measure of the amount of turn from one direction to another. You can also think of it as the difference in direction between two lines meeting at a point. Angles are measured in degrees.
See *degree*.

ANTICLOCKWISE
Going round in the opposite direction to a clock's hands.

AREA
The space inside any 2D shape. Area is measured in square units, such as square metres.

AVERAGE
The typical or middle value of a set of data.

AXIS
(1) One of the two main lines on a grid, used to measure the position of points, lines, and shapes. (2) An axis of symmetry is another name for a line of symmetry.

BASE
The bottom edge of a shape, if you imagine it sitting on a surface.

CIRCUMFERENCE
The distance all the way round the outside of a circle.

CLOCKWISE
Going round in the same direction as a clock's hands.

COMPASS
An instrument used to draw circles and parts of circles.

CONE
A 3D shape with a circular base and a side that narrows upwards to its apex.
See *apex*.

COORDINATES
Pairs of numbers that describe the position of a point, line, or shape on a grid, or the position of something on a map.

CYLINDER
A three-dimensional shape that has a circle as its cross-section.

DATA
Any information that has been collected and can be compared.

DECIMAL
Relating to the number 10 (and to tenths, hundredths, and so on). A decimal is written using a dot called a decimal point. The numbers to the right of the dot are tenths, hundredths, and so on. For example, a quarter (¼) as a decimal is 0.25, which means 0 ones, 2 tenths, and 5 hundredths.

DEGREE
A measure of the size of a turn or angle. The symbol for a degree is °. A full turn is 360°.

DENOMINATOR
The lower number in a fraction, such as the 4 in ¾.

DIAGONAL
A straight, sloping line that isn't vertical or horizontal.

DIAMETER
A straight line from one side of a circle or sphere to the other that goes through the centre.

DIGIT
A single number from 0 to 9. Digits also make up larger numbers. For example, 58 is made up of the digits 5 and 8.

EQUATION
A statement in maths that something equals something else, for example 2 + 2 = 4.

ESTIMATING
Finding an answer that's close to the correct answer, often by rounding numbers up or down.

FACE
Any flat surface of a 2D shape.

FACTOR
A whole number that divides exactly into another number. For example, 4 and 6 are factors of 12.

FORMULA
A rule or statement written using mathematical symbols.

FRACTION
A number that is not a whole number, such as ½, ¼, or ¹⁰⁄₃.

INTERSECT
To meet or cross over (used of lines and shapes).

LINE GRAPH
A diagram that shows data as points joined by straight lines.

LINE OF SYMMETRY
An imaginary line through a 2D shape that divides it into two identical halves. Some shapes have no line of symmetry, while others have several.

MULTIPLE
Any number that's the result of multiplying two whole numbers together.

NEGATIVE NUMBER
A number less than zero: for example -1, -2, -3, and so on.

NET
A flat shape that can be folded up to make a 3D shape.

GLOSSARY

NUMBER
A value used for counting and calculating. Numbers can be positive or negative, and include whole numbers and fractions.

NUMERATOR
The upper number in a fraction, such as the 3 in ¾.

OPPOSITE ANGLE
The angles on opposite sides where two lines intersect, or cross over each other. Opposite angles are equal.

PARALLEL
Running side by side without getting closer or further apart.

PERCENTAGE
A proportion expressed as a fraction of 100. For example, 25% is the same as $^{25}/_{100}$.

PERIMETER
The distance around the edge of a shape.

PERPENDICULAR
Something is perpendicular when it is at right angles to something else.

PLACE VALUE SYSTEM
The way of writing numbers. The value of each digit in the number depends on its position in that number. For example, the 2 in 120 has a place value of 20, but in 210 it stands for 200.

POLYGON
Any 2D shape with three or more straight sides, such as a triangle.

POLYHEDRON
Any 3D shape whose faces are polygons.

POSITIVE NUMBER
A number greater than zero.

PRIME NUMBER
A whole number greater than one that can't be divided by any whole number except itself and one.

PROBABILITY
The chance of something happening or being true.

PROPORTION
The relative size of part of a thing compared with the whole.

PROTRACTOR
A tool for measuring angles.

QUADRILATERAL
A 2D shape with four straight sides.

RADIUS
Any straight line from the centre of a circle to its circumference.

RATIO
Ratio compares one number or amount with another. It's written as two numbers, separated by a colon (:).

RECTANGLE
A four-sided 2D shape where opposite sides are the same length and all the angles are 90°.

REFLECTIVE SYMMETRY
A shape has reflective symmetry if you can draw a line through it to make two halves that are mirror images of each other.

REMAINDER
The number that is left over when one number doesn't divide into another exactly.

RIGHT ANGLE
An angle of 90° (a quarter turn), such as the angle between vertical and horizontal lines.

ROTATION
Turning around a central point or line.

SEQUENCE
An arrangement of numbers one after the other that follows a set pattern, called a rule.

SPHERE
A round, ball-shaped 3D shape where every point on its surface is the same distance from the centre.

SQUARE
A four-sided 2D shape where all the sides are the same length and all angles are 90°. A square is a special kind of rectangle. See *rectangle*.

THREE-DIMENSIONAL (3D)
Having length, width, and depth. All solid objects are three-dimensional – even thin paper.

TRIANGLE
A 2D shape with three straight sides and three angles.

TWO-DIMENSIONAL (2D)
Having length and width, or length and height, but no thickness.

UNIT
A standard size used for measuring, such as the metre (for length).

VERTEX
A point where two lines meet.

VALUE
The amount or size of something.

WHOLE NUMBER
Any number such as 8, 36, or 5971 that is not a fraction.

INDEX

Numbers in bold are the pages with the most information.

2D shapes 50, **52**, 93
  fortune-tellers 18
3D drawings 140–143
3D shapes **54**
  chocolate boxes 115
  impossible triangles 81
  popcorn cones 121

A
abacuses 12–17
addition 23
algebra 9, **11**
angles **155**
  bird feeders 152
  clocks 144
  dreamcatchers 33, 34
  friendship bracelets 100
  marble runs 135
  optical illusions 141
  origami jumping frogs 68
  pop-up cards 83
  wrapping paper 56
architecture 49
area 114
averages **97**

B
bags 56–61
bingo 22–25
bird feeders 150–157
bisection 70
block printing 56–61
boxes 114–117
bracelets 98–105

C
cards 82–87
cars 90–97
charts **156–157**
chocolate boxes 114–117
chocolate truffles 110–113
circles 34, **94**
  illusions 141–142
circumference 100
clocks 144–149
collages 26–31
concave lines 141
concentric circles 142
cones 121
convex lines 141
coordinates **48**
cubes 115, 143

D
da Vinci, Leonardo 31
data collection **156–157**
decimals **16**, 133
density 106
diagonal lines 100
diameters 33, 114, 118
division 23, 41, 114
dodecahedrons **50–55**
doll's houses 67
doubling 127
dreamcatchers 32–37
drinks 106–109

E
equations 9
equilateral triangles **79**
estimation 130, 133

F
Fibonacci sequences 26–31
footballs 55
fortune-tellers 18–21
fractions **40**, 41, 144
fridge magnets 8–11
friendship bracelets 98–105
fruit drinks 106–109

G
graphs **156–157**
grid references 48, 63–67

H
halving 40, 127, 152
horizontal lines 101

I
illusions 140–143
impossible triangles 78–81

J
jumping frogs 68–71

L
lolly stick bird feeders 150–157
looms 100–105
lucky dip 130–133

M
magnets 8–11
marble runs 134–139
multiplication **21**
  abacuses 12
  bingo 23
  fortune-tellers 18

N
natural patterns 31
nets 115

O
optical illusions 140–143
origami 18–21, 68–71

P
paper construction 82–87
parallel lines 59, 103
  abacuses 12
  bird feeders 152
patterns 26, **59**, **103**
  dreamcatchers 37
  tessellating patterns 72–77
  wrapping paper 56
percentages 113, 133
picture balls 50–55
pizzas 38–41
place value 12, **16**
polygons **52**
polyhedrons **54**
popcorn sale tray 118–125
pop-up cards 82–87
potato printing 56–61
pricing 124, **125**
printing 56–61
probability 132–133
protractors 85
puppets 126–129

Q
quadrilaterals **93**

R
racing cars 90–97
radius 33, 118
ratios 26, 31, **109**
  fruit drinks 106
rectangles 68
reflective symmetry 46, **47**

right angles 26
rotation 49, 76
  fortune-tellers 18
  tessellating patterns 72
rubber band racing car 90–97

S
scale factor **65**, **67**
scaling up pictures 62–67
sequences 26, 100
shadow puppets 126–129
scale factor 67
shop prices 124
sizes 62–67, 129
speed trials 90, 97
spirals **26–31**
squares 68
straight lines 101
subtraction 23
sweetie boxes 114–117
symmetry **44–49**

T
telling the time 149
tessellation 72–77
textiles 61, 105
times tables 18–21, 33
tracking birds 156–157
trays, popcorn 118–125
triangles 68, 78–81
truffles 110–113

V
variables **97**
vertical lines 100
vertices 46

W
weaving 105
wrapping paper 56–61

ACKNOWLEDGMENTS

The publisher would like to thank the following people for their assistance in the preparation of this book:
Elizabeth Wise for indexing; Caroline Hunt for proofreading; Ella A @ Models Plus Ltd, Jennifer Ji @ Models Plus Ltd, and Otto Podhorodecki for hand modelling; Steve Crozier for photo retouching.

The publisher would like to thank the following for their kind permission to reproduce their photographs:

(Key: a-above; b-below/bottom; c-centre; f-far; l-left; r-right; t-top)

17 Mary Evans Picture Library: Interfoto / Bildarchiv Hansmann (br). **25 Getty Images:** Jonathan Kitchen / DigitalVision (bc). **31 Getty Images:** Universal Images Group (br). **49 123RF.com:** Maria Wachala (crb). **61 Alamy Stock Photo:** Karen & Summer Kala (br). **77 Getty Images / iStock:** Elena Abramovich (br). **92 Dreamstime.com:** Stocksolutions (tbl). **97 Dreamstime.com:** Stocksolutions (bl/notebook). **Getty Images:** Anthony Wallace / AFP (crb). **103 Getty Images / iStock:** Tatiana Terekhina (bl). **105 Dreamstime.com:** Ukrit Chaiwattanakunkit (br). **108 Dreamstime.com:** Stocksolutions (cb/notebook). **109 Shutterstock.com:** SeventyFour (br). **124 Getty Images:** Westend61 (bl). **125 Dreamstime.com:** Stocksolutions (notebook). **129 Alamy Stock Photo:** Pacific Press Media Production Corp. (bl). **Dreamstime.com:** Stocksolutions (cra/notebook). **133 Dreamstime.com:** Stocksolutions (br/notebook). **149 Getty Images / iStock:** chasmer (crb). **152 Dreamstime.com:** Stocksolutions (bl). **157 Dreamstime.com:** Stocksolutions (notebook).

All other images © Dorling Kindersley
For further information see: www.dkimages.com